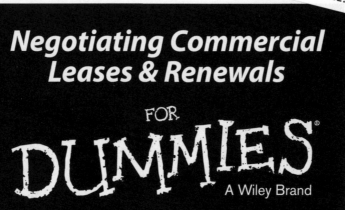

Negotiating Commercial Leases & Renewals

FOR DUMMIES®

A Wiley Brand

by Dale Willerton
and Jeff Grandfield

Jenny,

Regards,

2016.

FOR DUMMIES®
A Wiley Brand

Negotiating Commercial Leases & Renewals For Dummies®

Published by
John Wiley & Sons, Inc.
111 River St.
Hoboken, NJ 07030-5774
www.wiley.com

For general information on our other products and services, please contact our Customer Care Department within the U.S. at 877-762-2974, outside the U.S. at 317-572-3993, or fax 317-572-4002.

For technical support, please visit www.wiley.com/techsupport.

Wiley publishes in a variety of print and electronic formats and by print-on-demand. Some material included with standard print versions of this book may not be included in e-books or in print-on-demand. If this book refers to media such as a CD or DVD that is not included in the version you purchased, you may download this material at http://booksupport.wiley.com. For more information about Wiley products, visit www.wiley.com.

Library of Congress Control Number: 2013933948

ISBN 978-1-118-47746-5 (pbk); ISBN 978-1-118-50252-5 (ePub); ISBN 978-1-118-50254-9 (eMobi); ISBN 978-1-118-50255-6 (ePDF)

Manufactured in the United States of America

10 9 8 7 6 5 4 3 2 1

About the Authors

Dale Willerton is The Lease Coach. Before getting into commercial real estate, Dale owned many businesses that required him to be a tenant. His interest in real estate led him to work for commercial landlords, managing and leasing shopping malls, office properties, and strip plazas. In 1993, Dale realized it wasn't landlords who needed help, it was tenants. He switched to the tenant's side and became The Lease Coach, creating a new niche in the consulting industry. Within a few years, the demand for professional consulting services meant expanding into a much larger team. Dale partnered with Jeff Grandfield, who is responsible for much of The Lease Coach's growth and success today.

Jeff Grandfield is a senior consultant with The Lease Coach. Jeff completed his honor's B.A. degree in business administration with a designation in marketing from Wilfrid Laurier University. It was the challenge of the real estate industry and satisfaction of working with business owners of all types and sizes that drove Jeff to pursue a career in real estate and join The Lease Coach in 2005.

Dale, Jeff, and The Lease Coach team have successfully complete more than 1,200 consulting projects for tenants. They have conducted hundreds of seminars, workshops, and webinars. They frequently provide real estate training for franchisors and franchisees. Speaking at industry tradeshows and for healthcare organizations, they've helped tens of thousands of business owners and tenants. The Lease Coach has offices throughout the United States and Canada, exclusively representing tenants with one-on-one coaching and consulting, new and lease-renewal negotiations, site selection, lease document reviews, midterm rent reductions, lease assignments, building acquisitions, operating cost audits, and space measurements. The Lease Coach never accepts any fees from landlords and works with small and large, independent and franchise tenants. For a complimentary consultation or to inquire about having Dale and/or Jeff do a live speaking presentation, webinar or training at your next event, visit www.TheLeaseCoach.com, e-mail DaleWillerton@TheLeaseCoach.com or JeffGrandfield@TheLeaseCoach.com, or call 1-800-738-9202 (ext 1).

Dedication

This book is dedicated to the most important people in Dale's and Jeff's lives — their families: Linda, Alana, Jessie, Jean, Elaine, Louise, Lester, Janice, Brie and Vaughn, Miles, Terry, and Cory

Authors' Acknowledgments

How does one say thank you when there are so many people to thank? Dale and Jeff want to acknowledge The Lease Coach team, including Pam, Lyda, and Rick, for their dedication, hard work, and loyalty. We also want to acknowledge the 1,200+ business owners, entrepreneurs, doctors, and tenants who have trusted their leases to The Lease Coach — and the many more to come. And to those thousands of business owners and tenants who attend our seminars, providing us with the opportunity to do what we love: help tenants.

Publisher's Acknowledgments

We're proud of this book; please send us your comments at `http://dummies.custhelp.com`. For other comments, please contact our Customer Care Department within the U.S. at 877-762-2974, outside the U.S. at 317-572-3993, or fax 317-572-4002.

Some of the people who helped bring this book to market include the following:

Acquisitions, Editorial, and Vertical Websites

Editor: Corbin Collins

Acquisitions Editor: Erin Calligan Mooney

Special Help: Sharon Perkins

Assistant Editor: David Lutton

Editorial Program Coordinator: Joe Niesen

Technical Editor: Brad King

Senior Editorial Manager: Jennifer Ehrlich

Editorial Manager: Carmen Krikorian

Editorial Assistants: Rachelle Amick and Alexa Koschier

Cover Photos: © teekid / iStockphoto.com

Cartoons: Rich Tennant (www.the5thwave.com)

Composition Services

Project Coordinator: Kristie Rees

Layout and Graphics: Carl Byers, Joyce Haughey

Proofreaders: Jessica Kramer, Evelyn C. Wellborn

Indexer: BIM Indexing & Proofreading Services

Publishing and Editorial for Consumer Dummies

    Kathleen Nebenhaus, Vice President and Executive Publisher

    David Palmer, Associate Publisher

    Kristin Ferguson-Wagstaffe, Product Development Director

Publishing for Technology Dummies

    Andy Cummings, Vice President and Publisher

Composition Services

    Debbie Stailey, Director of Composition Services

Contents at a Glance

Table of Contents

Part V: The Part of Tens... 267

Chapter 18: Ten Leasing Tips, Tactics, and Strategies for Tenants 269

Chapter 19: Ten Questions to Ask the Landlord's Real Estate Agent 277

Chapter 20: Ten (or So) Warnings: What No One Ever Tells Tenants.....................................285

Introduction

● ●

*W*elcome to *Negotiating Commercial Leases & Renewals For Dummies*!

Over 10 million business owners, entrepreneurs, retailers, and healthcare and franchise tenants lease commercial, retail, and office space across North America. Prior to 1993, Dale worked for landlords, managing shopping centers and leasing their space. In 1993, Dale realized it wasn't the landlord who needed his help — it was the tenant — and that's when he became The Lease Coach. As a professional lease consultant, Dale brought on Jeff Grandfield as his partner, and both of your authors consult with and negotiate leases exclusively for tenants throughout North America.

Based on our two decades of experience in the commercial real estate industry, Dale and Jeff have developed keen instincts for which business concepts will have longevity and which are likely to struggle or fail, especially when we factor in their location and the lease deals being signed. Business owners need to start their business with the end in mind. That means looking forward *now* to be able to better predict the future.

In his book *Outliers*, Malcolm Gladwell talks about the 10,000 hours it takes to become a recognized expert or authority in your field. That is exactly what your authors have done, and its all been worth it. Working with business owners is extremely fulfilling. Dale and Jeff get to meet tenants all over North America as they travel and speak at conventions and tradeshows. A great business in a poor location at a high rental rate may never achieve its full potential, if it survives at all. Often it takes a professional lease consultant who is working for you, and not the landlord, to actually steer you in the right direction and get you the deal you need.

About This Book

This book and its stories and cases studies are a compilation of over 1,200 successful leasing projects that the authors have completed for tenants to date. You don't have to read it from beginning to end; instead, if you're in the middle of negotiations and need certain information right now, use the table of contents or index to turn right to the part of the book where that info is found and start reading. And you can keep returning to the book whenever you need a quick education on certain aspects of the leasing process. If you're more the orderly type, you can certainly read straight through from beginning to end. You'll find that the information is presented in a natural, logical way that leads you from one step of the process to the next.

One of the most popular seminar presentations The Lease Coach delivers is called "Thirteen Costly Mistakes Tenants Make Negotiating Commercial Leases and Renewals." Readers of this book, like many of our seminar attendees, come to realize that they've already made many lease negotiating mistakes.

But don't let that realization discourage you! This book will strengthen your negotiating position for all future dealings — and if you're in business, there will be more chances to negotiate. This book opens your eyes to what tenants need to know.

Feel free to take out your highlighter when reading the book and use it profusely. If you're like Dale, sticky notes come in handy too. This book will not only improve your negotiating skills as a tenant, but also raise your consciousness about commercial leasing.

Conventions Used in This Book

To help you navigate this book, we follow these conventions:

- ✔ **Boldface** highlights key words in bulleted lists.
- ✔ New terms and words are emphasized in *italics*.
- ✔ Web addresses appear in `monofont`.

When this book was printed, some web addresses we mention may have broken across two lines of text. If that happened, rest assured that we didn't include extra characters (such as hyphens) to indicate the break. If you want to visit a website, and the URL has been broken, just type exactly what you see in this book, as though the line break didn't exist.

What You're Not to Read

Sometimes we have to mention things that are interesting but aren't crucial to your understanding of the topic at hand. Sidebars contain discussions of "side" topics that you may find useful but that aren't necessary for you to get what we're talking about. Read these or not, it's up to you.

Sometimes we can't help ourselves and go into specialized detail that you don't have to read to get our main point. When this happens, we place a Technical Stuff icon to mark those paragraphs as skippable. Like this one.

Foolish Assumptions

Your authors at The Lease Coach have written this book with the assumption that you're either about to open a business that requires space for lease or that you already own a business for which you're leasing space. Sections of the book are written toward first-time tenants, whereas other areas are dedicated to existing or more experienced tenants who may have already negotiated a commercial lease or two.

We assume that our readers are from all industries and professions and are interested in leasing all types of commercial space, including strip plazas, office buildings, shopping center space, and even industrial space.

We also assume that you're prepared to invest the time that's required to negotiate thoroughly. That means doing your homework and spending the time to create competition for your tenancy rather than jumping at the first deal that falls into your lap.

Finally, we assume that you're prepared to embrace the role of the negotiator or delegate the task to a professional lease consultant who's more experienced and capable than yourself.

How This Book Is Organized

The leasing process is a just that — a *process*, not an event. The process has a predictable beginning, middle, and ending, whether you're dealing on a brand new location or a lease renewal. Lease agreements sent to us from all across the United States and Canada are quite similar in structure and format. We try to present the business terms and lease clauses in the order they commonly appear in the lease agreement, from beginning to end. We've also organized the material into various sections in our attempt to cover every leasing scenario for every type of tenant. There is some intentional content overlap to make each section complete unto itself, because you may want to pop in and out of the book to find the critical information you need at the appropriate time in the leasing process.

Part I: Leasing 101 for Tenants

In Chapter 1, we explain why negotiating a great lease is important to the tenant's financial well-being. Chapter 2 outlines the beginning of the leasing process. In Chapter 3, we explore the different types of properties for lease. Chapter 4 involves site selection and the proper method for conducting it. Using a real estate agent is dealt with in Chapter 5, and Chapter 6 outlines the professional assistance a tenant can hire.

Part II: Negotiating the Offer and Key Terms

Chapter 7 explores presenting and negotiating a lease proposal. In Chapter 8, we go over negotiation of the core business terms. Chapter 9 gets into negotiating the rental rate. In Chapter 10, we explain how area or square footage can affect your bottom line and how to measure your space. Chapter 11 deals with commencement dates and construction matters, and Chapter 12 includes negotiating the lease deposit and how to keep get it back when your lease term expires.

Part III: Reviewing the Formal Lease Agreement and Dealing with the Landlord

Chapter 13 is dedicated to understanding and negotiating the rest of the lease. In Chapter 14, we're finalizing the formal lease agreement. In Chapter 15, we explore methods for dealing with landlords including strategy and practical negotiating applications and wisdom.

Part IV: Negotiating Your Lease Renewal

Chapter 16 is especially relevant for existing tenants facing a lease renewal negotiation. We go deeper into the lease-renewal process in Chapter 17, exploring various clauses in the lease agreement that need to be negotiated.

Part V: The Part of Tens

In Chapter 18, we include many of the tips, tactics, and strategies we've developed for tenants. Chapter 19 is a list of pertinent questions that tenants should ask the landlord's real estate agent when going through the site-selection and lease-negotiation process. Finally, Chapter 20 alerts you to warnings and situations to avoid.

Icons Used in This Book

Icons are those little pictures you see in the margins throughout this book. They're meant to draw your attention to key points that help you along the way. The following are the icons we use in this book and what they signify:

 Some things are so important that they need to be set apart for emphasis. This icon — like a string tied around your finger — is a friendly reminder of stuff you should remember and use over the long haul.

 When you see this icon in the margin, the paragraph next to it contains a valuable, practical tip about the lease-negotiation process.

 This icon highlights things you want to avoid. An important part of achieving success is simply eliminating the mistakes; the information marked by this icon helps you do just that.

 This icon highlights information that may be interesting if you want to really drill down to another level of technicality, but it can be safely skipped without jeopardizing your understanding of the topic at hand.

Where to Go from Here

Although we recommend reading everything in this book eventually, chances are you might want to jump in and then move around from one section to another. Every section stands alone and contains all the information you need for that segment of lease negotiation.

First-time tenants will get the information they need most by starting with Parts I and II. Existing tenants may benefit most by starting with Part IV.

When The Lease Coach is presenting a seminar or running our Leasing Bootcamp at a convention or tradeshow, we often survey the audience to determine why specific attendees are present. Invariably, some attendees are at the beginning of the leasing process, and others are at the end of it. Many are facing a lease-renewal negotiation. Chances are the readers of this book are also at different stages of the leasing process.

Our goal is for you to use as much of the content as you can to improve your negotiating position and the entire lease agreement. In a few years, you might be starting the process all over again — so keep this book handy for that eventuality.

Part I
Leasing 101 for Tenants

The 5th Wave   By Rich Tennant

"See if this is covered in our lease agreement."

In this part . . .

Whether you're looking for a place to open a new business or searching out a new location for your existing business, you've got questions about the process. The location you choose and the terms of your lease can have a major impact on whether your business flourishes or folds. In this part, we help you weigh all the factors that determine whether a location is right for you. We also explain the role a professional leasing agent or real estate agent will play in your success or failure during the negotiating process.

Chapter 1

Yes, You Can Negotiate a Great Commercial Lease

In This Chapter
▶ Making the most of this book
▶ Starting the commercial leasing process
▶ Seeing the leasing process through the landlord's eyes

*T*he business terms of a commercial lease agreement, combined with the location, represent the platform that your business or company is built upon. Your business may be able to change its products, services, pricing, and marketing — but once you've signed a long-term lease commitment, you've got to make the location work. It's do or die time. And the more money you spend building out your location, fixturing it, and stocking it with merchandise or inventory, the more capital you have invested in the success of that business.

If we could have one wish come true, it would be that business owners take the leasing process more seriously and realize that when the dust settles, they better have gotten it right, because profit is king. And it all starts with the location and lease agreement.

This book aims to spell out how you can successfully negotiate a great lease. But first, a few preliminaries.

Understanding What a Profitable Lease Agreement Is

A *profitable lease agreement* does two things:

✔ It lets you the owner, operate a successful business, drawing a good salary from the company while servicing the bills, loans, and debts of the company. It gives you the privilege of employing people, and possibly allowing for future expansion, and thereby becoming truly rich and profitable at multiple levels.

✔ It enables you to acquire equity and goodwill, possibly leading to selling the business, recouping the investor's capital, and either retiring or allowing you to open another business.

The future salability of the business is often overlooked by business owners. The Lease Coach is often hired to work with entrepreneurs and business owners when buying or selling a business because a commercial lease agreement is involved.

Too often, The Lease Coach sees business owners not only struggle to take home a salary, but at the end of their 5- or 10-year lease term, they end up closing the business because no one wants to buy it. There was a story in Dale's local newspaper about a family-run business that after 30 years simply closed its doors for retirement. No one wanted to buy the business, which was a shame. You can assume that the owner of the business didn't get rich running his business or it would have had many suitors willing to buy it. If you spend all those years building a business and then you can't sell it, you can't get those years back.

Avoiding bad leases and knowing what makes them bad

A bad lease agreement may hold you back from making a good profit. A bad lease agreement could mean a bad or mediocre location. Dale and Jeff see this all the time. Great retailers, superb restaurateurs, exceptional service businesses in poor or mediocre locations do less business than they could in a better location. On the other hand, perhaps you picked a great location, but leased too many square feet (or too few), this can be a problem as well.

Combine a poor location with a high rental rate and you have a recipe for disaster. Your business will never succeed, let alone sell for a profit. Too many entrepreneurs are shopping for cheap space, but for the most part, you get what you pay for location-wise. This isn't to downplay the need for skillful negotiation; you don't want to pay too much for a good location — it's all relative. In many of the larger plazas and enclosed malls, the property in general may be recognized as an excellent location, but getting stuck in a quiet area of the property may make your business less visible than you would like.

A lack of adequate parking for your customers can make for a bad lease. A multi-unit restaurant tenant The Lease Coach is currently working with for a midterm rent reduction has come to the unfortunate realization that their newest location is parking starved. Just when people are hungry and want to come to their restaurant, the parking lot is already full of vehicles. Customers come in to complain that they can't find a parking space even close by — and many times cancel their reservation, go back to their cars, and drive away.

High rental rates — especially if combined with restrictive terms that make running your business difficult, if not impossible — can also hamper your future success.

Making a good lease a great lease

Brevity in a lease agreement is the enemy of most tenants. A good lease agreement is longer, not shorter. Never assume that what the lease doesn't say will play out to your benefit later — it won't. As the tenant, you want everything that could possibly be an issue addressed in your lease agreement.

Often it's what's missing from a lease agreement that really comes back to hurt the tenant.

For example, if a business owner wants to sell their business and assign their lease agreement to the buyer, the lease must have a comprehensive lease-assignment clause. However, landlords often include conditions controlling or potentially prohibiting the lease assignment (unless suitable wording is added for the tenant's protection). Another example is that most lease agreements have a *permitted use* clause stipulating what products or services you can sell — or perhaps not sell. If you open a ladies clothing store and realize you also want to sell shoes, handbags, watches, and other accessories; you may not be able to sell them if your lease agreement specifically states that your permitted use is ladies clothing. Anticipating what items you may want to stock or sell will allow you to negotiate and add appropriate wording to the permitted use clause.

Making a good lease great requires anticipation of what may change in your industry, in the economy, and with future competitors, and then capturing all that into the lease agreement.

Making a good lease great means removing, deleting, or negotiating restrictive clauses in the lease agreement that will hold your company back. For some tenants, the renewal-option clause can be the difference between whether you get to stay in your location for several renewal terms. A demolition clause can force you to move out of the premises if the landlord wants to knock down the building and put up a different type of building. A relocation clause can force you into a costly relocation. All of these are scary scenarios requiring proper guidance from a professional lease consultant who is working for and being paid by you to protect and serve your needs — the tenant.

Negotiating a truly profitable lease agreement

A profitable lease agreement may include an exclusivity clause preventing your indirect competitors or neighboring tenants from selling your primary permitted use products or services. A profitable lease agreement would include a clause allowing you to operate the days and hours of your choosing. This can also mean the right to close or open early/late hours on days where it is unprofitable to remain open. One landlord wanted to require that an optometrist tenant (our client) open on Sundays. We negotiated so that the doctor was allowed to close on Sundays and holidays.

Try to think in terms of whether you'd buy this business based on its current lease agreement. As a prospective buyer, what parts of the lease agreement would you not like? Would the rent seem high? What about the operating costs? Would a shortage of parking or an undesirable neighboring tenant drive away both your potential customers and buyers of your business? Thinking about these issues beforehand can make all the difference to your decision-making process.

Seeing yourself from the landlord's perspective

Business owners often fail to understand that a landlord doesn't just want any tenant; they want the best tenant possible. Most landlords prefer to have national chains and companies with locations and offices across the country. One of the jewelry store chains The Lease Coach works with has several hundred stores in 19 different countries with a strong presence and track record for both success and for paying percentage rent. The jewelry chain started with corporate stores and once success was imminent, they began franchising. As a landlord, you can see why this type of jewelry store concept may be preferable to a mom and pop operation or independent tenant.

Whether you're launching a new concept or copying a successful one is relevant to the landlord. Your business plan, your financial status, and your background are important to the landlord. If you're a respected mechanic with years of experience, you may be successful running an auto repair business because that business is one you know. But if you're a schoolteacher who suddenly receives a large inheritance, and can now quit your job and open the business you've always wanted — a personal fitness business, a cupcake shop, or a restaurant — the landlord may not be as certain about your future success.

Landlords love to lease space to national chains and franchisee tenants who have bought into large, proven franchise concepts. They really desire to lease space to healthcare tenants like dentists, doctors, and chiropractors. The doctors are professionals in their field who make for very stable and dependable rent paying long-term tenants.

If you know your tenancy or background isn't likely to look attractive to a landlord, then take heed and get better prepared. If you know you and your concept will be well received, then you're set. Some of the larger national landlords with hundreds of properties can likely size up any business concept or owner very quickly, so be prepared before you contact them. The first impression you make is a lasting one.

Leasing 101 for Tenants

Starting the leasing process in the right direction is critical if you want to achieve the best results. If you take the wrong path or veer off in the wrong direction, you may not achieve your goals or your business's full potential. That's how important the leasing process is. Errors, miscalculations, and bad advice at this stage can be difficult to fix later on.

To make the best leasing decisions, you need an inside and outside view of the different types of buildings or properties available (Chapter 3 can help you there). Then utilize a checklist to help you determine the pros and cons of different sites. The goal should be to lease the premises that will provide the most profit. On the surface, it seems that picking the best building would be advantageous; however, your particular business may not be able to afford or even justify paying the higher rents in more expensive properties. The last thing a tenant needs or wants is to find out that they've signed a long-term lease agreement in the wrong property. Chapter 4 can help you avoid this mistake.

During the initial leasing process, tenants invariably encounter and deal with commercial real estate brokers and their agents. We estimate that approximately 95 percent of all commercial real estate is listed with commercial brokers, so the chances of not dealing with one are slim indeed. Find out what the role of the real estate agent is, how to properly use a real estate agent, and how to conduct yourself in your dealings by studying the information in Chapter 5. Whether you're negotiating on shopping mall space, an office tower, industrial space, or a retail plaza location, it is necessary to navigate carefully as you negotiate with commercial real estate agents.

When it comes to negotiating a new lease or lease renewal, turning to professionals can save you time, aggravation, and money. Professionals you may choose to work with include a real estate agent, lawyer, or professional lease consultant. Investigating and evaluating the right professional to help you (the topic of Chapter 6) can be the difference between success and failure.

Negotiating the Offer and Key Terms

If you've never negotiated a commercial lease before, chances are you won't find this process easy or enjoyable. There's a steep learning curve when it comes to presenting lease terms and negotiating an offer to lease or letter of intent. Even if you have experience with hard negotiating, chances are you're not looking forward to locking horns with the landlord or their real estate agent — opponents who have experience on their side. This chapter explores ways to make you look and sound like a pro at the leasing table, even if you're a rookie.

Negotiating the business terms is one of the most critical aspects of the lease-negotiating process. The business terms include the rental rate, length of lease, deposit, personal guaranty, and a dozen other details that may not have occurred to you.

The rental rate is one of the most focused-on business terms, perhaps rightly so because it is one of the biggest factors determining the success or failure of your business. We look at how the landlord determines the rental rates, how to determine what you can afford to pay, and how to negotiate the best rental rate. The rental rate goes beyond one simple number — it can include additional rent often called operating costs and perhaps percentage rent, which can dramatically increase the total payment you make each month.

Knowing how important the rental rate you pay is, and that this number is calculated on a per square foot basis, means that understanding how much space to rent and how to calculate this size is crucial.

We also explore choosing the right commencement date — how to position yourself to take possession of the premises once the lease agreement has been signed by both parties. Traditionally, a tenant would spend one to three months building out their space prior to opening to the public. A lot can go wrong during that time. Tenants must know how to hold the landlord accountable and how to ensure and protect their rights in advance when the unexpected occurs.

Deposits are a misunderstood component of the leasing process. Many tenants are misled into believing that deposits are mandatory and pushed to provide larger deposits than may really be required or justified.

Reviewing the Formal Lease Agreement and Dealing with the Landlord

This part of the book deals with the remainder of the lease agreement — beyond the initial offer and key business terms — and discusses how to properly review and finalize the formal lease agreement.

Finalizing the formal lease agreement is a negotiation unto itself. Yes, the business terms have been agreed to, but now a 30-50 page formal lease document is looming and requires consideration. Understanding and negotiating the formal lease agreement should be done with the help of a professional — ideally, a lease consultant. Many clauses in the formal lease agreement require negotiation, amendments, or deletion. Adding certain phrases and clauses to the lease agreement also helps protect the tenant. Smart business owners realize that with any contract, it's better to be safe than sorry.

Dealing with the landlord and their representative, whether it's the property manager or a commercial real estate agent, is definitely a challenge. There are many different types of landlords with different motivations for owning property. Some landlords are billion-dollar corporations, and other landlords are small and accessible to a tenant. Understanding your opponent before you get into the ring makes a big difference in the outcome of your lease negotiation.

Negotiating Your Lease Renewal

Approximately two million commercial lease-renewal transactions take place every year in North America. Whether you're leasing space in a strip plaza, office building, shopping mall, or industrial warehouse, and whether you're a retailer, wholesaler, service provider, or healthcare professional, you eventually have to face a lease-renewal negotiation with the landlord. Once again, starting with the end goal in mind and planning far enough in advance, this process becomes easier, as we explain in Chapter 16.

Most landlords push for a rent increase on a tenant's lease renewal. This is normal and something you should anticipate. A lot can transpire in a 5- or 10-year lease term between when you moved in and when you need to negotiate your lease renewal. The lease-renewal negotiation is a familiar process to Dale and Jeff and gives these professional lease consultants an opportunity to re-address or fix a lot of the lease problems existing from the tenant's initial deal.

This part of the book also covers whether it is necessary to exercise the lease-renewal option clause, the best process for assigning your lease agreement if you're selling or buying a business, and how to prepare for the negotiating process. The difference between a rent increase or decrease on your lease renewal has lot to do with the homework you do and which professional helps you through the process.

The Lease Coach authors explain why many successful lease renewal negotiations include the return of the deposit to the tenant, removal of personal guaranties, and may also include leasing inducements and tenant incentives. Although you may not be able to pull this off on your own, experienced lease consultants like The Lease Coach specialize in negotiating lease-renewal rent reductions for all types of independent, franchise, healthcare, and office tenants. If you already own a business and desperately need a rent reduction on your lease renewal, pay special attention to this section.

The Part of Tens

In the Part of Tens portion of the book, we hope to throw some bite-sized nuggets your way that are both easy to understand and fun to discover. Turn to Chapter 18 for leasing tips, tactics, and strategies for tenants. In Chapter 19, we provide an easy checklist of ten questions to ask the landlord's real estate agent on prospective locations.. We also include ten or so warnings for tenants to heed in Chapter 20; these warnings will help you avoid leasing pitfalls and confrontations when dealing with your landlord.

The authors of this book welcome your comments and questions by e-mail or phone (see "About the Authors"). If you have a great leasing story to share or even a nightmare experience, we want to hear it.

Chapter 2

Starting the Leasing Process

. . . .

In This Chapter

▶ Knowing what to do before you get started on the leasing process

▶ Planning to make a great impression on landlords

▶ Creating business plans and other tools for a successful lease negotiation

▶ Scouting out locations for lease

. . . .

*W*e admire business owners and entrepreneurs who thoughtfully prepare themselves before getting started on the leasing process — preparation often separates the successful from the failures. The vast majority of tenants find a location and dial the real estate agent's phone number to make a listing inquiry without first preparing for the call. After asking a few questions about the property, they casually reveal too much about themselves and often give the agent the upper hand.

In this chapter, we stress the importance of preparing yourself, taking your time, and making thoughtful and calculated moves. The leasing process is just that, a process — not a race. You must control your impulse to rush through it.

Getting a Few Business Ducks in Order

Why is it important to get your business ducks in a row before reaching out to landlords and their agents? Because everything you say and do will be judged and weighed. The landlord's first impression of you and your business concept is critical. You may think to yourself, "But you told me the tenant is king, the tenant is the customer … and the customer is always right, right? So why is this first impression nonsense so important; if I pay the rent, they're happy."

Not so fast, innocent friend. Although vacancy rates may appear high across the country, and many spaces may be available for lease, there's still competition for the best locations. We get many phone calls from tenants scratching their heads about being rejected or passed over by a landlord and losing their favorite site to another tenant. This sometimes happens because the landlord has come either to the conclusion that you weren't prepared, or that the other prospective tenant was more prepared. Getting your business ducks in a row is good for a lot of reasons, including that it never hurts to impress upon the landlord that you do indeed know what you're doing. The next sections explain how.

Preparing a detailed business plan

A good business plan serves many purposes. It can help you get organized, avoid mistakes, secure financing, and persuade a landlord that you're a tenant worthy of leasing a great location. Often, the landlord won't expect to see a business plan, nor will they ask if you've prepared one. But if you're a startup concept, if you appear to be underfinanced, or if space is at a premium where you want to rent, a business plan can make the difference.

A detailed business plan shows the landlord that you've thought through every step of the business, including the real estate. One of Dale's clients just sent him a great-looking floor plan of their new healthcare office. It was particularly impressive that most of the tenants who take the time to design a space plan do so in 2D. This tenant's space plan was in 3D, and it really popped.

But having a business plan isn't enough. You need to do it right. Here are a few mistakes in your business plan that can hurt you and why.

- ✔ **Don't put the name of the plaza or property where you want to lease on your business plan if you're still negotiating the lease terms.** This screams that you've made an emotional commitment to that property, and the landlord may recognize how much you want the space and try to charge you a higher rental rate or provide fewer inducements.

- ✔ **Don't use the exact dimensions of the property's Commercial Retail Unit (CRU) for your space plan.** This will again show that you have set your sights on leasing that location only. A draft space plan should initially be based on a general size CRU that you require. If you need 3,600 square feet, use a dimension sample of 100 feet deep by 36 feet wide to get started and see if all the moving parts fit into that area. The design can be refined and detailed later when you've selected a specific unit to lease.

- ✔ **Don't include your financials.** You may have to eventually show some detailed financials. Some landlords want to know the source of the money for your venture But don't just lay it out in your business plan for the real estate agent, property manager, and landlord to see. The financial segment of your business plan should be separate and held back. If they think you're undercapitalized or underfinanced, you may not get past first base.

Forming a corporation to become the tenant entity

A businessperson only has a couple choices about the tenant entity in any lease agreement. Knowing up front what you plan to do is vital:

- ✔ **Corporations and Limited Liability Companies (LLCs)**: Forming a corporation or LLC to become the tenant entity is almost always the best choice for a business owner. Corporation and LLCs can limit your personal liability in the event you can't pay the rent or go into some other form of default. Remember, that these things can happen through no fault of your own.

- ✔ **Personal name:** Too many entrepreneurs allow their personal name to creep onto the offer to lease page. All landlords want business owners to list their personal name as tenant because that's the equivalent of giving a personal guaranty and gives the landlord more security. Having a corporation or LLC already formed and ready allows you to put that entity forward officially and technically as the tenant during the lease documentation process.

- ✔ **Professional corporations**: Doctor and healthcare tenants often list their professional corporation as the tenant entity. This is both fine and standard, although some doctors form holding companies to become the tenant entity.

- ✔ **Co-tenancies:** An example would be where three partners all list their personal names on the lease agreement as co-tenants. John, Mary, and Ben all sign the lease agreement, and all three are all responsible (both jointly and severally) for performance of the lease terms. In most cases it is better for these partners to all own shares in the tenant corporation. Their limited liability provides an easier exit strategy should one partner want to leave the business.

Putting your financing in order and checking your credit score

You'll either finance your business startup from cash or liquid assets you already have available, or borrow the funds. Your financing source is extremely relevant to the landlord. On the one hand, they like to know that you're personally and financially committed to making the business work. On the other, if you have limited resources of your own and plan to borrow most or all of it, this can work against you if the landlord finds out.

We recommend that you check your own credit score (before the landlord does). Some of our more savvy clients, knowing they have great credit scores and credit history, pull a credit report on themselves and provide a copy to the landlord, or include it in their business plan.

More importantly, by checking your credit report first, if you find inaccuracies on your credit history, you can do something about it now — before you need to show it.

Three business tools to have now

For first time business owners having some business tools ready in advance can serve you well going into and through the leasing process. You may think this section is simply too much homework, but we assure you that it's not a waste of your time to set these tools up before starting the leasing process.

Business cards

You don't need to wait until the lease agreement is signed or your business is open to print business cards. Being able to hand the landlord or their real estate agent a business card prior to viewing space will make you look professional and committed to launching your business. The business card can include the name of your company, your trade name, and a slogan or some product info. Including your home address, phone number, and e-mail address (and even a website under construction) will make you look ready to become a tenant.

But you're thinking, "Isn't that a waste? I'll only use a few cards and then have to print new ones when I get a business address." Take our advice. Suck it up and splurge. Dale's business cards look totally professional, and he can get 500 (the minimum run) for about $35. Make the investment.

Website and e-mail addresses

Yes, your company needs a website and the sooner the better. A website can help or hurt you, so get it right. You know the old saying that a book is judged by its cover? A business is often judged by its website. If your website looks like an amateur effort, then that's how the landlord will see you. They'll look at your website, whether you know it or not. And if your website looks great, it may have a favorable impact on your leasing.

When landlords are absentee, it's much easier for them to obtain information about your business and your concept from a website than any other way. Think of your company website as your company business plan in action. Include relevant pictures of yourself and/or your product/service along with a profile of your experience in this field or industry.

When it comes to e-mail addresses, leave cute or negatively descriptive e-mail addresses at home. I've seen e-mail addresses that were sexual, referred to drinking, or just plain unprofessional (probably from a more immature time). Your e-mail address should be formed like Dale's: `DaleWillerton@ TheLeaseCoach.com`. Your full name @ your business name .com, ideally with no other punctuations or abbreviations. Keep it simple, classic, and easy to remember.

Business telephone numbers

Using your cell phone number or printing that number on your business card is fine if you like getting lots of calls at all times of the day or night. We don't print our cell phone numbers on our business cards. We prefer that people call us at the office on the office phone. Many business owners have an office number, a store number and their mobile number all on their business card If you're one of those people who love to live on their cell phone, have multiple locations, or spend a lot of time away from your desk, then by all means proceed — it's your prerogative.

Preparing to Begin the Leasing Process

You may not be ready to start the leasing process, but truth be told, whoever is? The thought that you want to keep in mind is that the more you know and understand about the leasing process now, the fewer mistakes you will make along the way. Your natural inclination may be to simply try to avoid mistakes, but you have to get a few swings in too. Going on the defensive won't get your very far; following the advice in this book and getting a good lease consultant to work with you will.

Reading and studying that will pay off

If the landlord knows more about your industry than you do, he'll out- negotiate you on the lease as well. The Lease Coach subscribes to more than 100 business magazines and trade publications covering almost all industries. If you start reading your top three industry news publications now, it can lead you to tradeshows, webinars, and cutting-edge leaders. Staying current with trends in your industry is vital.

If we get a call from an entrepreneur planning to open a tanning salon, spa, or restaurant, we ask them if they've attended any good industry tradeshows recently. Most of them admit that they haven't attended any tradeshows. You don't have to wish that you could learn more; you can, if you're willing to invest in yourself and your company. Dale spent a few minutes on the phone last week talking with an entrepreneur who plans to open an upscale coffee house. Not only does this entrepreneur work in a coffee house, but he had just attended a coffee shop tradeshow. Dale was impressed by his effort, and many landlords will be too.

Visiting your competition or even going to work for them

Yes, that's right — working for your competition can be the cheapest and most effective way to get an inside education to the industry you want to open a business in. One of our clients looking to open an authentic Brazilian steakhouse spent over a year in Brazil working at different steakhouses to perfect his trade before opening his own steakhouse in North America. Why is this important from a leasing perspective?

- ✔ **Landlords feel you have a better chance of success if you've worked in your specific industry — and they're correct.** To some degree, the landlord is taking a chance that you'll be successful. Every lease deal is different, but both parties are taking risks.

- ✔ **You'll see things about the business operation that help you create a better business.** For example, if the clothing store you work for doesn't have enough changing rooms (and they never do), then perhaps your new store will have more of them. If customers where you work complain about insufficient parking, then your site selection process will focus on properties that can give your customers all the parking they want and need.

Opening a New Business — But Where?

The *where* in site selection can mean which city, which side of town, which property in that area, and even which unit in that building. *Where* is the million-dollar question. Every tenant wants to know where to locate their business and become profitable. We're paid a great deal of money to help tenants secure exactly the right location for their business. Why? Because it's just that darned important.

Making a mistake by picking the wrong location for your business is the equivalent of taking the wrong fork in the road; you'll never reach your ideal destination.

Mapping out your future location

We've given this advice to thousands of startup business owners, but only a few times per year do we see entrepreneurs actually do what we're about to share with you. Just a few weeks ago, a veterinarian came in to The Lease

Coach office to discuss getting help with her lease. She had been practicing animal medicine for many years doing locums. Loosely, a *locum* is a doctor filling in for another doctor to keep their practice running, usually when the practice owner takes a leave or sabbatical (health, family, vacation, and so on). This veterinarian had a large city map with a red dot on every location where there was an existing vet clinic. This revealed certain areas that were over- or underserved. She also had put small stickers on sites where good leasing opportunities existed or new commercial properties that were to be constructed the following year. Although for most of us this mapping process would seem a chore, she appeared to have really enjoyed doing the advance research. You can be sure this extra effort will provide her the peace of mind that she chose the best location for her practice.

Franchise tenants are often restricted to specific territories for which they've been awarded (or have purchased) the rights for that particular concept. The smaller the area, the more finite the site selection and leasing process should be. A territory can be a single street or an entire town. If you're getting involved as a franchisee, pay special attention to what territory you ask for. We've seen many franchisees have to switch territories when they can't find a suitable space in their originally chosen territory.

Searching the Internet

Searching the Internet can provide you with much detailed information about sites for lease, without your having to call the listing real estate agent — at least not right off the bat. Most medium-sized and major commercial brokerages post their real estate listings on their websites, indicating which units in a plaza are available or are coming up for lease, plus the rental rates, sizes, and much more.

Sometimes a landlord requests or is searching for a specific type of tenant, such as a medical doctor, retail, restaurant, or office type tenant, which is good to know. We made a leasing inquiry for a client, and the landlord turned the restaurant concept down flat, stating that they can't lease space to any more food tenants, they wanted more retailers.

Some landlords who are well organized or who have 25 or more properties may have a dedicated website for all their commercial real estate holdings. The information may not be current, but it's there for the casual or serious prospective tenant to research.

Don't assume the leasing contact person stated on the website is current. The last thing you want to do is to start divulging information to an agent that lost the listing weeks ago or an employee who doesn't handle the property anymore.

Scouting out prospective locations with drivebys

Drivebys are critical to scoping out any particular location. You don't even leave your car; you simply drive to retail plazas and look them over for available units and suitability to your concept.

We recommend doing nighttime drivebys as well —when it's dark outside, the interior is partially illuminated, and you can sometimes see more than during the daytime.

Resist the temptation to make lease inquiry phone calls from your car while sitting on the parking lot in front of a great location you just discovered. This is a rookie mistake.

Jeff and Dale recently met with a new client, a tenant who was planning to lease a specific unit inside a light industrial property that had just been built. Following the meeting with their client, Jeff and Dale drove to the potential new location to view the property. After viewing the space through the windows and pulling on a couple doors, one of them opened, and they were able to walk right in and speak with the construction crew on site.

When you can get into a space and talk to construction workers and other tenants, you can gather inside information without the real estate agent being there. When we're looking for office space in a high-rise office tower, we walk the hallways of every single floor, especially if the client has indicated a preference for that particular building. We've seen tenants in the midst of moving out and moving in — and plenty of unlisted vacant space.

These vacant units are often not promoted or advertised for lease on the listing agent's website because they're available for sublease by tenants who have moved out. You can get some great sublease deals if you can find them.

Knowing what to look for

Here's a checklist of the most important things to look for when driving by a property:

✔ Look not only for vacancies, but for weak tenants whose business is failing, and who may gladly give up their location if you showed an interest in leasing their space.

✔ Assess the physical aspects of the property, the condition of the asphalt, the landscaping, the awnings, and the general appearance. We took a medical doctor to see a space in a property that showed terribly. Weathered awnings that needed replacing, dirty sidewalks, garbage here and there, and more. We had to explain that even though the land-lord said they would take care of the issues, we pointed out, this level of property management and maintenance was what the prospective tenant had to look forward to if they leased space there. If a property looks bad on the outside, you may want to just keep driving.

✔ Notice whether the parking lot is congested. We like to count how many Mercedes, Lexus, and Cadillacs are in the parking lot if the client is a higher-end retailer — or, say, a dentist who specializes in cosmetic dentistry. Are the pylon signs damaged or missing panels? Are there pul-laway signs on the side of the property, creating unsightly clutter? How does the exterior signage look — fresh and attractive or worn and dull? These all send subliminal messages to shoppers telling them to stay away.

✔ Pay attention to *For Lease* signage on the property. Taking a picture of the *For Lease* signs for future reference can be helpful. Yesterday Dale drove by a property where two competing real estate brokerages had signage displayed. One brokerage was representing the landlord trying to lease vacant spaces in the property. The other brokerage was trying to sublease a space for an existing tenant wanting to move. If you're interested in a property with more than one *For Lease* sign, you should contact both brokerages directly to find out what they're offering.

Allowing Time for the Leasing Process

The leasing process can take differing amounts of time, depending on whether you're opening your first location or your fifth. You can discover a lot during your first few lease deals that you can carry forward, potentially saving you money and time. The key is to give yourself ample time so you can recover from setbacks and delays without it costing you more capital or rent.

Many tenants tell us how pressured they feel by real estate agents who keep pushing them to make a deal or sign a letter of intent. Many have regretted caving in to that pressure and making hasty decisions. Often you'll get a call from the agent saying that someone else is looking at the space you looked at last week, so you better hurry and sign an offer to lease. Don't let stuff like that sway you. Pace yourself. Go at your speed and get it right.

Buying versus Leasing: Pros and Cons

The most common reason tenants lease space instead of buying a location is that 95 percent of all commercial, retail, and office space is for lease and not for sale. There are several opportunities in which you may be able to purchase property: a business condo where you occupy the one unit, a strata title unit, small strip plazas or centers where you're now a landlord to other tenants as well, or standalone buildings on a small piece of land. Major factors that impact this decision for the average tenant are the long-term commitment of purchasing a building and the ability to obtain the financing.

For those tenants in the enviable position of being able to purchase, here are a few pros and cons of purchasing to consider, starting with the pros:

- ✔ Paying a mortgage is better than paying rent. Lease payments are forever, but your mortgage will eventually be paid off (hopefully). Often, your mortgage payment may be very close to your rent obligation.

- ✔ In most cases, you will gain equity in your property; over time your property may double or triple in value. This increase in value is in addition to the value of your business contained within the property.

- ✔ You're in charge. You don't have to deal with the hassles of a landlord or property manager.

Now for the cons:

- ✔ There may be some sacrifice on location, because many of the prime locations may not be available for purchase.

- ✔ If you're vacating an existing location, you may be leaving a great opportunity for a competitor to move into your location.

- ✔ Being in charge is a con as well as a pro. You're the one responsible for all maintenance and repairs issues that a landlord would normally take care of.

When making the decision to purchase or lease, don't make the decision to purchase simply for the sake of owning real estate. Only consider purchasing a space or property if you would be prepared to lease that same location anyway.

Chapter 3

Choosing the Building Type that Best Suits Your Needs

*F*inding the right location or building for your business is one of the most important decisions you can make, but it's not always easy to figure out where your business will do best. You can find the same types of businesses in strip malls, light industrial spaces, and in old quaint downtown houses. Why choose one over the other?

This chapter aims to help you understand the thought processes behind picking the most suitable building type to optimize your sales.

Influences on Your Choice of Space

Too many business owners take a shoot-first, aim-later approach to choosing the right property for their business. Often, serendipity seems to have more to do with the location than serious thought. For example, The Lease Coach has dental tenant clients who are in major malls, strip plazas, office buildings, and even light industrial areas. We also see restaurants, martial arts schools, and even retailers located in every imaginable property.

What makes two tenants in the same business or industry want to locate in such different types or extremes of properties? The reasons are many:

✔ **Available space:** You can only put your business in a building that has space available for lease. And if a competing or similar-use business has already located in that property, then the landlord may not want two of you in such close proximity. If the primary use (service or products offered) for your type of business is already taken in a particular building, you may need to go farther afield to find a location available for your use.

✔ **The hours you plan to keep:** We have restaurant clients who intentionally gravitate to downtown locations for lease because they want to run a Monday-to-Friday type of business. Often downtown cafes don't open on weekends because they cater to employees in downtown office buildings who work weekdays.

✔ **Long-term potential:** Ideally, a tenant should pick a suitable location that they can successfully operate their business from for 10 to 20 years. But often tenants end up moving or relocating several times over the years as they realize they picked the wrong location altogether, the wrong unit within that property, or the wrong size space in that building. These mistakes are costly and can often be avoided by having a long-range time horizon or vision for their business as well as some professional help from a lease consultant.

Analyzing and Comparing Building Types

There's nothing like a pro and con checklist to help you compare one property to another. The site-selection process is where many business analyses fail. To properly compare various properties, it's advantageous to deal on all available leasing opportunities simultaneously. Looking at buildings one at a time gives you no opportunity to compare what's out there. Moving the deal-making process ahead with multiple properties is the key. This section discusses selecting the right type and style of property for lease.

Searching multiple sites before making a single call

When we talk with tenants about how they go through the site selection process, the answers vary.

One thing we can absolutely tell you not to do is to drive around making leasing inquiry phone calls from your car when you're sitting in the property's parking lot. Resist this temptation, no matter how excited you are about a property.

We use site selection sheets to help make our decisions. Use one sheet of paper for each site, and begin gathering the data you need. It's okay to drive to properties and take pictures — but resist the urge to call the listing real estate agent or landlord until you're sitting at your home office, kitchen table, or existing place of business. During the driveby site-selection process, you can often find several properties of interest listed with the same agent or brokerage. If you phone that agent three times about three different listings, in one afternoon, you'll look like a rookie — the equivalent of a tire kicker. You want to be organized, well prepared, and deliberate in your leasing intentions.

By the time The Lease Coach is driving an area looking at properties for our clients, we may have found and discarded several locations that looked good on the Internet — until we drove farther up the road and found better ones.

Speaking of searching for properties on the Internet: Search, look, search, look, and *then* make your call. Website pictures of properties are often limited and can be deceiving.

Seeing the site plan for the property is helpful. The site plan is a diagram or view from above. Poorly done site plans are often not correctly proportioned. If the site plan showing the various units for the property is drawn to scale, the plan will be accurate and easier to work from as you move forward.

Demographic factors that must be considered by area

You need to consider building types by area — but also the demographics and other aspects of the area itself. Information that goes into area analysis includes:

- ✔ **Population density:** The more people living or working in a general area or vicinity to the property you plan to lease, the better. Future growth plans for the area are also important. Many newer properties will be in the suburbs on the outskirts of town. A great plaza may be built on one side of the street where homes are located, but across the street is an empty field that won't be home to families for many years. Waiting for a newer area of the city to mature and become populated can mean a lot of macaroni and cheese years, if your business attracts enough customers at all.

- ✔ **Age and family status:** A commercial property may not physically change much over time, but the age and family situation of local residents can. Daycare centers are a good example of businesses that can boom and bust as the community's ages shift. Just look at what the local residents are driving and how many cars are parked in the driveway — it's not that difficult to get a read on a community.

- ✔ **Income range:** Generally, the higher the income and the more family members earning a wage, the higher the family's disposable income will be. When Dale was doing real estate training for Auto Zone, he realized the company was not trying to open locations in affluent areas where the homeowners drove late model cars. The business model focused on mid- to- lower income areas, where the residents drove older cars and were more inclined to fix those vehicles themselves with parts they bought from the local Auto Zone store. Affluent communities are often surrounded by premium shopping centers or plazas because that's what the residents demand and expect.

✔ **Disposable incomes:** The problem with some affluent areas is that the homeowners are house rich and cash poor, meaning they have less disposable income than you may think. A commercial property near apartment buildings can be a good location or a bad one, depending on whether they're owner-occupied condo apartments or all renters in single bedroom apartments.

✔ **Shopping patterns:** Have you ever considered *when* people buy wine, pizza, or milk, or rent a movie? It's usually on their way home from work (a common shopping habit or pattern). If your business is located on the wrong side of the street of a busy intersection with no ease of access, the consumer may drive right past and pull in where it's more convenient. A retail type business will want to locate where the people are already shopping more so than where they hope the people will come to shop.

✔ **Economic factors:** An oil spill in the gulf, a large plant or factory closure, or an election can all affect the economics of an area. The property where your business is located becomes doubly important when economic times are tough. Tourism can make or break some businesses especially during certain times of the year or peak seasons.

Thinking out of the box

We live in an anything goes or whatever works society, and that philosophy often applies to business locations as well. Near The Lease Coach office, a major restaurant chain went under. The freestanding building was quickly snapped up by a group of orthodontists for their new office. A gas station may close and be converted to a restaurant. A big box store moves and is replaced by a sporting goods anchor that gets one-tenth the traffic. A liquor store opens where a restaurant closes. A chiropractor moves in where a fitness facility failed. And so on.

There are both conventional and unconventional leasing opportunities for every business industry. Perhaps a trophy location will make sense for your business. This is a specific unit that outshines all the other spaces for lease in a property because of its prominence and visibility. Because they are scarce trophy locations do not rent cheap but for some companies it can put their business on the map. Do all dentists need to be located in strip malls? Do all office tenants need to be located in office buildings? Of course not. You need to evaluate every type of building or property that is available because its unique qualities can represent the 20 percent advantage you need to be successful over your competitors.

Evaluating Various Building Types

Not all buildings or properties are created equally.

The more you can think like your customer, the more likely you are to choose the right location for your business.

Although the fundamentals of negotiating leases remain the same, each property has unique aspects that you must factor in. Because the perfect property or site only exists in a fantasy, the challenge for the business owner is to lease a space with the most advantageous set of criteria they can find.

This section goes through the advantages and disadvantages of different locations.

Retail strip plazas

A retail strip plaza may exist with or without anchor tenants. Anchor tenants are large, well-known, heavily trafficked businesses. Unanchored strip plazas are those consisting of small, mom-and-pop type stores. Sometimes several strip plazas are clustered together. Neighborhood plazas typically have a well-rounded mix of tenants, but it's not uncommon to see just four to five tenants in a small strip plaza. Larger landlords typically own the larger plazas, with or without local management.

Typical unit sizes in strip plazas are around 1,200 square feet, depending on the depth of the property. Most retail tenants in a strip plaza want at least 18 to 20 feet of *frontage* (width). If the property is 60 feet deep, then a unit with 20 feet of frontage would be a 1,200 square foot space.

The type of strip mall or plaza you select for your business and its location will determine how far you can expect your customers to travel to your place of business. Consumers like to be able to do multiple tasks on any shopping trip: grab some groceries, pick up the dry cleaning, and stop at the bakery, for example, and possibly without moving their car.

Not every unit in a strip mall is created equal. *End caps* (end units) are the most valuable units for lease; often you'll see a 24-hour convenience store leasing that space and probably paying a premium for it as well. Some advantages of end caps are proximity to the road, plus front and side windows. End cap units are also desirable for drive-through coffee shops, quick service restaurants, and the like. End cap units often have more parking adjacent to the building (if there's no drive-through). Having signage on two sides is also extremely desirable and possible with an end cap unit.

Typically, each retail unit in a strip plaza has a heating, ventilation, and air conditioning (HVAC) system on the roof, with a suitable capacity to properly heat and cool the space below it — but do not take that for granted. Always ask to be sure that your unit comes with a properly working HVAC unit.

If your retail concept or business requires less than 1,200 square feet, you may have trouble finding a space small enough for you in most plazas of this type.

Unanchored strip plazas

When Dale and his wife, Linda, built their first home in the suburbs, unanchored strip plazas popped up at two different entrances to the community. Unanchored plazas are often occupied by independent or even franchise tenants who live in the local area and want to run their businesses for that local community. There are at least a hundred thousand of these small strip plazas located across North America.

Fewer shoppers visit unanchored strip plazas, and therefore rents are usually lower than in anchored plazas. Seeing five to seven stores side by side is common, but the building may also have an L shape. Typical tenants include a convenience store, hair salon, a healthcare professional like a chiropractor or dentist, and maybe a coffee shop, café or dry cleaner. Unanchored plazas are also located and scattered around any community.

Anchored strip plazas

Lots of soon-to-be business owners don't understand the tremendous importance of locating and leasing space within a well-anchored strip plaza. The traffic that the anchors draw to the plaza is part of the reason landlords can typically charge higher rents for these types of properties. The anchor tenant may actually be getting a fairly sweet lease deal from the landlord because of the reciprocal benefit to other regular tenants and the landlord.

If the anchor tenant is set off with its own building and parking lot this will be less advantageous to the rest of the smaller tenants. Ideally for the smaller tenants the anchor tenant will physically comprise part of the plaza, and they will all share a common parking lot making walking from say the grocery store to the dry cleaner easy.

But bear in mind that not all anchor tenants are created equal or provide equal benefit for your business. You must use some good old common sense when evaluating anchored strip plazas. A high-end ladies clothing store located in a property anchored by a home improvement big box store may not benefit from the traffic that the anchor generates.

A strip plaza can qualify as an anchored plaza even if the anchor store is not attached to the plaza. The Lease Coach frequently locates its clients in properties anchored by well-known big box stores or grocery chains, where the main anchor store is freestanding or attached. Where multiple buildings are located on the same property in close proximity, rental rates for specific units will vary by as much as 50 percent. This can depend on each unit or building's proximity to the anchor tenant and access to various roadways. Visibility and accessibility count when it comes to putting a rental value on each building or unit.

The size of the anchored strip plaza (along with the attractiveness of its premium location) will often dictate whether national chains and franchise systems will find their way in as the dominant tenant type. Some plazas are two stories high, with residential or conventional office-type tenants on the second floor. This can put stress on the available parking, but it's generally good for business to have more people working in, living in, and visiting the property.

Enclosed shopping malls

There are several different kinds of shopping malls. Neighborhood shopping malls may have 100 or more tenants and a couple major anchor stores, including a grocery store. A regional shopping center may have 200 or more stores with 4 or more anchor department stores, plus a movie theatre. There are a few super regional malls across North America that dominate and stand out from the rest of the pack. Mall of America in Minnesota and West Edmonton Mall in Alberta are a couple good examples. Whether you are looking at space for lease in a Fashion or Specialty Center, a Lifestyle Center, Outlet Mall, Theme Centers or Power Centers, the leasing process for the tenant is more similar than different.

Most of the tenants in a shopping mall are national and regional chains. Independent tenants are much less common because the landlord wants to lease space to high-volume tenants who will not only pay the base rent but also a percentage rent on top of that. Due to the additional amenities and maintenance that come with an enclosed shopping mall, the operating costs of such malls are typically higher than retail strip plazas.

Rental rates can vary by as much as 300 percent in a shopping mall, depending on where each space or unit is situated relative to entrances, food courts, anchors, and so on. When Dale was a shopping mall manager over 20 years ago, he remembers implementing a traffic counter technology at each mall entrance so mall management could measure the number of shoppers or visitors entering and exiting the property. This allowed the landlord to set rents accordingly, based on traffic counts through the most popular entrances.

Shopping center tenants typically are required to report their monthly sales to the landlord. The landlord can then calculate the average annual sales for any specific category. The higher the average annual sales, the more popular the mall, and, often, the higher the rent. Most major shopping malls are owned by larger sophisticated landlords who may control a hundred or more properties across the country. There's commonly an onsite mall manager and staff to run the day-to-day activities and look after the tenants and shoppers.

Specialty shopping centers and malls often have a much higher mix of independent stores. Dale's sister, Louise, used to operate a mid- to high-end ladies fashion store in a specialty fashion mall located downtown (a common location for specialty malls). Although the mall is small, it does have one major department store anchor and several levels of retail. The specialty mall is both beautiful and enjoyable to shop in if you're looking for variety and personal service because the ratio of independent tenants to chains is often higher in these types of properties.

Office buildings

Office tenants can choose from simple one-story buildings right up through downtown high-rise properties. The variety of office buildings and their locations is quite extreme. Some office buildings are so large they're almost communities unto themselves, with their own food and service tenants. These office buildings may be linked to other properties with pedestrian walkways. Typically, downtown office properties are more expensive to lease, and the operating costs are commensurately higher as well.

A major factor when determining which office building to lease space within may be the parking — both availability and cost. Also, public transportation to the office building is part of the decision-making process.

For a smaller office building in an outlying area, you may be able to have signage on the building or the property to identify your company, but this isn't so common downtown. The building and property amenities vary greatly. The larger, high-rise properties often have shared common washrooms, meeting rooms, and nightly janitorial services for the tenants. Even having a café tenant inside the building can be considered an amenity that allows for greater productivity and comfort to the business owners and their employees.

Industrial properties and warehouses

There are both *light* and *heavy* industrial properties, depending on the area and nature of what tenants need. Some office type tenants will locate in light industrial buildings. Having a couple thousand square feet of retail space out front and several more thousand square feet of warehouse space at the back can be ideal for many tenants.

Many industrial buildings have very high ceilings, allowing tenants to partially or completely develop a mezzanine level. Mezzanine space may or may not be determined a rentable area, meaning your mezzanine space may not be calculated into the rent for the unit. If the mezzanine level is undeveloped or much smaller in area that the main floor, this may justify a lower rental rate per square foot — or no base rent at all. Perhaps operating costs will be waived on the mezzanine level as well.

Sometimes you can calculate rent for industrial units using a combined or blended method. For example, the front retail area of 2,000 square feet may be at $10 per square foot. The warehouse area of 6,000 square feet at the back may rent for $4 per square foot. And the mezzanine area may be at $6 per square foot (with no operating costs). Using a blended rent formula like this may help justify or equalize the value of one unit compared to another when those units are dissimilar in design, layout, or interior build-out.

Although landlords typically have standard rent application practices for their own properties, there's no absolute rule in how different areas are calculated as rentable: It's essentially negotiable.

Typically, light and heavy industrial tenants are particularly interested in the loading area at the back of their space and whether there's a raised or ground level loading dock. This may determine whether the tenant needs to buy a forklift, depending on the amount of shipping and receiving.

Mixed use properties

One of the first properties Dale managed for a landlord was a mixed-use property. It was a three-level retail shopping center with a ten-story office tower. A food court, retail tenants, and office tenants were all under one roof. Such properties are most commonly found downtown or in higher density areas. Sometimes there is even a residential component to the property. One accountant The Lease Coach used for itself had their office space located on the main floor of a mixed-use property and lived in one of the high-rise residential apartment units above the main floor restaurant and other commercial tenants.

Stand-alone buildings & pad sites

A stand-alone building can be situated on a single parcel of real estate or located on a multi-tenant piece of land. Leasing opportunities exist for stand-alone buildings on these pad sites where the landlord has designated certain pad areas for stand alone tenants. Many quick service restaurants (QSRs — formerly called fast-food restaurants) and even fine dining restaurants are built on pad sites. They may be leasing the land or pad site and/or the building itself. Some tenants lease a pad site for a 20-year term and construct their own building — essentially paying rent on the land only.

If the tenant is leasing the pad site land only — and spending their own money to construct the building, then the key is to have a long 20 year lease term with renewal options in order to have enough time to recapture their investment.

Other types of locations and properties

There are endless places to locate a business outside the usual strip plaza or shopping center location. Consider which type of property works best for your specific business or use before starting serious negotiations on any of the following types.

Discount centers

Most discount centers were not built originally as discount centers. Discount centers are usually older properties or malls that are no longer attractive to most shoppers or prime retail tenants. The right tenant in the right discount center can do quite well but, there is a tipping point where too many vacancies create an uneasy atmosphere for shoppers, and they simply don't come there to shop. As you can imagine rental rates in discount centers are often much lower than newer retail properties.

If an enclosed mall has been converted to a discount center and has a location and entrance that is shopper accessible from the outside of the building (from the parking lot), this is much more attractive to shoppers who don't want to walk the whole mall. One of The Lease Coach clients is a large Christian retail and gift store in exactly this type of situation. If shoppers had to enter the main entrance of a partially vacant mall then continue walking farther to enter this tenant's store, it would discourage many would-be shoppers who are not willing to make the effort.

Discount centers are sometimes unpainted and unkempt, with broken up parking pads, and other unappealing features. A discount store in a discount center may make sense for some retailers, but mainstream modern chains or franchises need to evaluate whether a center with a tired look will reflect poorly on their brand.

Power centers and big box centers

Power centers are open-air big-box shopping destinations that attract consumers from 20 or more miles away. Large parcels of land, often developed over many years, include various recognizable big box tenants and smaller retail tenants as well. Most tenants are national or regional multi-unit tenants including department or large big box specialty stores that may be considered category killers for their particular use or type of business.

Because these properties are so large, and driving around from store cluster to cluster is part of the shopping requirement, picking compatible or complimentary neighbors is desirable, not just within power centers but within your cluster of tenants. A dress shop beside a shoe store beside a jewelry store makes perfect sense and maximizes the ability to share and draw common profile customers with neighboring tenants.

Factory outlet centers

In a factory outlet center, larger, often well-known name brand stores move in to sell both current and discounted or last season merchandise. A handful of developers own and control most of these factory outlets, which is why you often see the same chain and franchise stores in these centers all across the country.

Regionally, the flavor of the centers change somewhat, but they are most typically open-air strip plazas clustered together for ease of walking, shopping, and dining. Most feature cavernous parking lots that can require a GPS to find your car after a long day of shopping.

Home improvement centers

These are not necessarily the properties anchored by the giants of home improvement; often they're strip plazas and clusters of properties that are leased to companies selling floor coverings, furniture, paint shops, tile and bath stores, and so on. Having complementary businesses all in one area allows customers to shop for everything they need for a home-improvement project without running all over town. The home improvement center near The Lease Coach office includes tenants specializing in floor coverings, windows, doors, lighting, and similar types of uses.

Airport space

With Dale's and Jeff's busy speaking schedules, they are on the road a lot, and they are very accustomed to spending money at airport malls and restaurants. Specialty tenants, especially those in the food service or restaurant industry, are often interested in space for lease at airports. Airports can be an extremely difficult opportunity to crack for an independent or franchise tenant, especially in larger airports.

With limited space available, the airport authority can pretty much choose the mix of tenants it wants. Some tenants appear to do well, but this is not always the case. Often airport tenants pay higher wages to attract employees to these remote locations. There can also be added delivery costs and storage requirements.

Just because an airport appears to have a captive audience of shoppers or diners doesn't mean these locations are licensed to print money. Your physical location within the airport mall or food court is just as important there as in any other property. Recently, a franchise tenant told us that his first quick service restaurant (QSR) failed in his airport location. So be cautious in locations where it's difficult to control your destiny; no amount of advertising will make anyone drive to the airport to shop or dine unless they are flying somewhere.

Storage space

Last last week our office received a flyer in the mail from a developer who was building a storage plaza. These were fairly good-sized units that could be leased or purchased for businesses requiring safe, permanent storage for products they were receiving and shipping. These are not locations where business is to be conducted but rather in most cases to house extra inventory. The higher the rent per square foot a tenant is paying in their primary location, the more sense cheap offsite storage or warehouse space makes.

Condos

A condo is not a type of building — it's a type of ownership. When a landlord condominiumizes a property, they are creating individual ownership opportunities. Condos can apply to any type of building, but not to just a portion of the building. A building is either all condos or none. This may not be self-evident if the landlord condominiumizes a property, sells off some units, and keeps some for himself.

Owning your own condo unit can be appealing for various reasons, including the following:

- Creating equity, which you can use for other business ventures and projects.

- Appreciating value in the condo or property can make you wealthier.

- Having greater control over what happens to the building and how you run your business is very appealing to many entrepreneurs and business people.

- The ability for long-term planning without worrying about what your landlord may do or if they will raise your rent can give you peace of mind and even fulfillment.

The Lease Coach frequently helps all types of business owners purchase or lease-to-purchase condominium units for their business. One of our clients not only did so, but when he sold the property less than ten years later, he was able to almost triple the return on his investment because property values had increased so much over that time period.

 The key is not to buy a location that you wouldn't lease anyway. This is critical if your type of business is location sensitive. It won't do you much good to own a property or condo unit if your business fails due to a poor location.

Kiosks

Whether you're shopping at the mall, the airport, or almost anywhere, you're bound to see kiosks. From jewelry to toys, or hair extensions, you can buy almost anything at a kiosk. There are two types of kiosks:

- ✔ **Temporary kiosks** at your local mall may include the space and or a cart that you rent by the day, week, or month. The landlord provides electrical power, and the tenant sets up shop. Although these kiosks can be profitable, the kiosk's location within the property is critical. Weekends tend to be where kiosk tenants do a good volume of sales; weekdays can be slower because foot traffic past the kiosk is reduced. Kiosk sales are largely impulse purchases, so shoppers must be walking by the kiosk to buy from you.

- ✔ **Permanent kiosks**. Often the lease term is three to five years. Although the rent per square foot may seem ridiculously high, the volume of potential business is high in the popular malls where traffic is plentiful. The tenant normally has to construct their own kiosk, hook into water, power, and so on. Every square foot counts when you're limited to a kiosk, so the design of the kiosk can be critical to fully maximizing your selling opportunity.

Home conversions

It's quite interesting how many houses, especially older homes in older areas, have been converted to businesses. There are entire streets or blocks where almost all the homes have been converted for business use. Sometimes the business owner is both tenant and property owner, but simply leasing these properties is also common. From dentists to travel agents, hair salons, and law offices, every conceivable industry has tried this type of location or property.

Not all prospective customers enjoy the type of atmosphere and feeling they get from walking into a business operating from a converted home or house. There can also be many more electrical, plumbing, and technology issues to conquer in a home renovation than in a regular commercial property. You may have such issues as a lack of parking or zoning in some areas.

Preleasing Undeveloped Property

The most potentially unpredictable lease agreement for a tenant to enter into is a *prelease of undeveloped property*. Why? Because you can't touch the bricks and mortar or visually assess the property. Often in these deals the tenant is required to make a long-term leasing decision and commitment based on design drawings from the landlord — which the landlord can unilaterally change. Additionally, there are no existing tenants to talk to about how their business is doing within the property, because none of them is open yet. In one such prelease deal, the landlord not only changed the color scheme and exterior look of the property (to save money) but did so against the wishes of the tenants who had already signed up.

On the other hand, some of the best leasing locations are preleasing opportunities or new properties under development, especially if the physical location or land is well situated. The Lease Coach has successfully completed many prelease deals for our clients, with excellent long-term results. Just keep in mind that landlords often reserve the right to make changes to your unit without tenant consent. This can affect the shape, size, even physical location of the tenant's demised premises, the building itself, or even grouping of buildings.

One trap to avoid is signing the lease agreement on the dotted line and then waiting months while the landlord tries to finish leasing up the property. Some landlords won't or can't afford to start construction until they hit a set percentage of done deals or leased space. The agreement with the mortgage holder may be that once the landlord gets signed lease commitments for 50 or 60 percent of the property, the funding package is approved and finalized, and the property can be built.

More than a few tenants have signed prelease agreements only to be kept on the hook waiting for a year or more. In some cases, the property never was developed. We talked last week to a client who earlier took our advice and passed up a prelease opportunity for various reasons. He reported that the property was not actually built for over five years because interest was not strong enough. You may get your deposit back, but that's little comfort if your business dreams have been kept on hold for years. And it's not all in the landlord's control — even an ethical, well-intentioned landlord can encounter problems and delays.

The more time-sensitive the opening date is for your business, the more you need to negotiate for a right to terminate if the landlord cannot or will not proceed with construction of the property. This is incredibly important.

Another trap to avoid is where the landlord is going forward with the development but has only secured a handful of tenants. Shoppers are not attracted to a property if every second unit is vacant. A proper tenant mix and synergy is required, especially for retail plazas and malls to be successful.

If you're one of the first tenants signing a pre-lease for a new development, you may be disappointed with who your neighboring tenants are. The marketing materials for the property may show a great mix of potential tenants, but this is only a wish list for the landlord. If a specific anchor tenant or other tenants never materialize, this obviously affects your site selection process and even the rent you're willing or capable of paying at that property.

The Lease Coach frequently negotiates for a longer rent-free period or a period of time where the rent is discounted if the rest of the property remains undeveloped or if the anchor tenant is not in place or open to the public. For example, a tenant may agree to pay $28 per square foot — but they only have to pay the proportionate percentage of that rent relevant to the occupancy level of the property. As the property gets fully leased (more specifically, as tenants open) a higher percentage of that $28 is paid. So if the building is 58 percent leased, our client pays 58 percent of $28 per square foot. You don't want to be the first tenant open and paying full rent if the common areas and parking areas are still under construction and unpaved. Shoppers don't want to navigate a construction zone just to get to your business.

Chapter 4

Selecting the Most Profitable Site for Your Business

• •

In This Chapter

▶ Choosing the right site

▶ Examining why different industries need different types of space

▶ Determining which site will make your business the most profitable

▶ Evaluating different sites

• •

*T*he location a business owner leases is like the foundation upon which every other brick is laid during the leasing process. Tenants understand this intellectually but often make poor site selection choices based on scarcity, timing, or other factors that positively or negatively influence them. Prospective first-time tenants need to adopt the mindset that if they don't find the right location, at the right rental rate, at the right time — they'll walk away and *not* lease the wrong location.

But this rarely happens in real life.

In real life, you want to open a business by a certain date or season. You start looking for sites, and you simply choose from what's available for lease at the time, in that area, in that rental rate price range. In some cases, tenants are simply leasing the best of the worst locations available, justifying their actions by saying there weren't many sites to pick from. This is the equivalent of telling your daughter that by her 21st birthday she must be married, regardless of whom she's dating. And if she's not dating someone, then she must go to the local pub and pick her man by midnight.

This is what can happen when you're working on a leasing deadline.

 It's better to live to fight another day than to lease a location that slowly kills your business concept and stifles your dream of running your own company — all for the sake of timing.

This chapter talks about how to avoid making this common mistake (and others) when selecting and leasing a site for your business.

Figuring Out Where Your Business Will Thrive, Not Just Survive

Just this week The Lease Coach met with a client who has over 30 locations — yet she candidly admitted that even at this stage, she didn't really understand the process for finding the right properties and locations to help make each of her businesses as profitable as possible.

The leasing and site-selection process is not easy or even enjoyable for most tenants. But predicable results can be achieved with a proper game plan and some help from a professional lease consultant who works for you, the tenant. This is an monumental decision that can cost you a small fortune if you get it wrong. Don't automatically turn to a real estate agent for site selection help — Dale and Jeff frequently get discouraging calls from frustrated entrepreneurs, franchisees, and healthcare professionals who were led by agents to easy deal-making locations versus the right or best location for that tenant.

The core reason tenants struggle with and fail to lease the optimum site for their business is simply the lack of knowledge that comes from insufficient experience. If you combine that with impatience, you've got a disaster in the making.

Making the location you lease a priority

This is the part of the book where we're obligated to use that old cliché, which you knew was coming sooner or later: *location, location, location.*

Because a location or commercial property is good for one industry or one type of tenant doesn't mean the property is universally as good or equally beneficial for all tenants.

When Jeff or Dale visits any of our 1,200-plus clients across the country (many of whom have hired The Lease Coach to negotiate their lease renewal), we ask why they thought so many years ago this would make a good property or location for their business. In their answers, not a single tenant emphasizes how much time or effort they put into site selection and how they carefully negotiated and shortlisted properties down to the right or perfect location. Rather, their location decision-making process took second place to idealistic plans of opening and running a quality business with fair prices, mistakenly thinking customers would beat a path to their door wherever that door was located.

Let's be clear here. We're not talking about your loving a property or feeling good or confident that a location is right for your business. We're talking about doing your homework to ensure that it's right. If your first priority is to find the right property, then you'll save time and energy by not working on lease deals that are better left alone because of their mediocre location.

Weighing rental costs and potential sales

When it comes to leasing commercial space, in general, you get what you pay for — and the more you pay, the better the location. But if that was an *absolute* truth, all a tenant has to do is find the most expensive location for lease and set up shop. But it's *not* an absolute truth. Tenants frequently sign long term lease agreements agreeing to pay rental rates that could have been negotiated much lower. Part of the reason The Lease Coach is successful in negotiating lease renewal rent reductions for so many tenants all across the country is because the tenant initially agreed to pay a rental rate that was too high in the first place. This is where the pastor at Dale's church would say "Can I have an Amen to that brother".

It's critically important to the business owner to crunch the rental numbers against the projected sales volumes for the particular business they plan to open. One entrepreneur couple in New Jersey we were coaching sent us their business plan, which clearly showed their anticipated sales volume. The locations for lease that were catching their attention and interest could have been considered either cheap or expensive, depending on the type of business and projected gross sales anticipated from that location.

We showed the couple that even if they achieved 100 percent of their projected sales volume, they would be paying approximately 35 percent of their gross revenues just to pay the rent each month. This formula simply cannot work; that percentage of gross sales to gross rent is far too high for any business, let alone the coffee shop/café they wanted to open. (See Chapter 13 for more help figuring what your business can afford to pay in rent.) Unless the couple in this case study realistically projects higher sales volume, they simply can't afford to lease these types of locations.

Most sophisticated retailers measure their success in *sales per square foot* not in gross sales for any particular location. A multi-unit chain tenant or retailer may report that one of their smaller stores is actually more profitable than their larger stores. Profit is king for a business, and if the rents per square foot are comparable, but the smaller store has higher sales per square foot, then smaller wins.

Looking at location variables

When you're looking for the right property, having a checklist of desirable criteria can help you stay on track. One of the reasons we like working with franchise tenants is that the good franchisors have a custom checklist of desirable criteria for their perfect location. These variables may include anywhere from 10 to more than 30 points the franchisee must address as part of the site-selection process.

Of course, one location may be desirable for one industry, but it may not score as high for another industry. The variables or demographic statistics don't change, but the value you credit to them for any particular use may vary. Whenever possible, we try to visit sites in person or at least see pictures or video of a property, because there's also an intangible component to site selection, which statistically cannot be captured on paper. Dale experienced this recently working with a tenant in Dallas, where he found that it was obvious that the local residents had made one nice property their go-to plaza and meeting place.

Demographics

You should weigh many demographic aspects when considering leasing a location in a certain area or territory. Just because you've found a new property with space for lease doesn't mean the demographics will fit your ideal criteria. Especially consider the following when searching:

- ✔ **Age:** The average age of the people living in a particular area is extremely important to many business owners.

- ✔ **Type of home:** Whether people are living in apartment buildings or luxury homes is truly relevant. For example, people living in apartments can't physically accumulate consumer goods like a large homeowner can.

- ✔ **Income:** As mean income and the proportion of two-income households vary, so do the ability and desire to spend disposable income at your shop.

- ✔ **Ethnicity:** Set up shop where your target customers already live if possible, rather than try to make them come to you. Leasing space for a new Italian coffee shop in an area populated by Asians who may be more inclined to favor tea over coffee could be a mistake.

Traffic flow and visibility

There were two movie rental stores in Dale's neighborhood, and he noticed that his wife always went to one but not the other. She explained that driving to one movie store required a few easy right-hand turns, but the competitor's location required her to make a left-hand turn against a busy intersection and traffic light and then cut through another parking lot, or she could loop around out of her way and cut in front of the police station — but either way it wasn't worth it.

If you don't think it matters which side of the street your business is located on, think again. Liquor and wine stores, for example, do better on the side of the street where most people are driving home after work. Most people don't buy booze on their way to work.

Traffic flow past a commercial property becomes more important when your product or service is generic. For example, to consumers it doesn't matter which store they buy their favorite name-brand cola at because the product is the same, although price may be a factor. Conversely, Dale's wife would willingly navigate any traffic maze to visit her favorite hairstylist, but not to rent a movie, because a hairstylist offers a very personal and unique service experience, but movies all look the same regardless of which store they are rented from (by the way, the hard-to-access movie rental store is now closed).

Lack of visibility for your store front can cause people to drive right by it, especially if traffic is heavy. Trees in a parking lot can block signage and restrict visibility for drivers passing by. Some landlords overbuild their pad sites near the road, blocking the visibility of the retail plaza behind it.

For some tenants, visibility and traffic aren't top priorities, and therefore paying premium rents for prime locations where these factors are strong can be a mistake. Second floor space in a strip center, space in the back or corner of a plaza, or out of the way office space can be appealing and suitable for many tenants if you don't rely on convenience factors or walk-by traffic to drive sales.

For tenants like dance studios, learning centers, and specialized medical professionals, factors such as being in the target neighborhood, an abundance of parking, or the correct tenant mix of the center may be more important than leasing the unit with the highest exposure, especially if it comes at a premium rental rate as well.

A few years ago The Lease Coach worked with a denturist who was looking at space in a retail strip center but was concerned about the high rent. When asked where most of his business came from, he revealed that the majority of patients needing dentures were referred to him by dentists and other customers or patients — which meant that a prime retail presence wasn't going to give or be a significant benefit to this type of business. Of course a prime location wouldn't hurt, but why pay higher rent than you need to if there is no corresponding benefit? The plaza we most preferred for this denturist was a two-level building with retail tenants on the main floor and a second floor dedicated to office and professional tenants, including a number of dentists he could also get referrals from. We ended up negotiating a lease for a space on the second floor at significantly lower rental rates than the retail space below or the initial strip center he was considering, while keeping him in the right neighborhood.

If you find a great property with space available for lease, look around. If there is a bare patch of ground between your desired unit for lease and the roadway, assume that someday the landlord will lease that pad site or construct a building there that blocks visibility to your signage and storefront.

Competition

If you don't know who your competition is and where they're located, you can't hope to compete with them.

Not only should you be acutely aware of your competitor's services, products, and pricing, you should have someone secret shop their business, try their services or products, and report back to you about the experience. As a bonus, have the secret shopper ask them about *your* business (if you're already open) to discover what your competitor is saying about your business — or if they're badmouthing you to their customers.

A personal fitness tenant decided to lease a quiet location on a back street with very limited visibility (against our strong recommendations to go with a more central and visible location). There were prime retail sites available on the main drag, but the higher rents scared her. She set up shop in a nice but out-of-the-way location. Just as we predicted, a few years later a competitor came to town and leased a prime space for their fitness center on the main drag and basically outmaneuvered her real estate wise with a superior location. Part of the site selection process is anticipating where your competitor may lease space or set up shop in the years to follow.

You also have to think in terms of *future* competitors. Check out which competing franchise systems are expanding within your city or planning to come to town.

There are two sides to the competition coin:

- ✔ **Join them:** Locating beside or near your competition to siphon off their customers is a legitimate site-selection strategy for some businesses. One mall had five stores that sold leather coats as their primary or ancillary product mix, which attracted many potential shoppers who wanted plenty of selection from a single destination. Dale shopped all five stores in less than an hour and one of them got his business. There are "restaurant row" and "fashion mall" areas that attract many more shoppers because so many similar tenants are close to each other.

- ✔ **Avoid them:** Locating away from the competition often makes sense to healthcare businesses like dental offices, chiropractors, veterinarians, fitness clubs, tanning salons, and any personalized businesses. Customers tend to be loyal to these businesses because they can only use one at a time. Many people have one hairstylist who gives them customized service, for example. But if you're buying an energy drink from a convenience store, you won't be loyal to that convenience store, unless there's some form of price advantage.

The tenant you want to cozy up to with your business could be planning to move or may even go out of business. You need to do a little due diligence here; talk to the neighboring tenants, talk to the landlord, and protect yourself as far as possible. Ultimately you may want to wait and lease that competitor's location when they close. The Lease Coach has done this for tenants and the key is to not wait until the tenant actually closes (and the *For Lease* sign goes up), but to approach the landlord in advance because the landlord could have another prospective tenant for that same space not knowing that you are waiting on the sidelines for your chance.

Distinguishing Sites That Make Sense for Your Business

Just because a developer bought some land and put up a building doesn't mean the site is automatically a winner. Perhaps 30 years ago it was a great neighborhood, but now it's gone downhill. Some areas are overdeveloped, meaning that another retail site isn't needed or justified from a tenant demand perspective. The *build it and they will come* mentality may make sense when the economy is booming, but it's amazing how many unnecessary retail plazas and marketplaces spring up when existing properties in the area have significant vacancies.

There are two ways to look at whether a specific retail site makes sense for you to consider leasing for your business:

- ✔ Are you planning to open a business that people will travel for miles to shop at? A good maternity store can attract shoppers from more than 100 miles away.

- ✔ Are you taking your business to where people already are, such as downtown or the suburbs or a large shopping entertainment development? A convenience store can only hope to catch customers within a small radius of its location.

Don't assume that franchisors and chain stores automatically know what they're doing when it comes to picking a retail site. Often these locations are selected for the franchisee tenant by an outside real estate agent who may see an easy commission with little work. Or perhaps the location was selected by an innocent or inexperienced franchisee or the franchisor's area manager or developer based on some weak criteria. A major submarine sandwich franchisee opened in a plaza near Dale's home. It was obviously a bad location choice for several reasons. The community didn't need another plaza, let alone another quick service restaurant in that particular area. Sure enough, though this chain had over 10,000 locations worldwide, this one opened and closed within the year.

Once a restaurant location, always a restaurant location

One of the most enjoyable aspects of being The Lease Coach is traveling and speaking at conventions and tradeshows. Dale and Jeff speak to thousands of restaurant owners each year all over the country — and even more if you include their leasing webinars hosted by restaurant associations. At least three out of four restaurant tenants who come up to speak with Dale after presentations and workshops admit they picked an inadequate or wrong location for their restaurant. Yet at the time of signing their lease agreement, they were all virtually certain they had found a gold mine spot, and hungry patrons would come flowing in as soon as the doors opened.

One of the special aspects about restaurants is that the diversity in cuisine, size, and concept means that they vary greatly. Every imaginable site or location has been leased for one of the half million restaurant operations in America. And when one restaurant closes or goes out of business in a specific location, often another restaurant opens in exactly the same space within a year. Restaurant locations that close and re-open in the same space repeatedly are often called *burned sites*.

Why does this happen? There's a logical reason. Building out a restaurant can be expensive. Think of all the plumbing and wiring that needs to be done. Grease traps, oven hoods, and extra power are usually added to the premises. So, if a restaurant entrepreneur wants to save startup money, they will open their new restaurant where another restaurant has vacated or failed. This isn't necessarily a good practice from a site-selection perspective, but it's why this scenario repeats itself over and over again. Note that landlords who are left with a vacant restaurant space often target or try to attract another restaurant concept (on their For Lease Sign) because of the industry infrastructure left behind and the potential to charge another restaurateur a higher rental rate because of the potentially low set up cost for their business. Trap or opportunity — you decide.

Choosing between inline space, end caps, and stand-alone pad sites

Inline space refers to a standard commercial retail unit (CRU), like you see in a strip plaza or shopping mall. The units are "in line" with each other. This type of space is most common and typically allows for both smaller and larger concepts. Often the landlord or developer will create inline CRUs that are about 1,200 square feet in size.

Quick service restaurants and convenience stores often lease an end cap unit. This is the end of the strip plaza often with a front and side set of windows. This is especially desirable to QSR's and coffee shop tenants if there is a drive-through window opportunity. End caps often lease for a premium or higher rental rate and though many types of tenant may try to get the end cap landlords often save them for the highest and best use tenant — who is also willing to pay higher rents.

Stand-alone or pad site space is often close to the street and has parking on all four sides of the building. This allows for more windows and a greater opportunity for patio space. One unique advantage to the stand-alone property is the ability to create an efficient drive-through business. Drive-throughs can be done with end-cap units that are inline as well, but not necessarily as effectively as with stand-alone buildings.

With pad sites the tenant has the option of leasing the land, say for 20 years, and constructing their own building. Or the tenant and landlord can agree to a more conventional lease deal that involves a landlord-constructed building, sometimes with custom tenant specifications. These pad site properties are often in positions closer to the road with greater visibility than the retail plaza located behind it.

Pad site tenants may not need extra pylon signage along the roadway if the signage on their building is large and visible enough — but can any tenant really have too much signage? It's a cost versus value consideration the tenant needs to make.

Looking for a franchise site

Prospective franchisees are banking on a proven brand for their success, but finding the perfect location for a franchise concept can still be quite challenging. One pizzeria franchisee told us that there was such fierce competition for good pizzeria sites that as the tenant, they didn't negotiate the rental rate and simply agreed to whatever deal the landlord wanted. This was not an isolated incident but in many market places the franchise tenant can still get a great lease deal if they know what they are doing.

There are approximately 3,000 franchise brands in North America, with food service being a dominate category, and most of them lease space for their business. Much of the same leasing philosophy given in this book applies to franchise tenants. The main difference is name or brand recognition. If you can throw out to a landlord that you are a franchisee of a famous and recognizable brand, the landlord or their real estate agent may show greater interest in your concept.

If the franchise concept you're buying into has a site criteria list, ask for it, and make sure you use it or include it in the leasing process. For example, a franchisor may stipulate that a good location is dictated by certain factors, such as age, population density, or income levels. A high-end frozen yogurt concept may do better in a more affluent or touristy area, for example.

A franchisor may have a lease addendum that it expects you to attach to the lease agreement that the landlord signs. This addendum may give the franchisor certain rights to take over your location and lease it for themselves or to another franchisee if you go broke. It will also state that the franchisor is to be notified if you're behind in rent, for example, or in any form of default on the lease agreement.

Using the franchise advantage during the leasing process

What is the franchise advantage? The depth and experience of the franchisor, along with the brand and name of the franchise concept, may open leasing opportunity doors for you that would be difficult to crack as an independent tenant. The fact is, for new developments, most landlords strive for up to 100 percent national and regional chains and franchise tenants. Obviously, the brand-name recognition of a franchise can influence a landlord's interest in you. When The Lease Coach is working with regional franchise brands that are expanding to another region of the country, the franchisor's success may not yet have reached the eyes and ears of the landlords in that area, but the advantage remains intact.

As a franchise tenant, you should be able to negotiate better lease terms and inducement packages than most independent tenants. The landlord's risk is lower when accepting a franchise tenant, and franchises bring greater prestige and value to the landlord's property.

Getting leasing help from your franchisor

A soon-to-be multi-unit franchisee told us that his franchisor had promised him extensive real estate support throughout the site selection and leasing process. When he and his wife went to the franchisor headquarters for the training program, they were surrounded by other wide-eyed new franchisees anxiously waiting to be trained so they could start opening locations. On the fourth day of training, the franchisee went out for a walk to escape the class-room claustrophobia. By the time he returned, the trainer had completely covered the real estate component of the course. Although there was plenty of reading material, there really wasn't any hands-on effort to help the fran-chisee during the actual leasing process — resulting in the tenant turning to The Lease Coach for that help.

Some franchisors are active in the site selection and lease negotiation pro-cess, but far too many simply introduce the franchisee to a local broker who supposedly works for the tenant. The problem is that the broker or agent is usually collecting a commission from the landlord. From most landlords' perspectives, any and all agents or brokers who are receiving a commission from the landlord are supposed to be serving the landlord's best interest, not the tenant's. While Dale is pro-franchising and is brought in by franchisors to speak and give their franchisees real estate training, this is a legitimate area of concern for many franchisees. How much hands-on help will they really get?

One franchisor with several hundred locations called The Lease Coach for advice about site selection for its franchisees. Dale explained that there was no magic bullet to site selection — you had to go there and do the site selec-tion hands-on. The franchisor said they did not have the money or the team to personally go to each franchise city (despite charging a $25 thousand dollar franchise fee).

One franchisee asked Dale why the franchisor's designated real estate agent was only showing her the agent's own listings. We explained that if she leased one of his listings, that agent would receive a full commission. She was unaware of commission splitting between agents and how it can be a deterrent to the tenant actually getting a great location. The franchisee said, "What about all the other locations the agent did not show me — don't I get to see those too?" A listing agent may try to protect their listing (so they can earn a full commission) therefore, if you as a franchisee let an outside agent introduce you to a property for lease your prospective tenancy may take second place to a tenant the listing agent finds for themselves. This is explained in more detail in Chapter 5.

If you want a professional to help you do site selection and negotiate your lease, expect to pay for their services. When was the last time you got anything of real value for free?

Note to franchisors reading this section: I like you, I admire what you have accomplished and the massive contribution your franchise system is making to the job market and the economy. Ideally, the franchisor can participate in all levels of the leasing process, from site selection, to lease negotiation, and finalizing the formal lease documents. However, not all franchisors have qualified and experienced in-house real estate people or resources to do that. I understand, your franchisees understand — all I ask is that you give your franchisees a copy of this book and give them a fighting chance. They will probably find this book online or in a bookstore and buy it anyway — so take a leadership role and make this book mandatory reading for all your new and existing franchisees — franchisees facing lease renewals need help too.

Finding a healthcare location worthy of your practice

The reason we say *worthy of your practice* is because most healthcare practitioners spend up to eight years in college getting doctorate degrees. For the most part, these are professionals who are dedicating their lives to keeping the rest of society healthy. These doctors deserve excellent locations allowing them to run profitable practices and to sell those practices when they retire. However, the demand for quality dental, chiropractic, and other health-related spaces, for example, is high. This means many doctors, dentists, chiropractors, optometrists, veterinarians, and others often mistakenly settle for lesser locations — resulting in a lighter patient load, less income, and a practice worth less money 25 to 30 years later when it's time to retire and sell it.

Doctors need to be very careful that the landlord's real estate agent doesn't try to charge them an artificially higher rental rate just because they are doctors. The perception is that doctors charge high professional fees, so they can afford to pay high rents. That's not necessarily correct. It is true that building out a healthcare office can be crazy expensive, which is all the more reason that doctor tenants need reasonable lease terms.

As negotiators, most doctors prefer to avoid confrontation and openly admit they need and want help with their new leases and lease renewal deals. Mistakenly, professional tenants often turn to attorneys for help thinking this is a legal process thereby not getting much help on the real estate side. If you know you're not a good negotiator or don't have time to handle the business side of your practice, hire the right type of help — get a professional lease consultant who is actually working for and being paid by you to represent you.

Getting the location right so you don't have to move your practice

Moving or relocating any business, let alone a healthcare office, is expensive. So if you don't get the location right when you sign a long-term lease agreement, you may be taking on the future expense of relocating at the end of your lease term.

Some of the same components of a good retail lease also apply to a doctor's space requirements for lease. Dentists, chiropractors, and optometrists need new patients to replace the ones they've helped and healed. So a strong location is often very important to these professionals, especially in the formative years of establishing their practice. Many dental offices, for example, are only open four or five days a week, while the retailers beside them are open seven days a week. So some dentists must do all their business in a shorter time period to pay the same rents that retailers pay while being open longer. Of course there are medical, dental, and chiropractic offices open every day of the week, but these are usually multiple doctors' offices that can share the work and the patient load.

Becoming the golden tenant to the landlord

The failure rate of medical, dental, and chiropractic offices is minuscule compared to the default-ridden food-service industry or retail sector. The landlord can literally bank on a healthcare tenant to pay their rent on time and to stay in that location for 10 to 20 years or more. The landlord's mortgage holder will often show preference to properties with healthcare tenants making you the golden tenant to the landlord.

If your office is only seeing a few patients at a time, your tenancy will take up far less parking than other tenants such as restaurants, bars, or retail tenants, and most landlords know that having a good mix of tenants from different industries with various uses is better for their parking ratios as well. If a landlord is trying to create a retail complex, they may reject healthcare tenants and hold out for retailers. Nonetheless, most landlords desire and need doctors to lease space from them.

The Lease Coach speaks at so many dental and healthcare conferences and events that both Dale and Jeff get to personally meet hundreds of fantastic doctors and other healthcare providers each year. As we tell those doctors, you're desirable tenants to landlords. Landlords want you and need you. It's nice to be wanted, isn't it?

Searching for good office building space

When it comes to leasing classic office space, location may not be so important. A typical office tenant can be on the 3rd or 15th floor of an office tower or building. The commercial office real estate marketplace is a completely different animal when it comes to office leasing. If you're an office tenant, you may be able to negotiate a more aggressive deal, because you can operate your business from almost any building.

It's important to check out days and hours of access for office tenants. One of our office tenant clients picked a great property and turned to The Lease Coach to handle the negotiations and the formal lease document. He was totally sold on the building — until we asked him how much business he did on Saturdays. With a quizzical look, he said about 20 percent of his clients came to see him on Saturday, why did that matter he was wondering. When we pointed out that the office building lobby doors were locked on Saturdays — and that the elevator was shut down and there was no air conditioning on the weekends — he immediately realized this was not the best office building for him.

Office building tenants frequently make assumptions that can turn against them. The Lease Coach gets too many calls from office tenants who are unaware of gross-ups and load factors (see Chapters 9–11). Some office tenants have faced over $1,000 a month more in rent because they didn't understand or negotiate on these clauses. One tenant was furious with his lawyer for not advising him about these extra rent charges. Dale spent years working as a commercial property manager for landlords before becoming The Lease Coach, which is why he advocates that tenants get help from a professional lease consultant with experience on both sides of the table.

High-rise office tenants typically don't receive any exterior signage, but their need for staff parking may be greater than a retailer's. Operating costs for common areas can be quite high for some office buildings. And then, of course, there's the view. It's typical for a landlord to charge higher rents for office suites with better views, more sunlight, or more glass. If demand for space on the side of the building with no view is low, the landlord may instruct the leasing representative to show that space first, hoping you don't realize what you're missing.

Insist on seeing all vacant units in that property if you want. And if you're prepared to take space that's less desirable, negotiate for a better lease deal.

Driving a little to save a lot

Although many business owners leasing office space prefer an office property close to their home — or that of their employees — other tenants realize that by being willing to drive a little farther to get to their place of business, they can often save a lot of rent money. This is especially true if your leased location isn't important to the success of your business. Almost every non-retail business can realize great savings on their cost of leasing space if they're flexible about where the business is physically located.

When we moved The Lease Coach head office from a first-class high-rise office building to a light industrial office complex, our rent went from about $6,000 per month to under $2,000 per month. We also reduced our square footage and took some cheaper storage space for all the client files and filing cabinets we accumulated over the years. By moving to this property, we also eliminated the need for paid parking stalls for the staff, saving another $1,000 per month. The operating costs were lower as well. True, it may be a bit farther for you or your staff to drive to work each day, but the cost savings on rent can far outweigh the inconvenience.

If your employees use public transportation to get to work, you must take that into account. If your employees are paying several hundred dollars per month for their own downtown parking, they're often happy to move to a property with free parking.

Chapter 5

Using Commercial Brokers and Real Estate Agents

In This Chapter

▶ Understanding and managing the various roles real estate agents play

▶ Determining whether using a real estate agent is best for the tenant

▶ Franchising and the use of real estate agents

C ommercial real estate brokers and agents do big business in North America; tens of thousands of them are out there buying, selling, and leasing commercial real estate. A tenant's first thought when you need to lease a commercial, office, or retail space may be to call an agent and have them start your site selection process and even take you to view various properties.

Not so fast. As we show in this chapter, working with just one real estate agent isn't always the best way to go about finding your perfect location. And it's almost never the way to get the best lease deal on a property.

Differentiating Between the Various Types of Brokers and Agents

Every brokerage or real estate agency has one broker in charge, who may or may not be the owner. Under the broker are the agents who work for that brokerage (note that in many areas, the title *agent* has been replaced with *associate* or *sales associate*). It's the broker's job (among other things) to take responsibility, to some degree, for the action of the agents and associates. Every brokerage is licensed, and every broker, agent, and associate is also licensed by a governing body to ensure uniform standards, codes of conduct, training, and accountability to the public.

Without brokers and agents, many landlords cannot fill their commercial office buildings, retail malls, or other properties. Landlords and commercial real estate agents enjoy a successful working relationship, no question about it — but that benefit doesn't always extend to you, the tenant.

In most parts of the country, a real estate agent or associate can trade in commercial (retail and office), residential, industrial, and land investment deals. There's a slow trend toward separating commercial from residential, and the majority of agents would identify themselves as working in either commercial or residential real estate. Real estate agents must cultivate relationships with the type of clientele they want to work with. It's pretty hard to be wining and dining commercial landlords during the week and homeowners in the evenings and on the weekends.

For your own protection, you need to understand how commercial real estate agents work and determine how you can get them to work for you rather than for the landlord. The next sections introduce you to the different types of agents and discuss how their business practices affect you.

Looking for the listing agent

When you see a *For Lease* sign on a commercial building, the first things your eye goes to are the name of the brokerage/agency and, usually in smaller letters, the name of the actual listing agent for that property. Most landlords turn to a commercial real estate brokerage to find tenants or lessees. The brokerage and the landlord enter into a listing agreement that defines the roles of the brokerage and the commission that is paid when a lease or sale deal is completed.

The listing agreement runs for a certain amount of time and describes the commission the landlord will pay. The agents for the brokerage are responsible for marketing the space for lease, advertising, showing the space, and ultimately negotiating and writing deals on behalf of the landlord.

We hope it's now clear that the listing or inside agent is working for and representing the landlord, who is paying their commission. What that also means is that this agent is *not* working for you, no matter what the agent says. If the agent was working for you a representation agreement would have to be negotiated and signed between the tenant and the brokerage. This is occasionally done but not often — and if the agent is still being paid commission by the landlord, the agreement may not benefit the tenant much anyway.

The listing agent or broker normally has a personal relationship with the landlord. Ask any agent, and they'll tell you that property listings are hard to get. The commercial real estate industry is highly competitive, and the agent's first loyalty is normally to the person who's paying him.

Some *For Lease* signs may list more than one agent as a contact. The agent's name that is at the top of the sign is usually the senior agent and the person most familiar with the landlord. By calling the senior agent, rather than a lesser experienced assistant who's name appears second or third, you may have better success getting solid information about the property.

Although a real estate agent may prospect for tenants as part of the sales position, tenants generally make the first call or leasing inquiry to the listing agent, often because they see the agent's name on the *For Lease* sign. The agent provides the tenant with rental rate information, shows the space, and ultimately hopes to make a deal with the tenant.

Far too many tenants think it's normal or even advisable to share the land-lord's listing agent, but nothing can be farther from the truth. The landlord has signed a representation agreement with the brokerage and is paying the listing agent to find tenants and to negotiate with them to get the tenant to pay the highest possible rental rate, to have the tenant provide a large deposit, and to acquire personal guaranties from the tenant. Your goals are the exact opposite. It's unrealistic to think one agent can serve two masters.

Contacting an outside agent

An *outside* agent is any agent who isn't the listing agent on a property. You may think, "Okay, the landlord has a listing agent, so I'd better get my own agent." But don't be too quick to assume that an outside agent (or any agent) is truly representing you either.

Although it may appear that the outside agent you contact and work with is representing you, who do you think is paying them? The outside agent receives a share of the listing agent's commission, which is tantamount to being paid by the landlord. This is perfectly legal and actually quite common. However, knowing that the agent's paycheck comes from the landlord, it may not be advisable for a tenant to let any agent supposedly represent them if there is no formal written representation agreement between those two parties. You may wonder how to get around this so that the agent is really working for you but without paying the agent out-of-pocket. You can have the agent sign a buyer's representation agreement, but we would estimate, based on over 20 years of experience in this industry, that less than 5 percent of agents who claim to be representing the tenant actually sign a buyer's repre-sentation agreement with the tenant. Nor does The Lease Coach endorse or recommend this process.

Understanding who's watching your back

Dale recalls running into one of his clients at an NHL hockey game. Sometime prior, Dale had done three lease deals for him that year. He wanted to open a fourth location, and the landlord was courting his tenancy hard, but the client wisely came to Dale first for advice and guidance. Dale could see from the sales volumes at the client's current stores that the property or leasing opportunity in question was far too large and much too expensive for him to survive, let alone make a profit, and essentially talked the client down and out of that lease deal.

For a few months, the client was disappointed because it was a prestigious location, but at the hockey game he shook Dale's hand and thanked him for convincing him not to lease that location. If he had been getting his advice or representation from a commission-driven real estate agent, would he have received the same advice? Who knows. But a real estate agent can only get paid if a lease deal is done, whether the deal is good for the tenant or not.

A buyer's representation agreement defines how your relationship is structured along with the agents' legal responsibility to you. This agreement also controls what information the agent can share with the listing agent or landlord. In the absence of a representation agreement between tenant and agent, the outside agent is more a freelancer or middleman.

Every tenant must decide whether they feel the outside agent can truly get them the best deal in the best location. One of Dale's clients asked, "Aren't all agents basically honest anyway? What does it matter who's representing whom?" Dale had to explain that indeed, for the most part, agents are honest, hard-working sales professionals, but it's not really an integrity question. Partly because so much of the deal-making process is subjective. Who decides if this is a good location or mediocre one? Who decides if the rent is too high? You see what we mean — these are not black-and-white decisions.

The very nature of the commission structure means that in most cases, *the agents earn a higher commission if the rental rates are higher*. Landlords may deduct inducements such as free rent and tenant allowance before calculating the commission. So, where is the motivation for the agent to get the tenant a lower rental rate or lots of free rent if doing so actually cuts into the agent's paycheck?

Trying a tenant rep

Many commercial real estate agents can refer to themselves as *tenant reps* (which is an oxymoron), specifically implying that they represent tenants in real estate transactions. This would be fine if indeed the real estate agent claiming to be a tenant rep were actually being paid by the tenant. In most cases, tenant reps are simply outside agents in disguise, and they still collect a commission from the landlord.

If you're considering getting the help of a real estate agent who claims to do tenant representation, ask specifically who is paying them. They may try to turn a potentially negative answer (that the landlord is paying them) to a positive one by saying that their services are free or cost the tenant nothing. Well, it can cost you plenty if you entrust your entire site selection process and lease deal to a real estate agent who essentially is being paid by the landlord.

Revealing the Real Estate Agent's True Persona: Friend or Foe?

A real estate agent can only truly serve one master. The saying *if you're not with me, you're against me* would loosely apply in this situation. This isn't an indictment of real estate agents — that's their job. If it weren't for dedicated and professional real estate agents, there would be a lot of empty, unrented space out there.

We think most agents do a really great job, but we also believe they're primarily doing that job for the landlord. This isn't to say they're doing anything inappropriate or trying to hurt you, but you have to ask yourself: Are they a friend of mine or a better friend of the landlord?

Uncovering myths about how real estate deals really work

Tenants would like to believe that all real estate deals are done in person with painstaking detail paid to every clause, and that the landlord and real estate agent are carefully discussing every point in the tenant's offer to lease. Occasionally that does happen — but more often than not, this is what happens:

1. The real estate agent calls the landlord and leaves a voice-mail message . The agent lets the landlord know that the agent has received an offer to lease or a letter of intent on a unit in the property. The agent may verbally convey a few highlights of the deal or warn the landlord in advance about aspects of the proposal that the landlord may not like.

2. The agent e-mails the offer to the landlord and waits.

3. The landlord (being the landlord) may or may not actually call the agent back to discuss the deal. The landlord may want some background on the tenant — but often the landlord simply counteroffers with less than 20 minutes of real thought invested. That's partly because it's a much bigger deal for the tenant than the landlord. Landlords are negotiating and working on lease deals all day.

In the minority of situations, the landlord may have phone or in-person discussions with the agent or even ask to meet the prospective tenant. Many times the landlord sends a *redlined counteroffer*. If the offer to lease is prepared as a Word document, then the counteroffer is made to the tenant in the same document with passages redlined out and new passages added in. Often the deals aren't even signed but go back and forth with no real commitment from either party (which we don't recommend).

A few deals are still being done old-school, meaning the offer is signed and presented first; the other party makes handwritten changes and then signs and initials all their changes. Either of these processes can go many rounds back and forth.

How real estate agents are paid

In the world of commercial real estate representation or commission agreements, there's no price fixing — every real estate agent can negotiate their commission or payment structure with the landlord. Here are a few common scenarios for how agents are paid:

- ✔ The listing agent for a property typically gets 5 to 6 percent of the base rent for all lease deals they complete or sign, typically for the entire 5-, 7-, or 10-year term. Some listing agreements or contracts state that the commission is also payable on lease renewals, or that commissions are reduced to half for years 6–10 on a longer lease. If an outside agent brings in a lease deal, the agents typically split the commission, meaning that the outside agent gets half the commission and the listing agent gets the other half.

- ✔ In some cases, the landlord and their listing agent may agree to a commission structure that pays the outside agent 5 percent and the listing agent 2 percent, so as not to discourage outside agents from showing other agents' listings. The commission is calculated on the total base or minimum rent (not operating costs). And if the deal includes free rent or tenant allowance money, often the landlord deducts these incentives or inducements from the cumulative rent before calculating the commission.

- ✔ In some parts of the country and on some types of property, the commission structure is based on the amount of square feet leased versus a percentage of the base rent. In this scenario, an agent may get paid, say

$1 per square foot (per year). On a 5-year lease term, that is a commission of $5 per square foot.

✔ The landlord pays all the commission to the listing brokerage, which then pays the agreed-upon amount to the outside brokerage. Then the brokerages pay a pre-agreed amount to its own agents. If the total commission on a lease deal is $30,000, it's split between two brokerages, with each brokerage receiving $15,000. Then each agent probably receives half ($7,500), depending on their agreement with the brokerage (and this does vary).

If an agent is supposedly representing you the tenant, and the offer to lease doesn't state the commission amount — ask. If the outside agent is trying to get a high commission from the landlord, the deal may be rejected by the landlord for that reason. Often the offer to lease simply says the landlord pays the agent a commission, but doesn't say how much. You're entitled to know this if you ask. If unknowingly to you, the agent is trying to squeeze the landlord for a 10 percent commission, this can be one of the reasons the landlord rejects your offer to lease (and accepts another tenant instead).

Realizing How Commission-Splitting Can Negatively Affect the Tenant

When using an outside agent, potential commission-splitting can almost certainly impact the deal-making process. When making the decision whether to use the services of an outside agent, it's important to understand how commission-splitting can affect which properties the agent shows you and how this may factor into the negotiations.

Splitting a commission and the outside agent

A franchisee for a major quick service restaurant (QSR) chain (previously referred to as fast food chains) called Dale one day. She said she'd just spent an entire day looking at space with an agent provided by her franchisor. The agent had shown her many properties. Later, after finishing the tour, she looked through the leasing brochures and realized that every plaza the agent had shown her was his brokerage's own listings. She asked why this was the case. Dale explained that if she agreed to lease one of the agent's listings, then that agent would get the full commission and not have to split a commission by taking her to another agent's listing. The tenant was understandably upset because she wanted to see all prospective sites.

Making a decision for all the wrong reasons

We want to make it clear that we have nothing against commercial real estate brokers and their agents. They provide a valuable service and play an important role in the economy of any city, state, or country. What we want entrepreneurs and tenants to realize is exactly what role any agent is playing in any particular lease deal.

In Dale's former life, when he worked for landlords in a traditional real estate agent capacity, he found out something valuable from one particular transaction. After completing a lease deal with a tenant (working for the landlord), he went back and asked the tenant why she

did that deal — why she picked that particular location. Her reply was very candid; she said that the property across the street had been her favorite, but that Dale paid more attention to her and been more helpful, and that she preferred to deal with him.

Unfortunately, this type of reasoning is far too common and doesn't contribute to good, long-term decision-making when it comes to leases. Yes, relationships are important, but don't base your leasing decisions on who treats you the nicest or which real estate agent is most responsive. You can respect good salespeople, but you don't always have to buy from them.

Now in all fairness, this is rarely the way it plays out. The agent who is showing you space all over town may show you other agent's listings, but they probably won't show properties where the landlord is hard to deal with or properties where landlords object to paying commissions (such as enclosed shopping malls).

Commercial real estate listings are hard to come by. They represent a finite inventory for any listing agent. Therefore listing agents may try to get exclusive listings from landlords or even protect their listings so that they can receive a full commission.

Splitting a commission and the listing agent

One reputable multi-location tenant told us he that couldn't understand why he missed out on a particular unit for lease, saying, "I sent in the agent to make an offer to lease on the space for me, but the space ended up going to another tenant." Turns out the tenant who got the location had been a walk-in — meaning they simply called the listing agent directly to inquire about space for lease. The listing agent dealt with the walk-in tenant instead, knowing that he could get a full commission if he did the deal.

In a similar scenario, we currently work with a tenant who wants The Lease Coach to inquire on space she is interested in. She told us the listing agent shared with her the existence of another interested party who was using an outside agent. In our initial conversation with the listing agent we inquired on the status of the other potential deal, to determine where it stood. We found out that the listing agent was waiting to hear back from the other party's agent. As the conversation progressed, the agent was up front in wanting to work with our client to get a deal done, essentially indicating he wouldn't pursue the other deal unless the other agent took action. In other words, once again a listing agent was motivated to push a deal forward that would result in a full commission.

Creating a commission on a renewal

Not only does using an outside agent create commission-splitting, but if you're about to negotiate a lease renewal and use an outside agent, it may create a whole new commission the landlord had not budgeted for.

The landlord pre-factors the real estate commissions into his lease rental rate for new leases or new tenants. For existing tenants, landlords don't expect to pay commissions, so if you let your agent negotiate your lease renewal, it can actually drive up your rent. You've now just forced your landlord to pay a commission, again.

You really don't need to use a real estate agent for lease renewal — hire a professional lease consultant instead.

Looking at Real Estate Agents from Different Perspectives

The majority of tenants have some interaction with a real estate agent when leasing space, so put yourself in the other party's shoes to understand this dynamic. Most tenants don't give much thought to how the agent benefits from or interacts with the other agent, the landlord, or the tenant.

Once you understand the benefits the agents may bring to you or the landlord, and what benefits the agents gets from you and the landlord, it's easier to understand the financial motivation of the agent and why they make certain suggestions or recommendations. For example, Dale and Jeff often get calls from tenants with this problem: The tenant wants to lease about 3,000 square feet but the space they like is 4,000 square feet. Remember there is a 25 percent greater commission for the agent if you lease the entire area. So the agent may try to persuade you to take it all saying, "you'll grow into it — you may need that space years from now." Because of physical limitations demising the space down may be difficult or even expensive, but so is paying rent and operating costs on 1,000 square feet you don't need now and may never need. When Jeff or Dale face this situation for a client, they either get the space size reduced or find the tenant the right space size elsewhere.

Using an agent, from the landlord's perspective

Dale was speaking at a business mixer that was open to the public; the room was filled with different types of business owners. He discovered that one of the people was a commercial landlord. Dale identified him and at the appropriate time in the presentation asked him what type of properties he owned. Mostly strip plazas and a few other buildings, the landlord said.

Dale asked him how he found tenants for his properties. The landlord said that he gave listings to real estate agents. When asked whom he thought the real estate agent was working for, without missing a beat the landlord said, "The real estate agent had better be working for me with all the high commissions I pay them." There you have it. That's pretty much every landlord's perspective. And you know, there is nothing wrong with that perspective; why would any landlord not want to get the best possible lease deal for them — after all, they're paying the agent to perform that service.

Using an agent, from the agent's perspective

We frequently get e-mails from commercial real estate agents telling us how wrong we are and how hard they work for tenants. They go on to say, "Yes, we get paid by the landlord but we want to help the tenant." We believe that they believe that. However, the majority of agents don't call us and don't claim they're trying to help the tenant. For better or worse, they're simply brokering the lease deal. Most real estate agents are happy to represent landlords and be in the landlord's corner.

One commercial broker whom Dale respects for his honesty said, "You know, Dale, in the commercial real estate industry, we brokers and agents eat what we kill." As you can imagine, it is the tenant being sacrificed. You can be sure that real estate agents don't bite the hand that feeds them, because landlords wouldn't work with them again or give them listing agreements on their properties.

Using an agent, from the tenant's perspective

Most tenants admit that the listing agent is representing the landlord, yet each year thousands of tenants mistakenly agree to share an agent or allow the agent to lead and take them through the entire leasing process. To the landlord and their listing agent, this is a perfect situation.

We estimate that at least half of all tenants still believe that an outside agent is also working for them. We get phone calls from tenants all the time wondering why the agent won't do this or do that for them. "Why won't the agent show me other sites; why won't the agent make multiple offers to lease? Why won't the agent try harder to get me a better lease deal?" By, now, you know the answer. All together now: *The agent's not really working for you.*

Franchising and Real Estate Agents

There are approximately 3,000 franchise systems operating in North America and perhaps 90 percent of them lease commercial space for their business operations. The Lease Coach works with many franchisors and their franchisees and have perhaps seen every possible scenario when it comes to how the franchising industry works, lease-wise.

The purpose of this section isn't to disassemble a franchisor's operational system. It's to specifically look at how agents fit into the franchisor's plan for their real estate site selection, lease negotiation, and lease document reviews. If you're a franchisee or about to become one, remember that your location and your lease deal can make or break your business.

Using an agent, from the franchisor's perspective

Franchisors who turn their franchisees over to local real estate agents tell us they do so for several reasons. It can be that the franchisor doesn't have the time, money, or in-house expertise to take on the enormous jobs of site selection, lease negotiation, and lease document review.

Some franchisors have specifically told us they don't want the liability for placing their franchisees into a poor location or a poor lease deal. By hooking the franchisee up with a locally licensed agent, the franchisor can pretty much wash their hands of the leasing process. Other franchisors say that it's for the tenant's own benefit, that the local agent will work hard for them and get them a great deal (a theory which of course we've debunked herein).

One franchisor said that the job of the franchisee's agent is to beat a good deal out of the landlord — which is hardly something any agent would say for themselves. How can an agent that is paid a commission by the landlord bite the hand that's feeding them? One franchisee said he didn't feel the agent helped him at all, but virtually gift-wrapped his tenancy for the landlord and just went through the motions to collect an easy commission. After all the franchisee said, I wasn't even given a choice which local agent I worked with — he was told by the franchisor that this agent would represent him — a pretty sweet arrangement for an agent, and I'm sure you agree.

Recently, we were hired by a multi-unit franchisee who was opening more locations. The franchisee outright rejected the local real estate agent referred to him by the franchisor, for various reasons. This franchisor even had an in-house real estate person to manage the agent/franchisee relationship, but that hadn't happened in the past, and the franchisee felt he received no benefit from this situation or the relationship created by the franchisor. Franchisees need to discuss these matters with their franchisor and ultimately look out for themselves. It's your name going on the lease agreement, and you, the franchisee, pay the rent after all.

Measuring the pros and cons of using an agent for the franchise tenant

You get what you pay for, right? Well, if the franchisee isn't paying the agent to represent them, then perhaps you really do get what you pay for. On the one hand, the agent is free of charge to the franchisee, so that's good, right? It depends on what you expect the agent to do for you. Can the agent negotiate for the franchise tenant to get the lowest rental rate, the most free rent, and tenant allowance? Can the agent negotiate hard so the franchisee doesn't have to put up a lease deposit or personal guaranty?

If the local agent you've been referred to has negotiated a lot of deals with a particular landlord, which relationship is more important to them — one deal with you or many deals and listings with the landlord?

Asking the Agent for Disclosure Information

Licensed real estate agents are required to be transparent. If the tenant asks for information, full disclosure is required of the agent. But most tenants don't ask the agents for anything. Tenants often think it's none of their business, or that they shouldn't care how much commission the agent charges the landlord. That's a mistake.

Tenants shouldn't be afraid to ask the agent anything.

This section gives you a few ideas on what you really should ask your agent.

Understanding where the deposit goes

Sure, the landlord is paying the agent's commissions. And often the main purpose of the lease deposit is to satisfy that commission so that the landlord doesn't have to reach into their own pockets to pay the agent. In a few commercial real estate transactions, it's the agent who holds the tenant's deposit in trust, not the landlord. If the deal goes forward and closes, then the brokerage simply deducts its commission from the deposit in trust, or, in some cases, bills the landlord for the shortfall. Make sure you read the section on deposits in Chapter 14.

Revealing what the agent won't or can't do for the tenant

The real estate agent typically doesn't go on record approving any location or piece of real estate. They don't want the liability in case the tenant's business fails. Although an agent may give a tenant their professional opinion, if you read the fine print of an agent/tenant representation agreement, you may see many disclaimers.

The agent may not tell the tenant if a landlord has a bad reputation in the marketplace, not even if asked outright, perhaps considering the question or answer to be subjective.

The agent may not reveal whether other tenants, including anchor tenants, are planning to move out of a prospective property or close down. Although the landlord may have inside information about certain tenants, they often strategically will not communicate any negative information to their listing agent. This gives the agent plausible deniability, sort of a real estate version of don't ask, don't tell. So it's up to the tenant to ask and demand answers of the landlord and their agent.

The agent won't review the formal lease documents, opting to advise the tenant to consult a lawyer for help on that matter. Even if the agent is aware of some nasty clauses in the lease documents, the agent doesn't want to get on the landlord's bad side by appearing to help the tenant.

Avoiding dual agency representation or such agreements

Dual agency means that one real estate agent simultaneously represents both the landlord and the tenant. This may be stated in a representation agreement, or more likely it simply appears on the offer to lease or letter of intent.

An unsuspecting tenant may not think it matters if you have dual agency representation, as long as the landlord and not the tenant pays the commission. However, if the agent misrepresents the lease deal terms, you may not be able to point a finger at the landlord — because you agreed to share a dual agent. From the tenant's perspective, dual agency is not a good idea.

Watching out for agent/tenant representation agreements

The Lease Coach was hired by a first-time tenant in New York to help him on a new location for lease. A few weeks prior, the tenant went out on his own, found a location, and looked at a space for lease with the landlord's listing agent for the property. The listing agent told the young entrepreneur that it was traditional to sign an agent representation agreement, which he did.

Later, the entrepreneur showed us the representation agreement, which essentially said that the tenant would exclusively use this agent for any and all lease deals, and that if the tenant didn't use the agent, the tenant would have to pay the agent's commission, regardless. When we pointed out to the entrepreneur what he had agreed to, you should have heard the crying — his and ours.

This same situation happened to another office tenant. After four months, the agent had not found the tenant a suitable location (even though space was abundant). The tenant turned to The Lease Coach, and we successfully got the tenant a great lease deal in a prominent office complex — but the tenant still ended up paying the agent over $60,000, because of the tenant/agent representation agreement.

Tenants must be careful what representation agreements they sign with agents.

Controlling the actions of the agent

You can and should do a better job of controlling the actions of an agent by not allowing yourself to be led through the process. Tenants sometimes have themselves to blame if they're not getting matters in writing. You can hold the agent accountable — if you're willing to take charge of your own destiny in the following ways:

- ✔ Set some ground rules and get them in writing. State a representation period such as 60 days rather than indefinitely.

- ✔ If an agent is verbally leading you to believe that a deal is good or that other points are reasonable, ask them to put their comments or opinions in writing.

- ✔ If you ask an agent a question, don't settle for a casual or verbal response, request the answer by e-mail so you have a paper trail.

- ✔ State that if the agent is working for you and being paid by you, that they don't milk both ends of the deal by also receiving a commission from the landlord. Don't be surprised if they won't agree to this, and here's why: The commissions paid to agents tend to be 4 to 8 times greater that the fee a professional lease consultant such as The Lease Coach will charge you. So, of course agents would rather work for commission because the potential payout is much greater.

Anyone can be fired, even a real estate agent. There are codes of conduct and standards for professional behavior. If you have a written representation agreement, and the agent doesn't fulfill their obligations, then you should be able to fire them for cause (but that needs to be stated in the agreement as well).

One final piece of wisdom: If a real estate agent prepares an offer to lease or LOI for you to sign and slips in a clause stating that the agent is representing the tenant, the landlord, or both parties, *stop*. Ask yourself, is this correct? Is this what I want, and do I fully understand what relationship I'm getting into? If you don't like what it says, take a pen and cross it out or change it. Take control of your destiny, or someone else will.

Chapter 6

Selecting the Right Professional to Help You, the Tenant

- -

In This Chapter

▶ Realizing why you may need professional help

▶ Determining who can best serve or help you the most

▶ Understanding the different roles professionals play

▶ Using a checklist to select the best professional to help you

- -

*T*he difference between success and failure in a business can easily come down to your location and lease terms, but if you're not an experienced and savvy negotiator, you may not stand a chance in negotiations against the landlord or his real estate agent. Bringing in someone who will go to bat for you or even take the whole negotiating process off your shoulders can save you money in the long run.

In this chapter, we look at how hiring a professional such as a lawyer or professional lease consultant can help you come out ahead in the leasing process.

Understanding Why You May Need Some Professional Help

Selecting the right location, negotiating the commercial lease terms, and finalizing the formal lease document can be daunting tasks for most virgin tenants going through the leasing process for the first time. Even seasoned business owners with existing locations are no match for the landlord and their team of property managers and real estate agents. Making a single mistake on a commercial lease deal can be so costly that five years later the tenant may still be struggling to make ends meet and not taking home a decent salary from the business.

To put this in perspective, compare your position with the landlord's for a minute. The landlord knows what every other tenant in a property is paying in rent, when their lease agreements are expiring, who's renewing or moving, and what their inducement packages were. You probably have none of this knowledge. Does that sound like a level playing field? The landlord has likely owned the building a long time and has relationships with real estate brokerages, meaning the landlord understands the local commercial real estate marketplace and prevailing rental rates for similar properties. The typical tenant usually does little homework, lacks experience and marketplace knowledge, which is why they're easily outmaneuvered by the landlord.

The easiest and most expedient way for you to level the playing field with landlords is to find an experienced professional, hire them, and listen to their advice. This section should educate you on how a professional can help you and how to find the type of professional best suited to your needs and leasing situation.

Saving money with a lower rental rate

Negotiating the lowest rental rate on any lease deal should be a primary objective for any tenant. The rental rate on a commercial property is negotiable in most cases, depending on where the landlord or their real estate agent sets the *asking rent rate*. A market rental rate can fluctuate dramatically, depending on the economy and many other factors, including the time of year. Reducing your rent per square foot can literally save your business from mediocrity or even failure and increase its profitability. A great location and low lease rate can make the business more valuable and eventually easier to sell for a good profit.

Unfortunately, when it comes to negotiating a lease rate with a landlord, tenants come up short on both knowledge and experience. Their lack of both leads to overly high rents, for the following reasons:

- ✔ Tenants typically don't know the market well enough to make an intelligent or competitive offer or counteroffer or when to walk away from overpriced property.

- ✔ They lack negotiating experience and are often timid or nonconfrontational. In a dogfight with the landlord or their real estate representative — both of whom are by nature more aggressive — guess who loses? The commercial real estate industry attracts highly competitive sales people who have to negotiate to win, because working on commission dictates that they won't make any money if they don't.

- ✔ The emotional factor makes the would-be tenant more susceptible to persuasion by the landlord's agent. As human beings, we make some big decisions based on emotions when no one is there to stop us.

A landlord knows exactly how much rent he needs to pay the property mortgage and make a return on his investment. Novice tenants don't know what level of sales they'll achieve and tend to think that if their expenses are higher (such as higher rent) that they'll just have to sell more goods and services — but of course this is a dangerous approach for an untried business.

To be on equal footing, any professional you hire to negotiate your rent must be knowledgeable and experienced, but also willing to negotiate verbally with the landlord. Hiring someone to write letters or lease proposals doesn't get the same result as getting in the ring and actually going a few rounds verbally with the landlord.

Avoiding lease clause mistakes

Most of the mistakes tenants make on commercial lease agreements can be attributed to their being new at the game, but plain old lack of knowledge and disinterest in becoming more educated about the leasing process also contribute. Many tenants simply don't know what they need to know. They don't read or understand the complex legalese in the lease and therefore make critical mistakes on their own. Dale and Jeff do a lot of lease renewal projects for tenants and continue to be surprised by what terms, conditions, and lease clauses tenants agreed to in their first lease that they did on their own.

It's the landlord's property, the landlord's lease agreement, and the landlord's real estate agent — talk about hometown advantage for the landlord! It's so easy for a tenant to agree to lease clauses that should have been deleted, anticipated, or negotiated if someone had been fighting for the tenant or had done some legwork first.

Saving you time

Time is the new money for many successful business owners, who can better spend their time doing what they do best or what only they can do for themselves and their business. Many business owners and healthcare tenants hire professionals in all industries to save them time, so why not use a professional lease consultant to handle the leasing process, too? The entire lease process can take 20 to 40 hours stretched over many months — time you may better delegate to someone who does it for a living.

Tenants who choose to delegate the entire leasing process to a professional need to be informed and advised about how things are progressing, but aren't responsible for the day-to-day details of putting a great lease deal together. You're freed from driving to the site, talking with other tenants, meeting in person with the landlord, and hardball negotiating.

One tenant who used The Lease Coach, a dentist, wrote to Dale stating not only how valuable using a professional had been, but how Dale had saved him over 100 hours of patient time.

Even if you feel you don't put such a high value on your time or you feel you have the time, will you actually dedicate yourself to all the processes, phone calls, meetings, and details that need to be handled? Based on thousands of coaching sessions with tenants, Dale has seen tenants use every shortcut or excuse in the book for avoiding the heavy lifting that comes with a lease deal. So don't kid yourself into thinking you will put in the time if you likely won't.

Choosing Between Professionals

When it comes to picking a professional who is well versed in the entire leasing process and lease agreement, you have three choices. You can

- Hire your own real estate agent, but unless you're paying his commission, he's still essentially working for the landlord. (We discuss real estate agents in detail in Chapter 5.)
- Hire a lawyer, but you'll need one who deals with landlords, leases, understands lease clauses — and who is willing to help with negotiations.
- Hire a professional lease consultant. In our minds, this is the best choice, because this is what we do.

Looking for a lawyer

Tenants who use lawyers are typically trying to make sure the lease agreement is legal, rather than trying to get a great lease deal. Consider that the actual leasing process is comprised of many steps or phases. You may feel safer using a lawyer to review your lease agreement but should that lawyer or attorney be used for every step of the deal-making process — not likely.

If you decide to involve a lawyer in your lease negotiations, find one that specializes in commercial real estate deals *for tenants*, because many lawyers actually specialize in helping landlords. The Lease Coach has worked with tenants in conjunction with their lawyer, and often the lawyer was not at all in tune with market rental rates or the negotiable business terms components that an industry insider like Dale understood so well. Don't assume your lawyer is a savvy negotiator either — many are not.

In some cases, a lawyer may be required at the end of the leasing process. Or you may simply want to involve one. But be selective of when and how you use one. Using a lawyer can also be unpredictably expensive; one tenant who became a client told us that they were only part way through their lease deal, and the billable hours from the lawyer were already at $11,000. It was like every speed bump along the way cost them another $1,000, with no end in sight.

Although attorneys may point out problematic lease clauses, they often overlook obvious issues such as overreaching operating cost clauses, rental rates that are too high, and locations that don't make sense from a business standpoint. Additionally, many landlords view lawyers as *deal killers* simply because of their overall approach to the leasing process. The landlord uses a real estate professional to lease the building for them, so don't assume your best line of defense (or offense) is a lawyer.

We have nothing against lawyers and attorneys. If you're suing your landlord, by all means get legal representation, but make sure you discuss your expectations and get a fee estimate in writing first. Using the wrong or an inexperienced attorney on your lease deal may cost you more than it's worth.

A lawyer may be helpful for fixing problematic clauses, but what good is fixing a lease agreement you never should have entered into in the first place?

Using a real estate agent

If you want to use a commercial real estate agent to represent you, that's your prerogative, but don't fool yourself into thinking the real estate agent is working for you if they get paid a big commission by the landlord. Even if the landlord has their agent and you have your agent — this may not be the most effective way to proceed if there is commission splitting involved. If the landlord is paying commissions to both agents involved then you may not have gotten professional help for yourself at all — you're simply sharing the landlord's representatives.

Chapter 5 covers all you need to know about using brokers and agents. If you're bouncing around this book from one part to another, remember to check back to Chapter 5 for an eye-opening section on using real estate agents.

Hiring a professional lease consultant

The best money a tenant can invest in the future of their business is using a professional lease consultant. A professional lease consultant truly represents you and is paid only by you. The lease consultant should not receive any fees or commissions from the landlord. It was in 1993 that Dale gave up a career working for commercial landlords and became possibly the first real lease consultant for tenants only.

There are a few real estate people out there calling themselves lease consultants who are actually trying to charge the tenant a fee while also collecting a commission from the landlord on the same deal. You must ask about this and take nothing for granted. Stay away from that kind of relationship because no one can serve two masters equally, and you're more likely to be the loser than the landlord. Watch out for wolves in sheep's clothing.

Typically hundreds of questions are raised, and they all require thoughtful consideration and discussion when negotiating a new lease or renewal. A professional who's willing to give you telephone time to answer questions, raise new questions, and provide experienced counsel can be worth their weight in gold and peace of mind.

For many tenants, signing the lease agreement is only the beginning of their new business. Frequently questions and leasing issues arise during the construction process and even after the tenant opens for business. A professional lease consultant will often provide follow-up services and help months or even years after your initial consultation.

Exploring the Services a Lease Consultant Can Provide

First-time tenants signing a new lease need a different type of help than an existing tenant negotiating a lease renewal. A lease consultant can evaluate your situation and requirements so that you can decide how much help you need and what you want to handle on your own. Although real estate agents or lawyers may be involved at some point through certain leasing scenarios, a lease consultant can provide you well-rounded assistance from start to finish with almost any lease deal.

Selecting your site

When we see some of the locations tenants have signed long-term lease agreements on, it almost makes us cry. Fifty percent of marriages end in divorce, meaning that half of all people can't pick a permanent spouse even with years of advance courtship. Yet entrepreneurs and would-be tenants and business owners think they can pick a great business location all on their own. When a tenant gets the site selection process wrong, none of the other lease deal pieces fit together properly.

For example, if a tenant feels that they can budget $27 per square foot per year for base rent, that assumption or calculation is based on getting a great location — if they pay $27 per square foot for a mediocre location that really should be going for $22.50 per square foot, it negatively effects their business forever. If a tenant selects a 2,200 square foot unit (because that's all that was available for lease), but they really needed 2,700 square feet, that also can hold back future growth and limit future profitability.

Combine several hundred thousand dollars of leasehold improvements to a mediocre or bad location, and it could mean an early end to your business dreams. If you're using a lease consultant paid by you (and they're not receiving a fee or commission from landlords), then you'll get to see *all* the spaces available for lease, even ones that are currently occupied but coming back on the market in a few months. Lawyers don't look for real estate sites for you, and real estate agents aren't really working for you (see Chapter 5). Even if a commission-driven real estate agent shows you many sites, the agent typically won't write offers to lease on more than one at a time, to avoid explaining to all the other landlords why the agent didn't bring your tenancy to their property after all — because you may look at 5 to 10 sites but ultimately only lease one.

When The Lease Coach conducts site selection, we're often presented with a few sites pre-selected by the tenant. The tenant may not know which is better for their business. So we fly into that city and do hands-on site selection work for that tenant. We've never seen a lawyer or real estate agent get on a jet and fly two thousand miles to help a tenant with site selection, but that's what's necessary in most cases.

Walking you though lease negotiations

Lease negotiation is where many tenants stumble and fall down financially without professional guidance. There are so many moving parts or important clauses in an offer to lease or letter of intent that it's easy for a tenant to make critical mistakes that carry through to the formal lease document. An experienced lease negotiator — working for and being paid only by the tenant — will not only save the tenant from making mistakes on their own, but will often earn their fee many times over by negotiating in the tenant's favor on both new leases and renewals.

- ✔ **New lease negotiations:** A first-time tenant is like a free agent who can shop around, take their time, and even postpone signing a lease agreement if the right deal and right location don't materialize. Leasing for the first time is a much longer process than renewing, but in most cases, you can use that to your advantage.

- ✔ **Lease-renewal negotiations:** The challenge many tenants face in negotiating a lease renewal is that they want to stay in their current location. You may have made a considerable financial investment in leasehold improvements. That doesn't mean the landlord has an advantage during the lease-renewal process unless you unwittingly give the landlord the upper hand by waiting too long to start the renewal process or tip your hand to the landlord. Landlords don't budget for paying real estate agents' commissions on renewal, so letting an agent represent them on lease renewals can cost you money because the landlord will probably add the commission to your rent. A lease consultant doesn't cost the landlord anything fee wise but can help you reduce your rent on lease renewals.

Reviewing lease documents

A lease document review is an essential part of the leasing process. This can include reviewing both the offer to lease or LOI and the formal lease agreement (see Chapters 9 and 11 for more about both). It's not just that tenants get tripped up on legal jargon or legalese — they also tend to think everything in the lease agreement is standard when in fact most of it is negotiable.

The average tenant can't tell a good lease agreement (on paper) from a bad one. And why should they be able to when that's not their area of expertise? Real estate agents almost never weigh in on the wording of the lease document, especially not the formal lease agreement. There's no money in it for them, and they lack real experience in that field. A lawyer may point out problematic clauses but generally doesn't offer much in the way of how to negotiate. Neither do they typically provide the practical coaching advice necessary for the tenant to persuade the landlord to make the lease changes recommended by the lawyer.

Most lease consultants do a point-by-point lease document review and inspection to ensure that the document is thoroughly vetted and no clauses are missed. With a concise written report from the lease consultant and a telephone consultation under your belt, you can decide whether you want to negotiate the recommended lease amendments on your own or turn it over to the lease consultant to negotiate for you.

Orchestrating mid-term rent reductions and early lease terminations

When you find yourself stuck in a lease agreement paying more rent than you can afford, you need to renegotiate your deal with more favorable lease terms. Doing so requires a specific set of maneuvers with the landlord, because no landlord wants to lower a tenant's rent.

Landlords don't lower rents for the sake of the tenant; landlords lower rents to help themselves retain a rent-paying tenant, because receiving 70 percent of the rent is better than receiving nothing at all, especially if there are vacant units in the property.

It's important to differentiate between a *midterm rent reduction* that includes an *abatement* (forgiveness of future rent or rent arrears) and *rent relief*, which means the landlord simply tacks the unpaid rent onto the end of the lease term.

In some cases, the tenancy cannot survive, and an early termination of the lease agreement needs to be negotiated with the landlord. Surrendering the space to the landlord is actually a reasonable and feasible alternative for both parties. Unless you're suing your landlord, its best to leave your lawyer out of mid-term rent reduction negotiations or lease terminations, because this is not a legal exercise but a true negotiation. Landlords need to be shown that keeping the tenant alive paying a lower rent or freeing up the space for another tenant is in the landlord's best interest, not just the tenant's best interest.

Handling lease assignment or transfer negotiations (buying or selling a business)

Tens of thousands of businesses are bought and sold each year. And they almost all require a lease assignment negotiation with the landlord. A landlord can deliberately or creatively sabotage lease assignments. They may do this out of fear that the new tenant who is buying your business may default. Or it could be that the landlord agrees to the assignment but wants a higher rental rate or a greater deposit or personal guarantee (or all of those things) from the assignee buying your business.

The landlord's actions could kill the sale of your business or make you rethink buying a business, depending which side of the tracks you're on. A professional lease consultant can help you navigate these potentially dangerous waters so that both you and the person you're selling your business to benefit from the terms.

While a lease assignment may appear to be a fairly straightforward process, frequently negotiation or guidance is required from a lease consultant to ensure that the buyer and seller (the tenant's) are properly represented.

Building acquisition negotiations

Buying a building or a business condo can be the right move for many business owners. Paying a mortgage for a specified period is often more desirable than paying rent forever. When The Lease Coach takes on any new client looking for space, we don't automatically assume they'll lease their space; we include properties for sale in the site-selection process.

Exploring any and all property purchase opportunities could lead to a purchase or solidify in the tenant's mind that leasing space is still their best option due to location, availability, or access to financing. Your professional lease consultant should be willing to accompany you in looking at locations for sale as well as those for lease.

Finding peace of mind

Knowing that you've got a good, solid lease agreement under your business is a great feeling, tenants tell us. If you can't or don't completely trust your professional advisor, you probably won't get much peace of mind throughout the leasing process, or after. So, picking the right type of professional — and the right person — is essential if you want to feel comfortable handing over the reins of lease negotiation to them.

Peace of mind is something tenants tell us they want and need when making a long-term lease commitment. How would you feel waking up Monday morning and finding out that your neighbors are paying less rent than you, or that another tenant got twice the tenant allowance, or more free rent? Peace of mind comes from knowing you didn't overpay on the lease rate and that you got the best overall deal possible. Having a go to consultant who is protecting your tenancy and is there for you in the future can make all the difference in how well you sleep at night.

Using a Checklist to Make Sure the Professional You Hire Can Do the Job

If you're serious about getting some professional help with your commercial lease or renewal, use Table 6-1 to determine the best type of professional to work with.

Table 6-1	Comparison of Professional Services		
Services for Tenants	*Lawyer*	*Broker/Real Estate Agent*	*Lease Consultant*
Understands market rents and comparable lease deals	Not usually	Yes, but may be biased toward landlord	Yes
Does tenant's site selection	No	Yes	Yes
Calls or speaks with tenants to gather market information	No	Not likely	Yes
Meeting with you in person at your business	Not usually	Yes	Yes
Calling other real estate agents to gather information	No	Yes	Yes
Meeting landlord on tenant's behalf	No	Yes	Yes
Reviewing formal lease documents	Yes	No	Yes
Writing an offer to lease or LOI	Sometimes	Yes	Yes
Specializes in commercial real estate for tenants	A few do	Mostly for landlords	Yes
How services are paid for	Billable hours to tenant	Paid by landlord's commission	Paid by tenant
Sets a project fee maximum to avoid surprises	No — billable hours	N/A — paid by landlord	Varies, but The Lease Coach does

Note: This chart is a guideline. Tenants are advised to ask plenty of questions. Don't make assumptions and get the service agreement in writing. This is commercial real estate, and no professional can guarantee a specific outcome. The Lease Coach has tried to simplify the process of hiring a professional lease consultant by creating a rate sheet of professional services along with a transparent fee guide and a standard engagement letter, available upon request.

Part II
Negotiating the Offer and Key Terms

The 5th Wave   By Rich Tennant

"Is there any wiggle room in that 'eternal soul' portion of the lease contract?"

In this part . . .

*O*nce you've grasped the basics of lease process, it's time to negotiate the initial offer and the key terms in your lease. The rent you pay will influence your bottom line, so we guide you through the negotiating process. We also focus on other important terms such as your square footage, when to open your business, the issue of deposits, and how to approach the negotiation of these terms.

Chapter 7

Presenting and Negotiating a Lease Proposal

In This Chapter

▶ Preparing for the deal-making process

▶ Understanding the role of the parties

▶ Working effectively with landlords and their real estate agents

▶ Picking the right tools for making an offer to lease

▶ Presentation strategies that work

There's more than one way to present and negotiate a commercial lease proposal or agreement; some ways are right for some situations and not for others. If this is your first rodeo, or if you've only negotiated a couple of leases, you're more likely to make critical mistakes at various junctures in the process. Whether you're a retailer, franchise tenant, office tenant, or healthcare professional looking for a place to set up shop, you can apply the fundamentals and leasing principles covered in this chapter to whatever type of transaction you're conducting.

One of the most popular seminars The Lease Coach presents at conventions or tradeshows is called "Thirteen Costly Mistakes Tenants Make Negotiating a Commercial Lease or Renewal." Unfortunately, far too many tenants tell us that they have made many of those mistakes or fallen into many of those traps. In this chapter, our goal is to keep you from joining their ranks.

Understanding the Players and Their Roles

Most people don't bother to make a game plan before they start negotiating a commercial lease, and this is a problem because the stakes are much too high and the consequences are long lasting.

One of the first things you need to decide is who will be in charge of the lease negotiations. In football terms, you're going to have the quarterback throwing the ball, the receiver catching the ball, and the coach telling everyone what to do from the sidelines. You might want to be the quarterback — then again, you might not. But if you don't decide these roles up front, your lease negotiations may become not only frustrating but also time-consuming and ultimately expensive.

Part of what you're deciding is whether you'll be negotiating on your own, using a real estate agent, sharing the landlord's real estate agent, or getting help from a lawyer or lease consultant.

Even if you go it alone, you'll be negotiating against someone. It may be the landlord, the landlord's property manager, an in-house leasing representative, the landlord's real estate agent, the landlord's lawyer, or perhaps even a landlord's relative. Our experience is that with the majority of commercial leases, a tenant negotiates their lease against the landlord's listing agent (especially on new leases) or in-house leasing representative, perhaps even a property manager. The more properties the landlord owns, the more likely you'll work with one of their employees or representatives.

Much of what we explain in this chapter is how to decide whether you should be pushing or pulling; in other words, whether you are making an offer to lease or are the recipient of a lease proposal from the landlord. These two situations may sound like they lead to the same end, but they can actually have quite different outcomes.

Getting your game plan together

Once you know who the players are in the negotiations, you can begin to decide how you want the negotiation process to unfold. Of course, you also need to know what you're negotiating *for* before you roll up your sleeves. Before you go into lease negotiations ready to fight for what you want, you need to have the following already determined:

- ✔ When you want to open your business
- ✔ How much rent you feel you can afford to pay
- ✔ How much it will cost you approximately to build out the space
- ✔ Where to buy your equipment
- ✔ Whether you will qualify for financing
- ✔ How much area you actually want to lease
- ✔ What street, community, or city you want to do business in

These are all issues that can come up in lease negotiations, and if you don't know the answers, the landlord or his representative won't take you seriously or may think you're wasting their time. When Dale worked for landlords as a leasing representative, he got good at evaluating what stage prospective tenants were at in their planning process. It's not that you can't start kicking tires on space for lease at the beginning just to see what's out there, but you only get one chance to make a first impression on the landlord or their agent. And if that impression is that you don't have a game plan, they may blow you off — or later on ignore you, even after you get your act together.

If you plan to open a new business, one of the most important ways to come across as if you've got your act together is to talk to the landlord and real estate agents about the business you *are* going to open, not the business you *think* you're going to open, or would *like* to open. That can make a huge difference in the manner in which they treat you.

Women in particular have to present a professional and organized front right off the bat. Approximately half of all new businesses are opened by female entrepreneurs and professionals. The commercial real estate industry is dominated (especially in the leasing field) by men. Every month we get calls from women making leasing inquiries on space for lease but can't get the real estate agent to return their calls, or feel they're being treated like second-class tenants. This is all too common, so be prepared for your first meeting.

Putting players in the right positions during the leasing process

You usually have no control over who you may negotiate against, be it the landlord, landlord's real estate agent, the property manager, or the landlord's unemployed second cousin. What you can control is who represents *you* and help you make key decisions during the negotiation and presentation of the offer-to-lease process.

Sometimes tenants think that if they go around the landlord's leasing agent and directly to the landlord, they can get a lower rent deal by helping the landlord avoid paying a commission to the real estate agent. This rarely works because the landlord and the listing real estate agent already have a contract. That listing agreement (most of the time) says the agent is paid regardless of who lassos the tenant. There are exceptions, but if the landlord gives a listing agreement to a real estate agent, they've already budgeted and decided to pay the commissions. Why would the landlord want to do all the work of negotiating directly with you, the tenant, if they have to pay the agent a commission anyway?

At The Lease Coach, we do a lot of work for healthcare tenants, such as dentists, medical doctors, and chiropractors. It's common for the doctor's spouse (who may be the office manager) to be actively or primarily involved in the lease-negotiation process rather than the doctor. This is neither right nor wrong, but an important distinction to make.

After Dale gave a seminar to a group of business owners, two of the attendees (partners) asked whether Dale would visit them. When Dale arrived at their office, he learned that three partners owned the insurance company. Two of the partners had attended Dale's seminar and clearly realized how much help they needed with site selection for their new location. Dale found it interesting that they designated the third partner — who was unfamiliar with what we were doing and who had not attended the seminar — as the spokesperson that Dale would work with and as the company representative for the negotiation process.

If you delegate the leasing process to someone on your team who is unqualified, they won't make much headway on their own unless they are also being coached or led by a professional.

Although you may be dealing with a property manager or landlord's in-house leasing representative (who is on salary), they may be a figurehead who has little power. One of the lease deals Dale is currently negotiating is through a professional property-management company; the landlord is a financial institution. The property manager Dale is negotiating against admitted that she had basically no power or authority and that she was only a conduit or paper mover to the landlord.

Negotiating against someone who can't give you a yes or can't make a firm commitment for the landlord can put you at a disadvantage. Asking the person you're dealing with to involve someone higher up who can make immediate decisions may produce better results.

Understanding the role of the real estate agent in the leasing process

Commercial real estate agents play an active and important role in the leasing process. Many landlords rely on listing agents to find them tenants, negotiate leases, and get the landlord the best deal possible. The landlord typically pays these listing agents on a commission basis. When a landlord gives a listing to a brokerage (broker or agent), the brokerage typically puts a *For Lease* sign on the building or on the property and waits for calls to come in, or even begins prospecting for tenants. Some agents still do door-to-door cold calling on tenants.

Too many tenants mistakenly think that the role of the listing agent is to help the tenant. Nothing could be further from the truth. This is not to say that the listing agent is trying to hurt the tenant, but rather that the listing agent's role is to get the best deal possible for the landlord. The landlord is the one who hired them — and is paying them. This is most clearly demonstrated when the listing agreement states that the commission paid by the landlord to the agent is based on a percentage of the rental rate. The landlord is incentivizing the agent with a higher potential commission if the agent can convince the tenant to pay a higher rent.

You can also use an outside real estate agent to represent you. The outside agent may claim to act as your representative in negotiations with the landlord or the landlord's listing agent. On the surface, it may appear that both parties are well represented by biased professional parties. However, the concern that arises is that both agents are typically sharing or splitting a commission that's being paid by the landlord, which is why we don't recommend this approach (see Chapter 5 for more).

Getting the Landlord to Pursue You

You're the landlord's customer; the rent money flows from the tenant to the landlord. You need to not only understand this, but also act accordingly. You don't want to conduct the leasing process in a way that makes it look like the landlord is doing you a favor by renting you space. If you're about to pay rent to the landlord for 5, 10, or 20 years, you must avoid looking like you *need or must have* any particular lease deal at any particular location. In other words, the landlord should be desperate for your business, not the other way around.

It's absolutely critical for you to handle the process in a manner that creates the appearance that you have multiple locations or leasing opportunities available to you if you want to get the best lease deal possible. The landlords you're dealing with should be pursuing you and trying to woo and convince you to move into their property. If you pursue or wine and dine a landlord, you're going to find yourself coming up on the short end of the lease deal.

Looking like a desirable tenant

One leg up that franchise tenants have is that landlords recognize that franchise systems are proven, well thought out, and often stay in business much longer and achieve much higher rates of success than many independent concepts. To some degree, the same desirability factor often applies to healthcare or dental tenants who spend a substantial amount of money building out an office and typically stay for 10–20 years in one location.

If you have an established business record of accomplishment, multiple locations, a franchise brand behind you, or you belong to an industry that's generally doing well, you need to make sure that the landlord sees and recognizes this. Color brochures, websites, and marketing materials can all help whet the appetite of a landlord for a particular tenancy. And if you play your cards well, this can translate into a superior lease deal all around.

If you're trying to rent in an area where commercial space is at a premium rate or multiple tenants are vying for the same location, the better you package yourself, the more attractive you'll look to a landlord as a long-term prospective tenant, and the more the landlord will pursue you for your tenancy.

Handling phone calls and personal meetings

When Dale negotiates leases for tenants, he frequently talks directly to landlords, property managers, real estate agents, or the landlord's lawyer. But he almost never calls a landlord or a real estate agent out of the blue. Why? A couple of reasons:

Dale likes to use e-mail to set a time for a phone conversation. This avoids playing time-consuming telephone tag and also avoids the situation where he leaves a message and the agent calls back when Dale's in the middle of another task (putting Dale at a disadvantage). By pre-establishing a telephone call appointment day and time, both parties are prepared to discuss the relevant issues and actually make some headway.

Meeting in person can have advantages, but many tenants become unnerved by the process, and their body language tells everyone in the room they're anxious or unfamiliar with this forum. The way the tenant dresses and the fact they may be meeting on the landlord's turf can put the tenant at a disadvantage. Some tenants are more comfortable and negotiate better at a neutral coffee shop or in their own place of business. Pick the battlefield where you perform at your best.

Going easy on the e-mail

As hard as it is, you or your representative need to resist negotiating important lease terms and deals by e-mail. You can't un-ring a bell, and you can't retract an e-mail or anything else you've written.

E-mails should be used to confirm items that have already been discussed verbally and to create greater certainty, but not necessarily for primary negotiations.

Most real estate agents and landlords who live, eat, and breathe commercial real estate for a living are good at reading between the e-mail lines and sizing up the tenant.

Just because you sign a lease proposal doesn't mean that the real estate agent or your representative will drive it over and explain it face-to-face with the landlord. Often these lease proposals are e-mailed back and forth with no real verbal discussions or negotiations taking place. Negotiation requires a verbal component that e-mail lacks. If the agents are only sending e-mails back and forth on your behalf, how much deal-making is actually going on? The written offer to lease should be the product of several conversations and some follow-up e-mails that put the terms of the offer into the proper context.

When negotiating for our clients, we frequently use the conversations with the landlord or their agent to probe for information on the landlord's position on certain points or lease clauses that may be sensitive or important to our clients. Asking questions such as whether the landlord typically provides free rent or how they might react to a certain rental rate proposal really lets you run things up the flag pole — something that's difficult to do in an e-mail or offer to lease. This process allows you to find out where there's room to negotiate and to test the waters on how the landlord may react to your proposal — before actually putting something in writing.

Creating Competition for Your Tenancy

Tenants who negotiate on only one location typically don't get a good lease deal. What we teach, preach, and do for tenants is *create competition* for their tenancy. Even if the tenant is absolutely in love with one location, we often locate and contact a couple decoy locations that we can use to create competition amongst these landlords. Ideally, these alternative locations are genuine or solid leasing opportunities, because having a soft place to land or true alternative sites is better than having fake ones. The next section explains how to leverage multiple sites to get the one you really want.

Negotiating on multiple sites

It's perfectly appropriate and even advisable to negotiate on multiple sites at the same time. The site-selection process, the viewing of the space, and the deal-making process should all advance at the same pace on all locations. You've got to put some effort into doing this rather than settling for the first suitable site you find.

Tenants who avoid looking at or dealing on multiple leasing opportunities often justify their lack of action based on not having enough time or interest or thinking it won't make a difference. Wrong. When we can tell a landlord that the tenant has viewed ABC Plaza and XYZ Plaza (as well as the landlord's), the competition the landlord faces becomes real to them. If we can say that we keep getting leasing calls from John Smith, the leasing agent for 679 Plaza, because they really want my client to locate in their property, it sounds more credible than bluffing with vague references to "other offers."

Dealing with multiple offers simultaneously

Collecting lease proposals or making offers to lease from multiple landlords simultaneously can be an extremely effective strategy for tenants. At The Lease Coach, our goal is to create a bidding war between various landlords for the same tenant. We can only achieve this if all the deals are progressing on the same timeline. Note that it's often best for the tenant if in the beginning you let each agent or each landlord think that their property is the only one you're considering, in order to attract a lease proposal from them. If you tell a listing agent too soon that you are viewing seven properties, they may not be motivated to prepare a letter of intent. Timing counts.

However, once we're holding three or four lease proposals, we don't hide the fact from these landlords that we're looking at multiple sites — just the opposite: We want the landlords to know that they have competition for our client and realize what other buildings we're negotiating on.

Landlords often know which other properties they're losing tenants to and may adjust their terms and conditions accordingly to attract your tenancy. You can't create the leverage you want as a tenant if the offers to lease aren't negotiated on multiple sites simultaneously.

Avoid working on one deal and when that falls apart working on the next one. Think and deal on multiple sites simultaneously.

Choosing the Proper Lease Agreement Format

Over the years, we've seen lease agreements of every imaginable format: some on legal paper, some on letter paper, and some on commercial real estate forms. Verbal lease agreements are generally legally enforceable if they're less than one year in length, so some lease agreements are not even recorded on paper (we don't recommend that).

Most landlords use standard leasing templates. The same applies to commercial real estate agencies. However, not all leasing templates are created equal, and the same clause may consist of two sentences in one lease agreement and four paragraphs in a different document.

When presenting or making an offer to lease to the landlord, three standard formats are commonly used, and we cover them in the next sections.

Using a letter proposal

A letter proposal typically is informal. It's not binding on the landlord or tenant but simply serves as an expression of interest. A letter proposal can be 1–4 pages, but typically shorter is more common.

A true letter proposal is not a casual e-mail — which should be avoided for the purpose of presenting and negotiating an offer to lease. A letter proposal is typically drafted on the tenant's, real estate agent's, or landlord's letterhead. If you haven't formed your company or don't have a business or brand yet, then your letter proposal will be on plain paper, but do it in a business letter format.

Considering a letter of intent (LOI)

LOIs are common. Often, real estate agents will draft an LOI for you to sign that they then present to the landlord. This isn't necessarily beneficial for you, because it makes it appear as if you're pursuing the landlord — the opposite of what you want.

On the other hand, a landlord's LOI to you is a desirable proposal or format. The LOI typically says that neither party is bound by the letter. However, you can't put a bullet back into a gun once it's been fired. If you're agreeing, stating, or proposing specific terms or rental rate in the LOI and you attempt to change or reduce that number at a later point, it looks like you're flip-flopping. Always carefully check any LOI the real estate agent drafts for you to send to the landlord.

If you simply neglect to put some important term or condition into the LOI, such as parking, signage, or renewal-option rights, then the landlord may well accuse you of negotiating in bad faith when you bring it up later. Sure, the LOI isn't binding, but once you put anything in writing, you've been backed into a corner and could get boxed into it.

One of the biggest problems with an LOI for new tenants occurs if you haven't yet created a business entity (no corporation or LLC has been formed). In this case, your personal name often appears as the designated tenant on the letter of intent. This gets carried forward onto more formal lease documentation, and before you know it, you have personally become the tenant (which you don't want — read more about this in Chapter 2).

Utilizing an offer to lease

An offer to lease is generally the best way to proceed when you're ready to enter into a formal agreement with the landlord. An offer to lease can be written from tenant to landlord or from landlord to tenant, but it's more common for the tenant to write or make the offer. But this isn't always right or the best thing for the tenant to do.

If you are going out to buy a car, do you take a purchase agreement with you to the car dealership? Of course, not; the car dealership has a purchase or sale agreement for you to sign if you want to buy the car. Tenants find themselves in a much stronger negotiating position if they require the landlord to first prepare and send them the landlord's standard offer to lease.

Even if the landlord's template document says that the tenant is making the offer to the landlord, as long as the business terms have been filled in by the landlord or their agent, this typically represents the landlord's opening position or offer. The point is to get the landlord to make the first bid, stating the rental rate and other details, so that the tenant is responding or in a position to counter offer the deal. Again, it's all about who appears to be pursuing whom.

The offer to lease *is* legally binding — which is why it's the preferred method. Of course, you can include conditions, such as attaining suitable financing in the offer (we deal with this in Chapter 8).

Presenting the Offer to Lease

If you've made the decision to submit an offer to lease to the landlord, putting it together and submitting it properly are important. This section explains what to include and how to present it.

The offer to lease shouldn't be used as a tool to justify why you should get certain concessions or incentives. The negotiation process should be verbal, but the offer itself should include just the facts, put down on paper.

Creating a checklist of business terms

A typical offer to lease will have approximately 14–20 business terms, including these, for example:

- ✔ Who the parties to the agreement are
- ✔ What the rental rate is
- ✔ When the agreement begins and ends

If you don't have a checklist to work from, there's a good chance that you may leave something important out of the offer to lease.

At a minimum your offer to lease should address the following:

- ✔ Name of tenant (this will be your corporation if you have one formed) and landlord
- ✔ Address of the premises (including the specific unit)
- ✔ Size or square footage of the premises
- ✔ Length of lease term (commencement and expiration date)
- ✔ Buildout or fixturing period
- ✔ Rental rates
- ✔ Additional rents (taxes, maintenance, and insurance estimates)
- ✔ Free rent (or rent-abatement period)
- ✔ Tenant improvement allowance
- ✔ Permitted uses and exclusivities
- ✔ Deposit amounts and terms
- ✔ Landlord and tenant's work for the premises

✔ Renewal options

✔ Lease assignment language

✔ Parking, reserved parking, and any charges

✔ Signage

✔ Personal guaranty (or indication of one not being required)

✔ Conditions and acceptance dates

Putting the terms in writing

Far too often tenants come to us complaining that some of the terms that they negotiated verbally as part of the lease deal either aren't appearing on paper or are appearing with a different context or meaning. Verbal negotiations often aren't captured on paper with the correct intent or detail; this is why you need a checklist to make sure that everything you negotiated shows up.

Sometimes a landlord or their representative may have selective memory, or the representative uses the excuse that they ran your verbal request up the flagpole, but the answer from the landlord was no.

Just because you discussed the additional signage, parking, or anything else doesn't mean it will be put in writing unless you ensure that it is. Generally the commercial real estate industry works on the basis that if it's not in writing, it doesn't exist (or that it was negotiated out of the agreement with no further verbalization or notification of such).

Formatting the offer

You may receive the offer to lease from the landlord in a word document that can be manipulated on any computer or as a PDF document, meaning that any changes or alterations you want to make need to be done without altering the original agreement. We typically go back and forth in negotiations with the landlord having each party making counteroffers and changes to the original document.

By using the original proposal for counteroffers, you can see what direction each party is moving in or countering, having initialed accordingly. The alternative is to create a new offer to lease for every round of negotiations, but it becomes difficult to follow that process after the third or fourth round.

It absolutely astonishes us when tenants call to say that they are going back and forth with a landlord on offers and counteroffers, but neither party is signing or initialing the paper each time. One tenant just told us that the agent he was using told him that in their part of the country it was customary to submit unsigned offers and counteroffers. This is one of the craziest ideas we've heard. Who would be so sloppy or careless as to spend time and energy negotiating with someone who hadn't signed their name or initials to a deal?

If there's no signature or initial, there is no deal.

Having the proposal reviewed

Tenants often come to us with their goose half-cooked. They've already signed a letter of intent or an offer to lease — then they want to get some professional help from The Lease Coach. We can still help them, but it could have been much more advantageous for the tenant had they come to us to review the offer to lease or LOI prior to signing and submitting. Whenever we ask tenants why they signed first and then brought it to us after the fact, their response is almost always, "Well, it's not binding."

Even if a lease proposal contains all the correct business terms and headings, it's often an insufficient or incomplete picture. Consider that the formal lease agreement will often be 30, 40, or 50 pages and drafted based on what the offer to lease terms state. If you didn't negotiate a point into the offer to lease, what makes you think that the point is included later in the formal lease agreement?

If you're going to have the lease proposal document or offer reviewed — and you should — do it before you sign it, period.

Submitting the offer to lease

Often a landlord or real estate agent sends an offer to lease or proposal to a tenant and stale dates it for a few days later. The tenant calls us in a panic, thinking that they must respond by that date or the deal will expire.

The truth is, stale dates or expiry dates in which the proposal is no longer open for acceptance are more of a sales tool than a concrete wall. If we receive an offer to lease on behalf of a client, we phone the real estate agent and talk with them, but typically resist responding prior to the expiry date simply to demonstrate that the tenant is the customer, and the tenant is in control.

Occasionally, a deal can be time-sensitive, but we determine that when we speak with the agent.

If we make the offer to lease or counteroffer, we advise the real estate agent that it's coming and book a telephone appointment to discuss it. If we can't be there in person, there is substantial phone interaction so that we can explain what terms we're offering.

Making Counteroffers

A good lease negotiation is like a boxing match, and a good boxing match lasts many rounds. It's perfectly acceptable and actually advisable to make multiple counteroffers, inching the deal forward and improving on it during each round.

Tenants tend to think that the leasing process is an *event*, but really it's a *process*. Speed is not conducive to getting the best deal possible for the tenant. A lawyer who hired us to negotiate his lease was amazed by the package deal we got for him by slowing down the pace of the deal making process rather than by speeding it up. If you have lots of time to play with before you want to open your business, and there's no real competition from other tenants for the same space (which is critical), time is your ally. You can often avoid costly mistakes or oversights by slowing down the negotiating pace. Don't be surprised if the landlord or the landlord's agent is trying to make you go faster. The listing agent is naturally motivated to complete deals quickly.

Somewhere during the leasing process, tenants often lose control to the real estate agent. Information is not being relayed completely or clearly, and the tenant often complains that the real estate agent isn't working for them. You're entitled to go as slow or as fast as you want through the leasing process. Granted, at times you must move quickly if multiple tenants are after a particular site. But in most cases, the tenant can pace themselves at a speed that is comfortable to them.

Facing the fear of rejection from the landlord

If tenants are afraid of anything, it is usually rejection. But rejection is simply an opportunity to revisit any term or condition in the lease agreement. When we're negotiating a lease for a tenant, we try to be assertive enough that the landlord objects or rejects the initial proposal. If we make an offer to lease or counteroffer on behalf of a client tenant, and that offer is simply accepted, then chances are we could have asked or negotiated for more.

It's important to temper your expectations and resist making a lowball offer to lease or counteroffer. The landlord may perceive you to be unable to afford the deal. Communication with the landlord's agent is critical to set the stage for the proposal. On the other hand, the more aggressive or assertive your proposal, the more you need to justify it. There's a balancing act to being bold enough but not looking foolish or uneducated about market rental rates and deals.

Knowing when the landlord is bluffing

Prior to 1993, when Dale started working exclusively with tenants, he spent many years working for landlords. He can tell you first-hand that landlords bluff their way through lease negotiations all the time. It may sound like they're drawing a line in the sand, or they may have instructed their real estate agent to do so, but landlords are almost always negotiable. Recently Dale spoke with a client who felt a bit exasperated by the many counteroffers back and forth with the landlord. The tenant asked Dale when he could expect to receive the landlord's best and final offer. Dale told him what all wise negotiators know: The best deal usually comes when you reject the deal, get up, and walk away from the negotiating table — if you have the guts to do so.

Don't take what you're being told or offered as the bottom line just because it was delivered with convincing rhetoric. If you've done your homework, you should know in advance what prevailing rental rates are and what comprises a competitive deal in that marketplace.

Timing the counteroffer for best results

Don't make a counteroffer too quickly. If you get a proposal from the landlord in the morning and you're modifying it and sending it back that afternoon, you're responding too soon. You need to pace the process for all the obvious reasons. Six or eight counteroffers are par for the course when we negotiate a lease for a tenant. This can take weeks or months, and also depends on the accessibility of the landlord's decision-makers.

Don't waste the other party's time. If you don't plan to make a counteroffer for a week, tell them that. Be forthright, communicative, and professional. It may turn out that you have to wait a few weeks for a zoning approval for your particular use. There are delays that you constructively create to get a better deal; other delays are just part of the real world.

Removing conditions

Once both parties have executed the offer to lease, there's often a period of time for either party to remove conditions. The landlord may want to check your credit, while you may require final approval from your franchisor or still need to finalize financing. Once both parties have removed their conditions, the deal can move forward.

However, if one of your conditions is your approval of the formal lease document, then the heavy lifting is about to begin. Reviewing and negotiating the 30–50 page formal lease agreement is not to be taken lightly. (We discuss the review process more thoroughly in Chapter 11.) Only after the formal lease agreement is executed by both parties can the deal truly proceed.

It's not common, but occasionally deals come unraveled over wording in the formal lease agreement. The sooner you can get a copy of this document, the better, providing it doesn't weaken your position by making you look too anxious.

Avoiding Common Negotiating Errors

Everyone makes mistakes, but some can be avoided in the leasing process. Watch out for some of the common mistakes mentioned in this section — they could cost you big in your negotiating efforts.

Knowing when to walk away

Sometimes, after weeks or months of negotiating, doing space plans, and completing other essential tasks, a deal doesn't look good from your perspective, but you've invested so much time (and possibly money) that you're reluctant to walk away. You're tired of the whole process and just want it over. So you stay with the deal, even though you know in your heart that you're making a mistake. And you really are: Don't do this, no matter how much easier it may seem to be.

Sometimes, weeks into the process, a landlord springs an unexpected clause or condition that you weren't expecting. You can avoid this in some instances by making it very clear which points will be absolute deal killers for you. For example, if you're vehemently opposed to providing a personal guaranty, then don't leave the negotiation of a personal guaranty to be discussed a month into negotiations. Get it out in the open at the beginning of the negotiation process.

One way that landlords or agents try to get around your objections is to state that the requirement of a personal guaranty is only subject to a credit check to be done on the tenant after the offer to lease or LOI is negotiated. Then, as you may or may not expect, the landlord simply claims the tenant is not financially strong enough, and a full personal guaranty is required. Novice business owners fall into this trap all the time, but we can see it coming a mile away.

Submitting a business plan

We're all for creating business plans, but in most cases you can do better in the negotiating process if you keep it general in nature. If your business plan is going to be shown to the landlord, and it contains the name of the landlord's property on the front or inside cover as the "chosen location," that tips your negotiating hand. We see tenants do this and lose all negotiating power because the landlord recognizes the tenant has emotionally made the commitment to leasing that particular property.

Consider what information your business plan provides to the landlord; your projected revenues or rent budget could impact how the landlord negotiates the deal. If your projected revenues look too low, the landlord may take this as a sign that you can't make it — at least not in his building at market rental rates.

Be cautious about who's reading your business plan and who may ultimately get their hands on it. That could include potential competitors the landlord or their leasing rep or real estate agent may be working with. You want to create a summary version of your business plan that will show the landlord that you've done your homework and provide them with insight on your business or industry — without giving away too much proprietary or confidential information.

Submitting financial information at the wrong time

It's not necessarily wrong or uncommon for a landlord to review a tenant's financials or do a credit check. The problem is that this should be done at the end of the negotiating process. If your financials are weak, the landlord may ask for a personal guaranty or larger deposit. Ideally for most tenants, this financial information should be submitted at the end of the process once the terms and conditions of the lease proposal have been agreed to. The landlord then has the right to decline or accept you as a tenant.

If your financials or credit score is strong, you can provide that actual info to the landlord in advance if you feel it is be beneficial. Use this opportunity to remind or inform them that a personal guaranty is out of the question.

Submitting a deposit with the offer to lease

Deposits are not legally mandatory and should not be submitted with the offer to lease. If you're negotiating on multiple locations, how many deposit checks can you afford to write at one time? The deposit should come at the end of the process, after both parties — not just the tenant — have agreed to the terms of the deal. An offer to lease can state that the deposit is payable within three days after the offer to lease or formal lease agreement is executed (by both parties — not just the tenant) and all parties have removed all conditions. Providing a deposit up front is a clear buying signal to the landlord. Don't fall for it. Read more deposit advice in Chapter 12.

Chapter 8

Negotiating the Business Terms of the Lease Deal

· ·

In This Chapter

▶ Using an offer to lease or letter of intent (LOI)

▶ Creating a checklist of the required clauses

▶ Negotiating tips and points

▶ Dealing with landlords and their agents

▶ Maximizing tenant inducement and incentives

· ·

*A*lthough it would be nice, it's highly unlikely that a landlord will hand you a proposed lease with terms that are worded correctly or are perfect in every way. It is still likely that you have to negotiate most of the approximately 20 primary or essential business terms critical to the success of your business. The offer to lease or the letter of intent (LOI) are the documents used to battle for those critical terms before moving on to the formal lease agreement.

Take the offer to lease or LOI negotiations seriously, because the business terms you agree to in these forms will carry over into the formal lease agreement.

In this chapter, we break down the lease clauses and terms you need to focus on with all the muscle you can muster.

Choosing Between an Offer to Lease or Letter of Intent

Tenants, landlords, and agents often use the phrases *offer to lease* or *letter of intent* interchangeably, but these initial lease documents often differ in the following ways:

✔ An offer to lease typically is more in-depth than a letter of intent and is binding, subject to conditions by the landlord and tenant.

✔ A letter of intent, often abbreviated to LOI, is often shorter and is also non-binding on either party.

Given a choice, The Lease Coach recommends using an offer to lease rather than an LOI when negotiating a commercial lease deal. Tenants are more easily persuaded by the real estate agent to sign an LOI if an agreement or proposal is non-binding, using the argument, "It's non-binding, so what have you got to lose?" Well, until someone can figure out how to un-ring a bell or put a bullet back in a gun after it's been fired, you have a lot to lose if you send in a hurriedly composed, poorly thought-out LOI or sign an LOI that's patently unfair to you.

Whichever method you choose as your opening volley, you need to follow certain guidelines:

✔ Create a checklist first of all the core points you want to cover in the LOI or offer to lease. Then create your document, following the checklist points to ensure you don't leave anything out.

✔ Make your offer to lease concise and comprehensive. The document typically ranges in length from two to five pages.

✔ Spell out everything, even if it's a point that's not applicable in your case. For example, if you don't want to give a personal guaranty, don't just leave it out. Under the *personal guaranty* heading, simply write *not applicable* or *none*.

The price of avoidance

The Lease Coach is currently coaching a franchisee for a major franchisor who didn't heed the advice to spell out everything. After several months of negotiating on a particular location and remaining silent about a personal guaranty, the landlord has now sprung it on him. The tenant didn't want to be the one to raise the guaranty issue, hoping that silence would serve him throughout the process. Now the tenant not only has 30 actual hours invested in the deal — having taken his contractor to the property and the franchisor — but has also prematurely paid a deposit. All that could have been avoided if the tenant had added the personal guaranty information right up front in the LOI the landlord's real estate agent prepared for him.

Determining the Parties to the Lease Agreement

Undoubtedly you know who you are and who the landlord is, but it's important to identify your corporate entities correctly on the lease form. The landlord's corporate identity is usually well established, but your own may not be.

You need to have your corporate identity, not your personal name, listed on the offer to lease or LOI. If you plan to form a corporation or LLC for your new business but hesitate (as so many tenants tell us), until you're sure you can find the right location, you're sending the landlords and their agents a signal that you're not fully committed to actually opening a new business. Don't be surprised if they don't take you seriously. Establish your corporate identity ahead of the negotiation process and have it ready to use on all your correspondence, because the name you use on the offer to lease will carry over into the formal lease agreement, unless noted that it will change.

Checking up on the landlord

Ninety-nine percent of all lease documents that we receive from landlords or their agents state that the landlord is a specific corporate entity. Many shareholders may be in that corporation, and many decision-makers as well. You need to do your due diligence and find out what you can about the landlord. You may even do some superficial investigation of the landlord, even if it's just an Internet search, before going too far into negotiations.

Talking with other tenants will reveal a wealth of first-hand information about any landlord.

Don't assume your landlord is strong financially, stable, or ethical in their business dealings, even if you see their name on numerous buildings around town. With a little digging, you may find the landlord is involved in multiple court cases with tenants or is on the brink of going into receivership. This won't necessarily change the desirability of the property for lease, but it can make you more wary during negotiations.

Deciphering the landlord's hierarchy in advance may also help you determine how accessible they're going to be if problems arise — and problems generally do, in one form or another.

Stating the tenant's name for the record

Most business owners and tenants that The Lease Coach works with have a corporation or plan to form one. Its name should be stated right up front as the tenant. If you allow your personal name to be stated as the tenant, you may have difficulty changing it later when you do want to incorporate. Some landlords want to see incorporation documents for a tenant, and that's perfectly acceptable and reasonable on their part. They want to know who the shareholders and players are in the tenant company. Both parties have the right to know who they're dealing with.

Would-be business owners and entrepreneurs would be wise to form a corporation or limited-liability company (LLC) in advance and present that entity to any landlords or agents. Your company will be the prospective tenant, and it's a non-negotiable issue. For both liability reasons and tax advantages, this only makes sense. If the landlord is pressing you to use your personal name on the lease form, remind them that the landlord has formed a corporation to be the landlord, and so do most savvy business owners.

Under no circumstances should you simply use your business trade name as your corporate name. We often see this situation. If your business is called something like Hillside Coffee House, and you put that name alone on a lease agreement as the tenant, you may find that the law actually deems you, the owner of the business, personally responsible for the lease agreement.

The name on the sign that customers see when coming into your place of business should not be the actual corporate entity. If you do use the same title, you need to add *Inc.*, *Ltd.*, or *LLC* after the name; which signifies that it's the corporation who is the tenant, not you personally.

Establishing the Location to Be Leased

It's also important to know exactly which property you're offering to lease. You may think this is no-brainer, but we've seen too many tenants confused about the exact location after dealing on several different units within a cluster of plazas located on a single piece of land. If the location of the property or the premises can't be easily identified in your paperwork, then the entire lease agreement can be considered null and void in extreme circumstances. This section reviews the importance of establishing the exact building, unit number, and square footage of the location being leased.

Naming the property on the lease document

Every commercial property has both a legal and municipal address. State both on the offer to lease or lease agreement. Furthermore, if the plaza, office building, or shopping mall has a name, it only makes sense to include that name on the offer to lease and LOI as well. This serves partly to establish which property you're dealing on, since there may be several properties with similar or almost identical names in an area, distinguished only by the descriptive words *plaza*, *shopping mall*, *shopping plaza*, or *shopping center*.

Stating the unit number of the leased premises

Typically, every individual unit within a plaza or property is assigned a unit number. A tenant may view several different units within the same property and perhaps negotiate on more than one unit within the same property simultaneously. These units are different sizes and shapes in different places within the property. You don't want to make a mistake by thinking you're leasing one unit but instead actually get a *different* unit. Yes, more than one tenant has accidentally signed an offer to lease on the wrong property or unit number in a building by being confused over which space they looked at last.

Tenants occasionally run into misunderstandings when one larger unit is being demised down to make two or three smaller commercial retail units (CRUs). If a single large commercial retail unit stated as Unit #12 is demised down, how do they number the smaller units? Normally they'd be called 12A, 12B, and 12C. If you want the middle unit (because that's where the previous tenant had installed washrooms), make sure you're getting the middle unit, 12B.

Attaching a site plan to the offer to lease or LOI visually indicates which unit the tenant is proposing to lease, for greater clarity. If the landlord or agent sends you an offer to lease or LOI that doesn't include a site plan, ask for one to be attached or attach your own, highlighting or crosshatching the correct unit.

Confirming the area or square footage of the premises

In most cases, the lease will state the area or square footage of the leased premises. This is important information for a few reasons:

- ✔ The base or minimum rent is calculated per square foot.
- ✔ The operating costs are also calculated per square foot.
- ✔ The tenant allowance may be calculated per square foot.
- ✔ Most business owners know approximately how much area or square footage they need to set up and operate their business successfully. If a business needs 1,000 square feet, and it turns out they're short 100 square feet, that represents 10 percent of their leasable area (100 square feet is relative, but 10 percent is huge).

When The Lease Coach is negotiating a commercial lease for a tenant, we often have the square footage measured and verified or recommend that the tenant do so. Just because the landlord states that a unit has 3,200 square feet doesn't mean it's correct. There can be phantom space involved due to measurement misassumptions about wall width or misplacement of new demising walls, for example. For office buildings, there's usually a calculation that also takes into effect the gross up and load factor for a property (see Chapter 10 for more on this topic).

In most LOIs and offers to lease (and even in formal lease documents), the landlord's language often includes the word *approximately* in front of the area. A few square feet here or there may not sound like they make much difference — but if your trade fixtures don't fit properly because you were told the space had 21 feet of frontage and you find out there's only 18.5 feet of frontage, you can see the potential design issues.

The correct area is not just about making sure you're getting the right number of square feet, you want to check the space dimensions as well. Sometimes if we're suspicious that space is going to re-measure larger than stated, we'll include language in the section of the offer dealing with measurements stating that if the area turns out to be larger than represented by the landlord, then the original lower square footage quoted remains the figure used in all rent calculations.

After all, the landlord should know what the correct measurements are — it's their building and their responsibility to represent the areas correctly rather than relying on *approximately* to save or protect them.

Knowing What Term or Length of Lease Is Best for Your Business

The majority of commercial lease deals are five-year lease terms. However, exceptions to a five-year lease term have become more and more commonplace. The Lease Coach frequently negotiates three-year, seven-year, or ten-year terms. A lease term can be stated in either years or months. It's important to factor in the start date and the expiration date of the lease term relative to what's best for your business. (We talk about when to start and end your lease more in the upcoming section "Stipulating the term or length of lease.")

Franchise tenants should make sure their lease term matches their franchise term to avoid issues later with the lease running out too soon. This happens when the start date of the franchise agreement is prior to the start date of the lease agreement — which may be several months later, when the franchise business actually opens.

The more money you invest in building out your space and setting up shop, the longer lease term you want.

Stipulating the term or length of lease

Starting or commencing the lease term when you go into your busy season and ending the lease term when you go into your slow season has its advantages for tenants in industries that are somewhat seasonal in nature. Therefore, choosing a lease term based on months rather than years makes sense. Many times a 64-month lease term or a 56-month lease term is better for the tenant than five years (60 months) would be, because certain times of year are more advantageous for opening or closing or moving a business.

Month-to-month leases have also become more common, especially for tenants entering into a lease-renewal term. If their business is not doing well enough to make a long-term lease renewal commitment, they may opt to try to negotiate the tenancy for a month-to-month term. This allows the business to stay open and the landlord continues to get rental cash flow from the tenant.

Establishing the commencement and expiration date of the lease term

The commencement date of a lease agreement can either be the anticipated date that the business will open to the public (which is most common) or the date the landlord hands over the keys and gives you access to the space. Where tenants frequently run into problems is that at the very beginning of the lease-negotiating process, they give the date they plan to open for business. This becomes the commencement date on the offer to lease — but then delays occur. A floating commencement date is often better, if possible. This means that the commencement date is triggered by the tenant actually opening for business, not by when they initially thought they would open.

So often, tenants who hire The Lease Coach to negotiate their lease renewals tell us verbally when their lease expiration date is. After reviewing their lease documents or speaking with the landlord, we see that the tenant is wrong. This can be due to misunderstandings or delays in construction and an opening that occurred 5 or 10 years ago. If, after the dust settles and you actually open for business, but are unsure about the actual commencement date, you can request a letter from the landlord stating the actual date. This knowledge or confirmation thereof will serve you well for future lease renewal negotiations or even to properly time your exit strategy.

Working in a fixturing period

Not all offers to lease contain a fixturing period. The purpose of a *fixturing period* is to establish how long a time period the tenant has to build out or renovate the premises. The fixturing period typically comes before the commencement date (where the anticipated commencement date is the day the tenant plans to open the business). During the fixturing period, you normally don't pay any base rent or operating costs to the landlord because you're not open for business yet.

The fixturing period can be stated as a set number of days, such as 90 days, or as certain months of the year, such as July, August, or September. The fixturing period can be one month or many months — it's negotiable. And whether you pay any rents during this period is also negotiable.

Asking for notice of vacant possession

Many of the leasing projects that The Lease Coach works on are pre-lease deals, where the property is still under construction. Sometimes the space is occupied, but there's an existing tenant that the landlord is attempting to evict, and the space isn't yet available for another tenant to occupy.

Don't be too quick to take the keys from the landlord if the property isn't really accessible yet. Because it will take you time to ramp up, plan your design, and hire your workmen, it's not necessarily advantageous for you to be handed the keys to the premises immediately. If the date of the transfer of the keys is the date the fixturing period starts, you may not have enough time to get the work done prior to when you need to open, since you don't actually have access to the property yet.

If the landlord is required to give you 15 or 30 days' notice of vacant possession prior to turning the space over to you, you have some time to get your ducks in a row and hit the start date of the fixturing period with some momentum. The same is true if the building isn't completed yet. This *notice of vacant possession period* can be well worth a tenant requesting or negotiating for, especially if the fixturing period is short or the amount of tenant's work is extensive.

Calculating the Base or Minimum Rent

Base rent and minimum rent are synonymous terms. *Base rent* is the portion of the rent payable to the landlord, excluding operating costs, and is the most negotiable portion of the rent you pay. Most North American landlords calculate their rent per square foot per year. However, throughout California and parts of the western United States, it's common for rent to be calculated per square foot per month. For example, $3 per square foot in California can be the same as $36 per square foot in the rest of North America.

Taking the number of square feet and multiplying it by the annual rent per square foot you can calculate the annual base rent. Dividing the annual base rent by 12 (months), you can calculate the monthly base rent for your tenancy.

Negotiating the base rent

It's common for the base rent to escalate over the lease term. Landlords are anticipating inflation, so they strive to set higher rents for future years. Of course, this is all negotiable and usually based on the landlord's wants and needs, not yours. Landlords don't necessarily set rental rates based on a projection of what the tenant can afford to pay, but based on the rate of return the landlord needs from the investment.

The landlord can or may attempt to get from a tenant the highest rental rates possible. That may appear self-evident, but many first-time tenants simply don't understand how negotiable landlords can be on the rent, given the right negotiating strategies. The number one reason more tenants don't try to negotiate a lower rental rate is because they think the landlord's asking price is set in stone. At The Lease Coach, we frequently achieve rental rates for our clients 15 to 25 percent lower than the landlord's asking or stated rental rate on new leases.

There's no absolute or set formula for how the base rent is structured. In some cases, rent can be the same rate or dollar amount over the entire term. The rent can increase by say $1 per square foot per year (or more or less, it's negotiable). Some landlords want a yearly 3–5 percent increase.

Negotiating the base rent is not unlike negotiating anything else in life. Dale and Jeff typically start negotiating at a lower base rental rate than the tenant is prepared to pay, to create some room to maneuver. The landlord or their agent probably sets the asking base rent higher than they expect to achieve and negotiate down from there. The tenant's leverage is based on knowledge of many things, including market rental rates, prevailing rates, vacancy rates, and many factors discussed throughout this book. It's important to remember that every piece of the lease puzzle is interconnected. The base rent you end up paying is relative to the length of the lease term, the incentive package, the economy, and other factors.

Annual percentage increases in base rent can compound each year, turning what seems like a small increase into a sum that can really add up over a 5- or 10-year lease term. Do the math to see the actual rent numbers you'll be paying years from now. (We talk more about negotiating your rent in Chapter 9.)

Adding up the percentage rent

In major enclosed shopping malls and some strong retail plazas, landlords can require tenants to pay percentage rent. *Percentage rent* is calculated like this:

An example of the terms of your lease:

Rent: $20 per square foot

Square footage of premises: 4,000 square feet

Percentage rent: 6%

Annual rent: $20 × 4,000 = $80,000

Natural break point: $80,000 / 6% = $1,333,333.33

To calculate the percentage rent to be paid:

Sales in year one: $1,500,000.00

Sales over breakpoint: $1,500,000.00 − $1,333,333.33 = $166,666.67

Percentage rent: $166,666.67 × 6% = $10,000.00

Total rent paid in year one: $80,000.00 + $10,000.00 = $90,000.00

We talk about percentage rent in more detail in Chapter 9.

Stating the Operating Costs, TMI Charges, or Net Charges

Every commercial property must pay real estate taxes, have insurance in place, and keep up with maintenance. These costs or charges may be referred to by a number of different terms but are borne by the tenants in the property. If you occupy 7 percent of the property, then you typically are responsible for that percentage of the taxes, insurance, and maintenance costs, which may include repairs to the parking lot, painting, roof patching, lawn maintenance, and even professional property-management fees.

Your lease agreement may use the term *triple net* charges, sometimes written as NNN (made up of taxes, maintenance, and insurance). In other properties, it may be based on *double net* (NN) or *single net* charges (N), meaning that one or two of those charges are included in the additional rent. Sometime these charges are called TMI. No, not *too much information* — TMI stands for taxes, maintenance, and insurance. In other cases, these additional charges or costs may be called *operating costs/expenses*. Regardless of what terminology is used, you should understand how much these charges are and what's included or not included in them.

Typically, these costs are calculated per square foot, much like the base or minimum rent. The only exception to a tenant paying operating costs is when a tenant is in a *gross lease*, meaning one rental rate covers all costs.

Stating the operating costs in the offer to lease or LOI

Make sure the operating costs for your property are clearly stated in the offer or LOI. Because operating costs are budgeted for a year, the landlord reconciles what they actually spend and either refund or charge the tenant extra to balance or reconcile the operating cost books. Don't assume the operating cost budget is correct. Negotiating to cap these costs in some cases can be a good use of your time.

Although operating costs are typically not negotiable, they are to some degree, in that not all charges levied by the landlord are necessarily recoverable operating expenses. If you're leasing space in a brand new property, the landlord will typically estimate the operating costs for the first year and then escalate them year after year as the building ages.

For a new property, operating costs may be budgeted artificially low, and tenants are often quite surprised how much the operating costs go up after the first or second year. If you're leasing space in a well-established older property, then typically the operating costs are reasonably stable, and yearly increases are predictably in the 5 percent-plus range. Although some landlords will try to get away with unreasonable operating cost increases, it can be a bit of a gamble.

Capping your operating costs

It's not unreasonable for a tenant to try to negotiate to cap operating costs to a maximum of 5 or even 10 percent increase per year. In a tight economy, tenants need to budget carefully and keep the landlord accountable for these additional rent charges.

The Lease Coach received a very nice but unexpected letter from one of our tenant clients who used us to negotiate her various leases. As an office tenant, she would lease a full floor or more in a downtown high-rise tower. In one lease, we successfully negotiated for a 10 percent cap on operating costs. A few years later, the landlord got ambitious and started sprucing the property up. The letter from this tenant went on to say how the cap on her operating costs saved her approximately $9,700 that the landlord could have charged back to her if the operating cost cap had not been negotiated for and included in her lease agreement.

Of course, landlords will resist capping operating costs, and why shouldn't they, as it affects their bottom line? If the landlord resists a blanket cap on all operating costs, you may want to try to cap *controllable costs* within the operating costs. Although the landlord can't, for the most part, control insurance costs or real estate taxes, they can certainly control how often they cut the grass, wash the windows, paint the building, and other discretionary costs.

Landlords are sometimes more receptive to capping controllable costs, which can certainly help control operating cost increases in some areas of the budget.

Using utilities

Utilities used for lighting the parking lot and watering the grass are covered in the operating costs because they benefit all tenants. But utilities being consumed by each individual tenant for their individual leased premises may be paid directly by the tenant— or paid by the landlord and recovered through operating costs. Larger enclosed shopping malls and office towers provide utilities to tenant and recover those expenses through CAM, whereas tenants in strip plazas and lighter industrial properties are typically separately metered and responsible for their direct consumption, since the utilities are in the name of the tenant.

Make sure you address utilities in the offer to lease and take nothing for granted. This expense or cost of doing business can range from a few hundred dollars per month to several thousand dollars per month for cooling, heating, and electrical services.

Including a Lease Renewal Option Clause

Whether a tenant is entering into a lease agreement for a 3-, 5-, or even 10-year term, including a renewal option clause is customary. Some landlords automatically offer this to the tenant, but in some cases you may have to request it and negotiate for the renewal option clause. Ultimately, the goal is not to exercise the renewal option clause but to keep it as insurance or backup in case the landlord tries to evict you or wants to take your space back.

In most cases, the rental rate for the renewal option clause is not pre-negotiated or pre-set, but there are exceptions. If you exercise your renewal option clause, you usually go through a negotiation process to determine the rent. If you and the landlord can't agree on a rental rate for the renewal term, an arbitrator is often used to settle the dispute. Chapters 16 and 17 deal with renewal options in detail and further reveal why most tenants should not need to exercise their renewal option clause.

Negotiating for Tenant Incentives and Lease Inducements

Negotiating for the maximum lease inducement package can make all the difference in the world to a startup business or tenant. A lease inducement package includes items such as a *tenant allowance*, money from the landlord to help build out your space, or *free rent* to allow you to open your business without paying all or some of your rent. Too often business owners approach the leasing process timidly, almost as if applying for the privilege of paying the landlord rent. Consequently, they leave a lot of inducements and incentives on the table.

Whether you're a first-time business owner or an existing tenant negotiating a lease renewal, tenant incentives and lease inducements offer plenty of potential gold in them-thar hills — if you're good at mining. This section aims to help you figure out where to dig to put more gold in your pockets.

Justifying a tenant allowance

A tenant allowance is money that the landlord pays to the tenant as an incentive to help offset the high cost of getting into business. A tenant allowance is used for leasehold improvements, such as paint, floor coverings, walls, washrooms, and other necessary additions. The tenant allowance is typically not used for trade fixtures, signage, or inventory you need to start or operate your business.

The amount of money a tenant spends on their space buildout, fixtures, and overall business setup is relevant to the landlord — the more money the tenant spends of their own money, often the more the landlord contributes. Whenever The Lease Coach is speaking at conventions, tenants ask, "How much tenant allowance should I try to get?" When we negotiate a lease, we often try to get the tenant an allowance that covers up to 100 percent of the leasehold improvement costs. Why go to the ocean with a spoon when you can take barrel? The more money you're going to spend renovating or building out a space, the more you can justify asking and negotiating for a large tenant allowance.

It's important to understand how the landlord pays you the tenant allowance. Tenants often mistakenly assume the landlord pays that money as soon as the deal is signed and before construction is started, but that's rarely the case. In most cases, you are reimbursed after you meet a number of conditions, including opening for business and proving that you've paid the contractors.

Have some short-term financing in place to carry you through if you're relying on the landlord's contribution to your build out. It's also possible to negotiate for some of the allowance up front in certain cases.

Securing some free or abated rent

In most cases, when a business owner is opening a brand new location or business, it takes a period of time to attract customers, build the business, and get the cash flowing. There may be very few customers coming in to a new business in the first few months. Therefore, you are justified in asking for some free rent period in order to offset your overhead expenses.

The most free rent The Lease Coach ever got for a tenant was the first 4 years' base rent free on a 10-year lease term. This was an exceptional case, but 6 months or even 12 months of free rent is not out of reach for a professional negotiator. If you're opening a brand new business, and you can get 6, 9, or 12 months of free rent, it can make the difference between whether your business reaches the moon or reaches the stars — or never leaves the launch platform.

Don't let the landlord fool you into thinking that the fixturing period should be your free rent period. It's only free if you're open for business. Sometimes we use the term *abated rent*, which sounds less one-sided to a landlord. Landlords who don't believe in giving anything away for free may still understand that the tenant truly needs an opportunity to get open and running, during which time the rent is abated to facilitate that process. Although free rent is often right up front, it can also be staggered throughout the lease term.

As with many areas of the negotiation, get creative with the free rent. Landlords may not want to give up substantial free rent at the start of the term only to have a business close down. And in some cases, the immediate cash flow and collection of rent is important to the landlord. There may be an opportunity to negotiate for every second month to be free for a period of time or a couple months of free rent at the start of each year or even paying 50 percent rent for several months. In some cases, extending from a five-year to a six-year term in exchange for a couple more months of free rent may be worth your while. These are common free rent strategies we try out on landlords to see which one they're more likely to accept.

Landlords may also lead you to believe that tenants don't get free rent on a renewal, because you're an already established business at that stage, but that's simply not true. Free rent on lease renewal deals is something The Lease Coach negotiates for our clients on a regular basis.

Dealing with Renovations and Construction

Whether you're an office tenant in the retail or healthcare fields, the cost of designing, creating, and building your new location can be expensive. Landlords often reserve the right to pre-approve all design and construction to be done by a tenant for a couple of reasons:

- It's often the landlord's tenant allowance money being spent on those leasehold improvements. The landlord wants to ensure if at all possible that the improvements you're making to the premises can live on and be used by the next tenant if your business fails or simply doesn't stay more than one lease term.

- It's the landlord's property, and they rightfully deserve to know whether your construction plans include penetrating a roof membrane or other structural changes. If your design plans reveal that you'll be using a disproportionate amount of utilities or installing a lead wall for an X-ray machine, the landlord may want some input on that, which is understandable.

In some cases, the landlord may include a review fee or charge for looking at and approving the tenant's plans. This review fee may not appear in the offer to lease but may instead come to light in the formal lease documents and is often negotiable. In one case, the landlord was trying to charge a tenant $1,500 to review their renovation plans, and we negotiated to eliminate the expense entirely because the plans were mostly cosmetic in nature — this was not a brand new buildout.

You never know until you ask, so don't be shy about negotiating to eliminate these types of design review expenses or at least to minimize them.

Clarifying landlord's work to be done

The landlord's work as listed in an offer to lease or formal lease agreement states very specifically any improvements to the property or the premises that the landlord will do, typically at their expense. This can be as basic as installing an HVAC system on the roof so the tenant has warm and cool air, right down to installing toilets, electrical work, plumbing, or other basic work. You can even negotiate to have the landlord *turnkey* a premises, taking most of the hassle, heartache, and anxiety out of the construction process for the tenant.

The lease agreement should also address the condition of the premises. If no or little landlord's work is being done, you can receive the premises *as is*, meaning you're left to pay for removal of all the previous tenant's leasehold improvements that you don't want. For our own office space at the Lease Coach, we negotiated to get a $3 per square foot allowance of $7,200 from the landlord for removal of old carpet and walls. This was in addition to the main tenant allowance we negotiated for our new leasehold improvements.

Establishing the list of tenant's work

Any work the landlord isn't doing is stated as tenant's work. Typically, this work is at your expense with the approval of the landlord. The more extensive the lease deal and buildout, the more likely the list of landlord and tenant's work is included in a separate exhibit attached to the offer or LOI.

Some landlords are casual about what leasehold improvements the tenant plans for the space. If it's a fairly conventional type of business, the tenant's work list may be relatively short. Make sure you include all plumbing, electrical, air distribution, lighting, and partition walls, and even window coverings because they're fixed or attached to the window sill. If the space is run-down, and you simply want to pop up a sign and open for business, the landlord may require you to at least replace floor coverings and paint. Make sure you're prepared to complete all the tenant's work on your list, or the landlord may force you to do so later.

Assigning or Transferring a Lease Agreement

The most common reason for assigning a lease agreement is to facilitate the sale or purchase of your business. The assignment clause is one of the vital organs of a lease agreement and should be included in the offer to lease or LOI. Read this carefully. Just because the landlord agrees to give assignment rights to a tenant doesn't mean they can't build in many tricky and dangerous conditions that can trip you up or cost you money later.

Landlords typically don't like it when one tenant sells a business and assigns or transfers their lease agreement to another tenant. As a best-case scenario to the landlord, the assignment or transfer of the lease agreement represents a lateral move. In the worst-case scenario, the tenant sells their business to a new tenant who runs it into the ground and can't pay the rent. This is the reason why landlords want to check out and approve anyone you sell your business and transfer your lease agreement to.

The second reason for assigning a lease agreement is that you want to move because you need to downsize your business or because you want to expand your business and get bigger somewhere else. If this is the case, then you can probably assign your lease agreement to a company in a different type of business altogether. Landlord approval and consent to the stated use or the change of use is essential in such a case. If you're a hair salon, don't assume you can assign your lease agreement to a butcher shop, or any other tenant for that matter, if the landlord doesn't agree to the *permitted use* change, too.

The key wording to include in an assignment clause is that *the landlord will not unreasonably withhold their consent* to the lease assignment. Another point to look at closely is the fee or dollar amount the landlord will charge to process the assignment. This can range from $0 to over $2,000, depending on the landlord. Finally, ensure that there's a timeline for the landlord to either grant or deny your assignment request. We've seen situations where the sale of a business falls apart simply because the landlord took too long to respond to the assignment request; 10–20 days is a reasonable timeframe, but much longer and the buyer might walk. This is all negotiable, so don't just automatically accept the landlord's standard assignment clause if the terms seem unreasonable.

Although there are a few basic points you want to ensure your assignment clause includes, be wary of other terms that may have major negative implications on your business or sale of your business. Here are a few common ones to watch out for:

✓ **Landlord's right to terminate:** In some cases, as an alternative to granting the assignment request, the landlord has the option to terminate your lease, simply for requesting an assignment. While this may be good news if you're assigning your lease because you're relocating to a bigger or smaller space, it can be devastating if you're selling your business, and you've now just lost your location.

✓ **Landlord's right to adjust the rent:** Your lease may also state that when you assign the lease, the rent can be adjusted by a certain percentage or index amount — or increased to a fair market value. Again, this can have a major impact on the sale of your business.

✓ **Requirement to sign a new lease:** The lease may require that the new tenant sign a new lease agreement, and depending on these terms, it can derail the process.

Deposit increase: The landlord may want the buyer of your business to increase or put up a substantial deposit or personal guaranty in order to gain landlord approval.

✓ **Removal of terms:** In some cases, an assignment results in the new tenant losing renewal options, exclusive use provisions, or other terms you negotiated for your benefit. This can again kill any deal to sell your business or even lead to lawsuits down the line if you represented these terms as part of your lease to the new tenant.

These are just a few of the many terms that can have a significant impact on you. Read this section carefully — or better yet, have a professional lease consultant review this for you. (See Chapter 6 for our recommendations about professionals reviewing your paperwork.)

Negotiating the Lease Deposit and Prepaid Rent

Commercial lease deposits are commonplace, but they're not legally required. We typically negotiate for no deposit on many lease agreements, or to have the deposit applied to first accruing rents. The landlord wants to collect as much up-front money from you as possible, partly to offset the commissions they pay to their real estate agents. A deposit or up-front earnest money sometimes demonstrates to a landlord that the tenant has the financial depth to build out the space and get the business open.

The most common argument landlords use for trying to collect a deposit from a tenant is that *All tenants are required to make a deposit.* This is simply not true, across the country or in real life. The amount of deposit and when it's paid are completely negotiable. In this section, we show you how to determine whether or not you pay a lease deposit.

Establishing the lease deposit amount, if any, and why

One to two month's rent is the industry deposit norm. Some landlords ask for both base rent and operating costs to be included in the deposit, whereas others only ask for base rent. In some cases, the deposit can be as high as four month's rent depending on the landlord or the tenant.

The amount of the deposit is fully negotiable. Furthermore, the deposit doesn't have to be paid when the offer to lease or the LOI is signed. In fact, it's a flawed strategy to pay the deposit at this time, because landlords often know that most tenants don't have enough deposit money to be dealing on multiple spaces simultaneously. Don't tip your hand this way.

If the landlord insists on a deposit, attempt to have this deposit applied throughout the term, especially if the deposit is several months' rent. In some cases, The Lease Coach negotiates to have the deposit applied to the rent in month 13, or month 25, or to have any remaining deposit applied to the last month of the initial lease term. At some point, you've proven yourself as a tenant, and the landlord should no longer require a large deposit, if any at all.

The offer to lease should state that the deposit be paid approximately three days after both the landlord and the tenant sign all documents and remove all conditions.

Stating whether any rent must be prepaid

Prepaid or *advance* rent is not the same thing as a deposit. A deposit or a portion of it is typically held for the entire lease term and returned to the tenant when they move out. Prepaid rent is additional good faith money that the tenant puts up front to close the deal. This prepaid rent typically applies to the first, second, or third month of the lease term once the tenant opens for business. Prepaid rent is not required or collected by all landlords and is even more negotiable than the deposit itself.

If you're opening a brand new business, you probably have better places to use your money than prepaying rent. Don't hesitate to negotiate on this point, especially if you're already committing a sizeable sum to open the business.

Anticipating a Personal Guaranty

If you're a startup corporation or don't have a lot of financial depth, you can expect the landlord to request or insist on a personal guaranty from you.

Sometimes landlords may also want a personal guaranty from your spouse or all the partners involved. A personal guaranty isn't mandatory. We frequently negotiate to either eliminate personal guaranties altogether or minimize them for the protection of the tenant.

Though a personal guaranty may seem like an unfair request; it's beneficial to look at it from the landlord's point of view. To a landlord, you're an unproven business risk. If the landlord is contributing tenant allowance money, free rent, and paying a real estate commission, then the landlord has some skin in the game. If the landlord's risk can be quantified — say $75,000 — then you shouldn't have to provide a personal guaranty for more than that amount.

If you can't eliminate the personal guaranty altogether, the goal should be to set a limit and reduce it over time. So, a $75,000 guaranty the first year may be reduced to $50,000 the second year, $25,000 the third year, and thereafter there is no personal guaranty at all. By that time, you've faithfully paid rent over all those years and have ideally earned the trust of the landlord.

Although an offer to lease or LOI may reference a personal guaranty as a point of the agreement, the personal guaranty details typically becomes a separate exhibit that's attached to the lease agreement and represented as its own separate agreement with the landlord. The tenant — which is actually your corporation — is responsible for the terms of the lease agreement, and the guarantor — in this case, you — is responsible for the tenant if the tenant does not fulfill the lease obligations. The guarantor is much like a co-signer on a loan. For that reason, you must focus carefully on this clause and be prepared to negotiate.

Protecting Yourself with Conditions

As an entrepreneur or a business owner, leasing commercial space is only one of the components necessary to bring your dream to fruition. You must also secure financing as well as bring all the other pieces of the puzzle together before you actually require the space for your business. In an offer to lease or letter of intent, both tenant and landlord include conditions that must be met in order for the deal to be consummated. For example, the landlord may make it a condition of the offer to lease that they're satisfied with your credit score or financial statements.

You need to include clauses for your protection as well, including the following items:

✔ **Business permits, including zoning:** Business owners are occasionally surprised to find that the property they want to lease isn't zoned for their type of use. This often has to do with parking ratios and how much traffic a business is creating to a particular area. Therefore, it's normal to make an offer to lease conditional upon getting a business permit, which of course, is issued only if the zoning for the property is acceptable.

✓ **Construction estimates:** If you qualified for a $200,000 loan, but the cost of renovating and improving the space far exceeds your initial budget, you may or may not be able to borrow more money. In some cases, the tenant is simply unwilling to borrow or put additional money into the project. One condition that you can put into an offer to lease is final approval of all construction estimate quotes.

✓ **Financing:** Dale recently spoke with someone planning to open a business. Although they were confident they could get financing for that business, the bank told them that final approval would not be forthcoming until the business owner provided the bank with an executed lease agreement. Therefore, it's perfectly normal to include a financing condition.

✓ **Inspection of the property or premises:** What you see isn't always what you get. A property can be loaded with patent or latent defects. There can be mold or termites, for example. Just because you negotiated a great lease deal doesn't mean that you shouldn't do a thorough inspection of the property, especially if it's an older building. Most lease agreements state that the tenant is accepting the premises *as is*. We've seen many tenants sign a lease agreement after visiting the property once. We recommend going back and looking at it several times with your partner or spouse or building inspector.

✓ **Partner or franchisor approval:** One of the advantages of having business partners or even a franchisor is that you have another set of eyes and ears to review various leasing opportunities. Not all partners will agree on which location constitutes the best place for their business. If one partner doesn't give their blessing to a location, you should have the right to rescind the offer to lease.

✓ **Satisfaction with the formal lease agreement:** A typical offer to lease or letter of intent is only a few pages in length. It's quite possible that a landlord and tenant cannot come to terms on certain sections or clauses within the formal lease agreement, which may be 30, 40, or 50 pages in length. Even though the landlord and tenant may have come together on the business terms, it's quite acceptable for the tenant to make their satisfaction of the formal lease agreement terms as a condition of the deal-making process.

Getting the Miscellaneous Points in Order and on Paper

There's no set rule on which business terms should be part of the offer to lease, but you'll have fewer nasty surprises if you address all financial terms and any other terms that are critical to your business as early as possible. Some of the terms important for you may include the following:

✔ **Acceptance dates:** There are often two dates on an offer to lease that are important to the tenant. A date should be applied as to when the agreement is created as well as when the agreement is signed. However, it's also advisable to stipulate that the offer to lease is only open for landlord acceptance for a certain period of time. This can be 4 business days or 10 business days, but there should be a window of opportunity for the landlord to respond. If the landlord doesn't respond within that time frame, you can move on or re-visit the opportunity with a revised proposal.

✔ **Consideration:** *Consideration* is the term given to the exchange of monies between the parties. That's why you may see a lease agreement stating *for $10.00 hereby paid and received.* A deposit, for example, can act as consideration.

✔ **Days and hours of operation:** Tenants shouldn't assume that they can control their days and hours of operation. In a popular retail plaza, the landlord may expect all tenants to be open seven days a week, from 9 a.m. to 9 p.m. But that may not suit your type of business. Office tenants who work on the weekend should recognize that landlords may not run the air conditioner on the weekends or provide public access to the elevators. Make sure you fully understand and negotiate your expectations.

✔ **Expansion right:** If your business is operating successfully, and you need to expand. It's quite possible that the unit directly next to you or elsewhere in the property will become available. You can negotiate now for expansion privileges in the future.

✔ **Parking:** Don't take parking for granted. Depending on the time of day you visit a property, there may or may not be sufficient parking. The location of the parking and whether the parking stalls are designated are all part of the negotiating process. In some cases, especially with downtown properties, parking is an additional monthly expense. All parking privileges should be stipulated as part of the offer to lease process.

✔ **Radius clause:** Landlords often attempt to restrict a tenant from opening too many stores in one area. Much of the reason for this clause is directed toward franchise and chain operations, who may or may not be paying percentage rent. You can either negotiate to eliminate the radius clause altogether or reduce the radius from 5 miles to ½ mile of your current location.

✔ **Signage:** A proper offer to lease or LOI includes very specific signage language. Don't assume that you have any signage rights unless specified in the offer to lease. This applies not only to fascia signage (on the front of the building), but also pylon signs and pull-away roadway signs. Some landlords may use signage as an additional revenue stream, so make sure you talk dollars as well.

✔ **Site plans:** At the back of an offer to lease or attached to the formal lease agreement is a site plan. Establish from a bird's eye view the parameters of the property and all the other buildings that may be included or excluded from this property. Having a site plan and the tenant's unit crosshatched on that site plan attached to the offer to lease is advisable.

✔ **Termination rights:** There are many reasons that you may want to terminate your lease agreement prematurely. You may simply be losing money running the business or you may have been so successful that you've outgrown your space and desperately need to expand. Whatever reason you can imagine for possibly wanting to terminate your lease agreement should be included in the offer to lease and formal lease agreement. Sometimes a penalty or an extended notice period may apply. Obviously, having a right of termination is desirable for you, but not for the landlord. Many landlords may not agree to an early termination, but you must decide for yourself how important this clause is to you.

Dating and Signing the Lease Agreement

Finalizing an offer to lease or LOI, whether on a new location or renewal, includes properly executing the lease documents. Tenants need to be sensitive to deadlines for signatures and condition removals as well as where and how notice is delivered to the landlord.

When making an offer to lease or LOI, it's wise to set a timeline or deadline for acceptance. Remember, it's not a deal until both parties have agreed upon the terms, signed the agreement, removed conditions, and made some form of financial consideration or financial transaction.

If both parties accept the offer to lease or LOI within any specified timelines, you can then remove any conditions and finalize the lease agreement. If conditions aren't going to be met by the deadlines, take the time to create a short condition extension letter or agreement, where both parties agree to extend these deadlines as needed.

Manage these timelines so that all your hard work isn't wasted because you miss a condition date. The landlord can then decide to back out of the deal. Or the opposite may occur, where conditions are removed because you didn't provide notice that the conditions weren't met.

Chapter 9

Negotiating the Rental Rate

. . . .

In This Chapter

▶ Understanding the value of a dollar (per square foot)

▶ Preparing for the negotiation

▶ Looking at the percentage rent

▶ Making offers and counteroffers

. . . .

*E*very tenant wants to pay the least amount of base rent possible. Every landlord wants to get more rent. In negotiating your rent, it's important to realize that not all tenants pay the same rent per square foot — that's negotiable based on many factors. It's equally important to understand that the landlord's asking rental rate is based on what they need to satisfy their mortgage and financial commitments — not necessarily on what you can afford to pay. This chapter walks you through the process of negotiating your rent.

Understanding the Importance of the Rent Figure

It should come as no surprise that rent can be one of your major three business expenses, if not the largest. Your rent is not only important as a big part of your day-to-day expenses — second only possibly to salaries and the cost of goods — but also as a major factor if and when you sell your business. Many retailers, entrepreneurs, restaurant owners, and even healthcare or office tenants have come to The Lease Coach over the years complaining that they're unable to sell their business because prospective buyers think the rent is simply too high. The buyer is essentially scared off by the overhead.

Never underestimate the importance of getting a property at the right rental price. Rent can make or break your business. If you're struggling to pay your rent, there are two possibilities: Either your rent is too high or your sales are too low.

Dale spoke with a brand new franchisee who was planning to open several locations in Texas. He did his homework and established that other tenants paid $30 per square foot in the property he was interested in, so he was prepared to pay $30 per square foot as well. Dale told him that he had done over 50 new leases and renewals for tenants in his industry, and that this amount was certainly pushing the limit and more than most tenants in that industry could justify or afford to pay.

Just because a house is valued at $1.5 million or a car is priced at $93,000 or the rental rate for a commercial property is set at $30 per square foot doesn't mean that you can afford to pay it — or should pay it. Negotiating the rental rate within the budget parameters for your particular industry is an important part of whether your business can be successful or not.

Exploring How Landlords Set Rental Rates

If your landlord is smart, they don't just pull a rental figure from the air. A typical commercial developer sets their rental rates based on a simple formula whereby the rental revenue from the tenants covers the mortgage and provides the landlord with a 10–20 percent *capitalization rate*, or return on investment.

Mathematically, this is an easy calculation for the landlord. The calculation involves two numbers or factors: face rate versus net effective rental rate:

- ✔ **The face rate** is the dollar amount of rent you pay and the amount that appears on the lease agreement.

- ✔ **The net effective rental rate** is the amount left after deductions for real estate commission, inducements and incentive packages, the landlord's work they do on the space, and so on. With a $24 per square foot rental face rate, the net effective rent the landlord is left with can easily be reduced to $17 per square foot after these deductions.

The next sections explain how the economy and other factors affect the landlord's rental rates and what you pay.

Looking at various economic factors

In the early 1990s, Dale did lease deals in his city for tenants at $0.00 per square foot. That's not a typo: The base rent was $0.00 per square foot. All the tenant had to agree to pay were the operating costs. The economy was at a low point, and commercial properties everywhere had numerous vacancies.

Landlords simply wanted to lease the space to help offset the cost of running buildings. The office Dale leased for The Lease Coach at $3 per square foot now commands rents in excess of $20 per square foot just ten years later.

The economy plays a big factor in commercial rental rates.

Successful business owners learn to read the economy and understand that there are leasing cycles. The goal, as they say in the stock market, is to *buy low and sell high*. For you, this translates into leasing your space when the economy is at the lowest. If your lease term expires when rents are high, and the economy is strong, it will hurt your business's bottom line if that translates into a substantial rent increase on your lease renewal.

Commercial leases are not unlike many other aspects of business, in that supply and demand play a major role in the landlord's expected rental rates. Even if the landlord gets their desired return on investment, they may raise rents based on the demand for space in the property or similar properties in the market.

Revealing why all tenants don't pay the same rent in the same property

Although knowing what other businesses in the building you lease space in are paying is a good idea, expecting their rent per square foot to be the same as yours isn't always realistic. There are legitimate reasons why various tenants pay differing rental rates in the same property:

- ✔ **Size:** The size of space the tenant requires (sometimes based on industry) or the size of the commercial retail unit can make a difference.

- ✔ **Term:** The length of the term or the number of years the tenant has agreed to lease can be a factor. A longer lease term doesn't necessarily mean a lower rental rate, depending on the current economy and occupancy of the property.

- ✔ **Strength:** The covenant and history of the tenant is relevant to the landlord from a rental perspective. Whether the tenant is a mom and pop startup or a national chain store, signing the lease corporately matters to the landlord and their mortgage holder.

- ✔ **Inducements:** The dollar value of the inducement package also impacts the rental rate. Although most landlords build some financial inducements into their asking rental rate, the two are connected.

- ✔ **Timing:** The timing of when the business becomes a tenant of the property matters. In a newly developed property, the first and last tenant may pay different rates.

✔ **Industry:** The tenant's industry is a factor. For example, hair salons are plentiful, but pet shops aren't. Pet shop owners have more locations not leased by their competitors to potentially choose from, so larger properties that want to attract a wider mix of tenants may have to charge a pet shop a lesser rent than hair salons.

✔ **Physical location:** The physical location within the location of the commercial retail unit relevant to other units in the property can make a difference.

Establishing where you are in the landlord's lease up plans or cycle

When a property is developed and under construction, the landlord launches a pre-leasing program to kick off or initiate leasing activity. The landlord's goal is to pre-lease as much space as possible and have the property and all the tenants open for business at approximately the same time. But landlords don't always achieve this goal; one of our clients told us that the property he occupies is six years old and that several units within the property have still never been leased.

If all the tenants open at the same time, most of them will have their lease renewals at the same time. However, over a 15- to 25-year period, some tenants will go broke, and some won't renew their lease agreement. The older the property is, the less likely all the tenants may renew their leases at the same time. Therefore, the landlord's leasing cycle changes as the property gets older.

Differentiating between asking rents and real rents

On the websites of the major commercial real estate brokerages, you can find thousands of properties across the country for lease, many of which include detailed leasing brochures. On those brochures, you may find stated rental rates. These are the landlord's asking rents with or without an inducement package.

Typically The Lease Coach can negotiate for a rental rate approximately 15 to 25 percent lower than the asking rental rate on the brochure. This varies from city to city and property to property and is affected by other factors. Keep in mind that most landlords and their real estate agents build room into the asking price of the rental rate to negotiate with the tenant.

What the rental rate may not include

Most leases are *triple net* leases; this means that all costs related to the property are passed through to the tenants. These operating costs or Common Area Maintenance (CAM) and property tax charges are typically stated as separate or additional rent, which the tenant must pay. In some cases, the operating costs are equivalent to or even more than the base rent.

The base or minimum rental rates stated per square foot probably don't include any charges the landlord wants for signage, storage, parking, utilities, and so on. Other costs indirectly related to the lease can be property taxes, business taxes, insurance, and so on.

 It's extremely important to have absolute clarity on what rents and related costs you have to pay. Many tenants, having negotiated their leases on their own, have come to us after signing lease agreements to ask and complain why these surprise related rental costs popped up. Always think *buyer beware* when you sign the lease agreement — or preferably before you sign.

In a *gross lease* (which is not that common), the operating costs are included in the *gross rent*. You may still have to pay extra for parking, signage, and other extras, but here again the onus is on you as the tenant to scrutinize this and negotiate accordingly. Contrary to what most business owners think, a gross lease is not better than a net lease.

Determining What You Can Afford to Pay in Rent

You can't negotiate your rent until you have some idea of what you can afford to pay. This would seem to be a basic business tenet, but it's one that many business owners neglect to figure out. This section explains how to come up with a figure that won't eat up too much of your business profits.

Knowing the average

A general rent range figure, encompassing all industries, is that tenants should budget to pay 5–12 percent of their gross sales in rent (provided their sales volume is high enough). Naturally, the exact number varies from industry to industry, depending on the type of product or services you're selling from the premises. The higher your sales volume, the more important every percent becomes to your bottom line.

Every industry has their ideal or maximum ratio. For example, Dale spoke at a private convention for a franchisor who brought The Lease Coach in to give real estate training to his franchisees. During the event, the franchisor told his franchisees that they should try to achieve rental deals in which their gross rent (meaning the base or minimum rent and the operating costs) was 5.5–6.5 percent of their gross revenue (sales).

A tenant we talked with recently was paying a 10–11 percent rent to sales ratio. They could barely afford this, let alone any higher percentage. Figure out what you can realistically afford before you sit down at the negotiating table.

Being realistic about your rental budget

The landlord doesn't generally set the rental rate based on what they think tenants can afford to pay. It's your job to figure that out.

If you're a startup tenant, you should have a business plan or sales volume figure in mind that you expect to achieve in any particular location. The amount of sales can vary depending on the location, of course; even franchisors have different anticipated sales volumes for smaller or larger model stores that are part of the same brand. So, part of being realistic about your rental budget begins with being realistic about your area and how much space you lease.

If your business plan estimates that your yearly gross sales may be $830,000, and you don't want to pay more than 8 percent of your gross revenue on rent, then, mathematically, you can only afford to pay $66,400 per year in gross rent. If the gross rent you're looking at is double that figure, there's no realistic reason for you to expect that you can magically come up with that extra money or sales revenues.

Examining what your competitors are paying in rent

A chiropractor (different from the one mentioned earlier) came to Dale and wanted help negotiating a new lease. He had found a jewel of a location, and Dale agreed it was an excellent property. But the rental rates were so high per square foot that Dale had to talk him out of the location because he would have been paying more rent than Dale's other chiropractic clients. It simply wasn't realistic for him to expect to open a new office in a new location by himself, just being out of university for two years, and think he would be able to pay more rent than any other chiropractor.

Whether you're in retail, food service, or any other industry, you need to look around to see where your competitors are located and estimate what rent they're paying in their locations, as well as how many square feet they're leasing. If your competitors pay a lot less rent than you do, then they have the potential to sell the same or similar products and services at a more competitive price than you do. This could eventually lead to the demise of your business concept.

You can pick an indisputably great location, but if you can't afford to pay the high rent, you can still fail, even if you're making decent sales, because your rent is siphoning off all your profits. Profit is king, not gross sales.

Comparing what you get to what you pay for

We often see tenants who get into trouble by agreeing to pay a rental rate within a property or plaza where their location is inferior to other units. End cap tenants with high visibility to the street and parking lot often pay the highest rental rates. If your premises are at the elbow of the plaza or in the shadow of a major anchor or at the quiet end of the plaza with side exposure instead of front exposure, you need to examine that closely and determine how it might affect your sales. A bigger space doesn't always equate into higher sales on an equal scale basis; remember the old adage: *location, location, location*.

Different units with the same property have a different value based on exposure, visibility, frontage, and other factors that draw traffic to your door. You need to be prepared to challenge landlords and their agents who make blanket statements that all tenants pay the same rent or that all the commercial retail units (CRUs) are equal. Even the depth and width of the CRU can make a difference in rental rates and desirability to the tenant.

Budgeting for annual base rent increases

Landlords anticipate that the cost of living or Consumer Price Index (CPI) may increase over time, and it usually does. This is called *inflation* by its simplest definition. Therefore, the landlord wants to build *steps*, or annual increases, into a tenant's 5- or 10-year lease term. This may be stated as a rent per square foot, such as $25.00 per square the first year with a $1.00 per square foot increase each year thereafter. Many lease agreements state that the annual rent increase may be calculated as a percentile factor, such as 3, 4, or 5 percent. You might see it written like this:

Year 1:	$18 per square foot
Years 2 and 3:	$19 per square foot
Years 4 and 5:	$20 per square foot

(Or like this)

Year 1 at $18 per square foot with annual increases calculated on the rate of CPI, or 3 percent, whichever is higher.

Fight like crazy on these annual base rent CPI and percentage increases. Every percentage point counts. In some parts of the country, landlords are satisfied to receive a flat rent or set rent for a full 5-year lease term. It's all negotiable.

Base rent can increases add up quickly year after year. Even if you can afford the rent in the first year, you may not be able to afford it by the time you get to the 7th, 8th, or 9th year of the term. You should actually calculate these compounding increases out into real numbers: Tenants are surprised by how quickly the rates increase when compounding over 5–10 years.

Preparing to Negotiate the Biggest Deal of Your Life

Considering the average business owner or tenant stays in the same location for at least ten years, it's easy to calculate mathematically the total rent that you may pay to the landlord over that time period. This is often more than you have ever paid for a house or anything else you've purchased. This is part of the reason you need to develop a grave respect for rent. On a monthly basis, it may not seem like such a big purchase, but most tenants aren't leasing space monthly, but for a 5-, 7-, or 10-year term. The economy can crash and rebound in one entire lease cycle or term. What you need is a long-term vision.

The Lease Coach continues to do a lot of work for the tanning salon industry. The industry has gone through and will continue to go through tremendous changes. Long gone are the days where you can only get a tan at one of these salons; now you can get teeth whitening, massages, bodywraps, spray tanning, manicures, and more.

When you also consider that tanning salons are often scrutinized by the media and the government over health concerns, we don't think anyone can accurately predict what tanning salons will look like ten years down the road. If you're in a similarly volatile industry, consider how much your industry may change over the course of a long lease term.

Dale remembers when there was a bagel shop boom. Independent and franchised bagel shops popped up everywhere. Then *carbs* became a dirty word, and in less than ten years, most of the new bagel shops closed, leaving only the previously well-established, highest-quality bagel shops in business.

The following sections tell you how to negotiate; do them in the order listed for the best results.

1. Gather rental information

Gathering information is the first step of the preparation process when get ready ready to negotiate a lease. Information provided to you from a tenant who signed their lease agreement several years prior may not reflect reality today. Market rental rates may have changed since then. Nonetheless, do your best and gather rental rate information from as many locations and sources as you can before and during the negotiating process.

If you're a casual note taker, this can get pretty messy and confusing. As basic as it sounds, get yourself a binder, some hole-punched paper, and dividers. Keeping yourself organized through the process is important especially if you're dealing on multiple locations.

Much of the rental rate information you acquire can be directly from the landlord, their real estate agent, or property manager. They may provide the information to you verbally or by e-mail, or you may get it from reviewing the real estate broker's website.

Of course, you can do what we often do: Talk with other tenants and gather information directly from the business owners who pay those rents. Make sure you check rental rates in surrounding properties too, not just the ones you're dealing on. You can find rental rate info and properties for lease on various websites. Local real estate brokerages and landlord websites are good places to start.

No two properties are exactly alike, no two units are exactly the same size, and rarely are two leases the same. This compounds the difficulty of making sense of it all. Don't focus so much on what the landlord is charging in rent, but rather focus on what you can reasonably afford to pay.

2. Compare rental rates

You understand that the rental rates from one property to another can vary based on all the factors mentioned: location, the visibility, accessibility, traffic flow, and twenty other things that can impact the attractiveness of your location. The newness of the building and which other tenants chose to lease space there are factors in what rents are justifiable for those properties.

That being said, if one location is $4 per square foot more and 200 square feet larger or smaller than another unit, you should be able to mathematically calculate how much more sales you need to achieve each month in the more expensive property to achieve the same profit. When The Lease Coach does site selection for a tenant, we don't necessarily look for the cheapest property; we look for the property where the tenant can achieve the highest volume of sales relative to ultimately making the most actual profit.

3. Work to get the lowest rental rate, not just a fair one

Does commercial real estate ever go on sale? Yes and no. A piece of commercial land near Dale's home just came down about 10 percent, or $100,000, in price. There are deals to be had and reasons for those deals; a landlord may be running out of uses and may realize that the last couple of units in the property need a reduced rental rate because they already have the top 25 industries or uses in place.

Don't sell yourself short when it comes to negotiating your rent. So often a tenant fixates on receiving a fair rent when there was an opportunity to get a reduced or below market rent due to various circumstances. Different industries can afford to pay different rental rates, and the more plentiful your type of use or tenancy is, the higher rents you may have to pay as you compete for good locations available for lease.

4. Ask yourself the right questions

What-if questions are great for exploring unforeseen or unexpected circumstances. Ask yourself, "What if the anchor tenant in the plaza moves out? What if the landlord sells the building? What if the landlord loses the building to foreclosure — will that affect me as the tenant? What if my aging parent requires me to stay home and care for them?"

Dale had a client who was doing site selection and looking for a place to lease for a new business. When her father became ill, it slowed her down, but when her father passed away, she actually shelved her dream of opening a business.

After speaking at a convention, a business owner came up and hired Dale to negotiate her lease renewal. Once Dale reviewed the formal lease agreement, he observed that her rent was not excessive or high compared to her industry competitors. When he explored this with her and discussed her gross sales versus gross rent, she admitted she was paying a below-market rental rate. Dale asked her, "What if the landlord tries to triple your rent — will that change your expansion plans?" In other words, don't assume you can afford to renew your lease if the landlord has plans to triple your rent. You may have to close or relocate. This is another reason not to exercise your renewal option clause willy-nilly without asking the landlord what their plans are for the renewal term rental rate.

Tenants need to ask themselves whether their rent is too high. When do you plan to sell your business? Will a pending divorce affect the future viability of the business if your spouse is one of the original personal guarantors on the lease? When one spouse signs a lease agreement and opens a business, it can all come crumbling down because of a divorce.

5. Negotiate the base rent (minimum rent)

One of the biggest choices you have to make is whether to negotiate the base rent up front, at the beginning of the leasing process or somewhere farther along in the process.

Because most landlords want to step or escalate the rent over a 5- or 10-year term, you're really negotiating your position both at the beginning and at the end of the lease term. Looking forward, the landlord may try to set your lease renewal rental rates based on the rental rates of the last year of your current term (which you are negotiating now).

Too often Jeff and Dale see tenants negotiating in dollar-per-square-foot increments when they could have potentially saved a ton of money negotiating at $0.25 or $0.50 increments over time.

6. Get your game face on for the leasing process

We can't stress enough the importance of preparation and getting ready for the negotiations. If you allow landlords and their real estate agents to lead you through the process, randomly calling you and sucking you into a negotiation or discussion, you can be caught off-guard doing five different things at once and be very unfocused. Decide to take charge of the process, timelines, and appointments.

Preparation is the key. Getting your homework done before you take the test is a great way to prevent failing. The more you can make it appear that you're all business when viewing properties and talking to agents, the more you'll be respected, and the more credit you'll get for knowing what you're doing. When viewing space with the landlord's agent, don't put your happy face on. Put your game face on.

7. Leverage your position by negotiating on multiple sites simultaneously

It's absolutely critical that tenants position themselves to negotiate with more than one landlord at exactly the same time. This is both permissible and ethical. It is also smart, necessary, and advisable if you want to get the upper hand.

We want to make an important distinction here. Sometimes when Dale and Jeff speak on this subject, a tenant may say, "Oh yes, I have three or four locations I really like, so I am doing exactly what you recommended." By digging a bit deeper, they learn that yes, they do have three or four sites picked out — but they're only negotiating on one of them. It doesn't matter if you have 25 sites; it only matters how many you're negotiating *simultaneously*.

The Lease Coach has perfected this process and actually creates a bidding war between several landlords simultaneously for their client's tenancy. Sure, Dale and Jeff are skilled negotiators in their own right, but why not make multiple landlords pursue your tenancy? Remember that the landlord can take multiple offers to lease on the same site from various agents and collect a deposit from each of them. So you've got to fight fire with fire.

8. Make the offer or receive their proposal — don't drop the ball

Determining in advance whether you'll be pitching or catching isn't easy when it comes to the offer to lease, but either way, it's important not to drop the ball. If you're pitching, submission of your offer to lease to the landlord requires more than sending a fax or e-mail. Setting the stage with a phone call or an appropriate cover letter is important. Don't use the actual offer to lease to justify your position or negotiate. The proposed terms of the offer should stand on their own. You can, however, use a cover letter or e-mail to set the tone or book a follow-up appointment (which we recommend).

If you're catching (receiving a proposal from the landlord), always send a professional reply acknowledging you've received it. Resist asking questions or replying too quickly with any form of negotiation. Check to see whether the proposal has an expiration date that you may or may not want to strategically consider. Tenants frequently respond too quickly and lose some of their strategic leverage.

Also, if you receive the landlord's formal written lease proposal, check for what may be missing or what new points they may have added now that the business terms are getting laid down on paper. It's not uncommon for Dale or Jeff to be giving a free consult to a would-be tenant who wants to counter-offer based on a verbal proposal or very casual e-mail from the landlord or their agent. If it's not on paper, it's not real.

9. Verbalize the lease deal terms

An important part of negotiating the base rent comes down to verbal discussions. In fact, more often than not, Dale is *discussing* matters with a landlord or their agent or property manager more than actually *negotiating*. He has to make sure his opponent understands his position, and verbalizing the details and discussing why certain points are important to the tenant client is critical.

It is unfortunate how many business owners substitute e-mail for verbal negotiations because of the tenant's shyness or lack of experience. You can't successfully accomplish the deal through e-mail or letter writing. Sure, you may think you're better off getting responses in trackable e-mails, but if you lose the negotiation over it, why bother? You must get on the telephone or go face-to-face with the landlord and discuss the rental rate. The Lease Coach does this process many times to achieve the best results.

10. Respond in writing

After you've verbally exhausted yourself, then you can put your position in writing. The way that a tenant responds to the landlord in writing tells the landlord a lot about the tenant's sophistication, education, and overall confidence in their position. Writing an articulate letter and looking intelligent is harder than writing a good e-mail. Whether you choose brevity or hundreds of words also affects the opinion the landlord develops of you.

Letters written by office tenants compared to, say, dance studio owners show clear distinctions in personal style. If you prefer text messages to e-mails — or faxing to mailing a letter — your methods reveal insights to the way you do business. By the way, texting with landlords and agents is not recommended as part of the actual negotiation process.

Whatever form of written communication you have with the landlord, be conscious that it reveals much about you, your sophistication level, experience, and business plans.

11. Send a counteroffer to lease

Counteroffers must be made in writing with a signature or initials where appropriate. Contrary to what you may have heard and experienced since the emergence of e-mail communication, signing documents is proper protocol. We would not take you seriously if you didn't sign something.

It's extremely difficult for the recipient of your counteroffer to know whether you're pushing or pulling or whether you're happy or angry with the offer. Once again, the cover letter or cover e-mail is important in setting the tone. For example, if Jeff finishes a negotiation or discussion with a landlord, he typically sends them an e-mail confirming the day he's going to make his counteroffer. Then on that day, he makes the counteroffer with a cordial, professional e-mail to pave the way with a scheduled conversation.

Verbal discussions do occur as well, but try to manage the process rather than be spontaneous. We're always trying to build on relationships — not tear them down. Relationships with landlords can be fragile, and handling them properly is important by respecting the other party's schedules, plans, and time.

12. Don't confuse compromising with negotiating

Compromising can best be defined as meeting in the middle with your opponent. If you want six months of free rent, and the landlord is only prepared to give you two months of free rent, and you both agree to settle on four months of free rent, that was a compromise, not a negotiation. They gave you more than they planned to, and you got less than you wanted. Ultimately, compromising is sometimes necessary, but don't make the mistake of believing that the other person is necessarily happy with the compromised position. They may feel they had to discount their position too far without justification.

In such an example, Dale or Jeff would negotiate not so much by giving in or compromising on the requirement for 6 months of free rent at all, but by negotiating for the tenant to receive months 1, 2, 3 free — then months 13, 14, 15 free. Yes, the benefit to the tenant is spread out over time, but the tenant did receive all six months free. The landlord may be satisfied with this because during that time period they did receive rent payments (cash flow).

13. Trade something they want for something you want

The give and take, back and forth nature of a negotiation sometimes requires both parties to trade off positions. Let's say the tenant wants and needs a larger tenant allowance, but the landlord is gun shy, thinking the deal is getting too risky. We might offer to increase the *prepaid* advance rent, which is similar to a deposit but applied to first accruing rents — or we might offer another form of security such as a letter of credit. Or we might even offer to pay a slightly higher rent for a few years.

In one case where our client wasn't location sensitive, the tenant agreed to take a lease on a less desirable space than the one we were dealing on. The landlord had been stuck with a particular unit that had been sitting vacant for years because it had less exposure. Although the tenant wanted to be in this property somewhere, the actual location didn't matter. We traded the proposed tenancy to a lesser location for more financial incentives, and both parties felt good about the trade and deal.

14. Recognize red herrings and create your own

A *red herring* is a kind of diversion. If the landlord wants to take your mind off the high rental rate, they may try to divert you by asking for a ridiculously high deposit or personal guaranty from not only you but also from your spouse or even your parent. You spend all your time fighting and negotiating the deposit and personal guaranty but then end up paying the higher rental rate because your attention was diverted.

Smart landlords know if they build red herrings and other obstacles into their lease proposals that give the tenant an opportunity to win a few rounds, then the landlord can have their way on the most important issues to them. By the way, Jeff and Dale do this for tenants in their lease proposals, too.

15. Walk away from the negotiating table

In all the years Dale spent working for landlords, they rarely gave a tenant their best deal when they were sitting at the negotiating table. The very best terms and conditions were given to the tenant when the landlord felt they were losing the deal because the tenant was walking away or leaving the negotiating table. This is a professional tactic that tenants can use on landlords, but beware: landlords can use it on you as well.

For many tenants walking away is a frightening thought because they fear they'll lose the location or deal to another tenant. This is one of those tactics that can backfire on you if you're inexperienced and turn away from the landlord for too long — or if you send mixed signals.

In the hands of an experienced negotiator the walk-away tactic is extremely effective, and we use it often.

16. Use other locations as leverage

By now you're so far into the negotiation process that you've probably forgotten to keep those other fires burning. You want to keep as many lease deals simmering as you can manage. Nothing makes you feel less powerful than dealing on just one location at a time. Make sure you follow up with other landlords and agents — don't let those deals go cold too soon.

17. Avoid rookie negotiating mistakes

Probably the biggest rookie mistake is telling the landlord and the agent exactly what you're thinking. Or exclaiming during a space showing about how much you love the space. Cutting a deposit check too soon or giving the real estate agent all your financial information up front with no thought to privacy or privilege or timing can set your negotiating position way back.

Negotiating the Operating Costs as a Rent

Although most commercial real estate professionals may tell you that operating costs are not negotiable, there are aspects of the operating costs that can indeed be changed to the tenant's favor. The landlord wants to make sure that the tenants pay for all the operating costs for the property. There's nothing unusual about that. But when we do operating cost audits for groups of tenants in a building, we frequently find that the tenants are subsidizing capital improvements that the landlord is using to enhance or increase the value of the building.

If a formal lease document uses sufficient detail to define what constitutes an operating cost, then the tenant has a fighting chance to at least examine, question, and negotiate each item. For example, one Florida landlord charged an annual fee to all tenants to have a pool of money available for hurricane damage not fully covered by insurance. Upon closer inspection, we noticed that there was no end to this billing or reserve fund. Tenants were required to pay it forever. If a tenant moved out at the end of their lease term, they did not get any of the money back that they had paid, even if there had been no hurricane damage. The landlord simply created a slush fund that they could use as they pleased.

So look for these types of odd clauses and scrutinize them carefully — after all, it's your money. This section shows you how to do this.

Looking at what you're paying for

The majority of commercial, retail, and office lease agreements may stipulate the specific or key components of the operating costs that the tenants needs to pay for. Typical examples include general maintenance, painting, lawn cutting, snow removal, insurance for the property, and so on. Almost every lease agreement has an operating cost clause and typically defines these common area maintenance charges in a short- or long-form manner. From a tenant's perspective, longer is better than shorter because it creates certainty.

In one property we noticed that the property manager's salary was included in the operating costs being paid by the tenants. But the landlord refused to reveal the amount of that salary. We forced their hand and discovered the salary was ridiculously high. It wasn't that the category or fact of the salary itself was inappropriate — just the amount.

Why proportionate share counts

If a tenant occupies 7 percent of a commercial property, they can typically be required to pay their proportionate share — 7 percent — of the operating costs as additional rent. But not all tenants use or consume operating costs proportionately. For example, which would use more water, a hair salon or a bookstore? Which would contribute more to parking lot trash collection, a convenience store or a bank? Who uses the elevator more, someone on the 1st floor or the 20th?

One dry cleaner felt it was unfair that he had to pay his proportionate share of trash removal. He claimed that the only trash he created was one bag of garbage per week, which he happily put in his van, took home, and threw away with his household garbage. Yet he was forced to pay his proportionate share of trash removal like the other tenants.

Have your proportionate share of CAM (as a percentage number) actually stated in the lease agreement. Don't be afraid to question the operating costs and your proportionate share.

Capping the operating costs

You've heard the old cliché that nothing's certain except death and taxes. Well, you can add ever-rising operating costs to that short list, too. Rarely do operating costs or CAM charges go down, and they most certainly rise over time. Many tenants fall victim to landlords who abuse the operating cost budget and use the tenant's money to polish their jewel — their property.

In some cases, a slothful or cash-strapped landlord may have skimped on regular maintenance, but after the property is sold to a more reasonable landlord several years' worth of deferred maintenance has to be caught up at the expense of the present tenants. If you're trying to budget costs for the year, and your overhead rents are important to you, you may want to negotiate a 5–10 percent cap on operating costs so that annually the landlord can only raise them that amount at a maximum.

Note that the landlord's response may be a willingness to cap *controllable* operating costs, meaning they won't cap property taxes or such items that are beyond their management control. Any ceiling or restrictions that you can put on rising operating costs will ultimately benefit the tenant.

Identifying your audit rights and keeping your landlord accountable

Over the years The Lease Coach conducts many operating cost audits for groups of tenants in commercial retail and office buildings. Typically, we get a phone call from one tenant who is disgruntled and wants to challenge the landlord. It's much more cost effective for that tenant to get his neighbors together and share in the cost of an operating cost audit. Although some lease agreements state that the landlord provide the tenant with access to financial operating cost records, many leases do not. Some leases build in a 90-day or one-year statute of limitations, drawing the line on how far back the tenants can go.

As a tenant, you have rights. The landlord is acting as a steward of your money. Operating costs should not become a profit center for the landlord.

Communicating with the landlord about CAM concerns

Operating cost discrepancies come in two flavors: honest mistakes or dishonest (deliberate, negligent, or fraudulent) calculations. In a building where the property is fully or close to fully occupied, the landlord may have less reason to try to profit from operating costs but may still try to enhance the property with the tenant's money. However, when a property has several vacancies, the landlord may want to avoid paying his proportionate share of operating costs for the vacant units. Therefore, the landlord may put language into the lease agreement stating that the operating costs will be calculated as if the property is 95–100 percent fully leased or fully occupied, whether it is or not. In some situations, tenants can be carrying a very heavy burden if the property is not fully leased.

Communicating with the landlord both verbally and in writing about any operating cost concerns you may have is imperative. And don't wait too long, because the lease may stipulate a statute of limitations on adjustments. Sometimes the problem originates with the property manager, but sometimes it comes from the owner or landlord taking advantage of the tenants. When Dale was a commercial property manager, one landlord told him to find creative ways to charge every penny spent on the property back to the tenants. If you catch your landlord with his hand in the cookie jar, don't be surprised if he's not cooperative or communicative.

Figuring Out and Negotiating Percentage Rent

Percentage rent is an additional rent you pay over and above your base or minimum rent and operating costs. It's calculated as a percentage of each dollar of sales over a set number or *break point*.

Not all tenants are subject to paying percentage rent, and of course it's completely negotiable. In fact, percentage rent differs from one industry to another. Typically, landlords with enclosed shopping malls and high-end plazas may try to collect percentage rent from their tenants. Many restaurants in standalone properties can also face percentage rent.

The reason landlords justify collecting percentage rent is simple. The landlord feels that their property is partly responsible for the success of the tenant. So if the tenant does better than expected with higher sales volumes, the landlord wants a piece of the action.

Doing the math to determine your percentage rent

Here's an example to help you understand how percentage rent is figured:

Lease terms

Base rent: $30 per square foot

Square footage of premises: 4,500 square feet

Percentage rent: 7%

Annual rent: $30 × 4,500 = $135,000

Natural break point calculation: $135,000 / 7% = $1,928,571.43

Calculating your percentage rent

Sales in year one: $2,500,000

Sales over break point: $2,500,000.00 − $1,928,571.43 = $571,428.57

Percentage rent calculation: $571,428.57 × 7% = $40,000 (payable in percentage rent)

Total rent paid in year one: $135,000.00 (base) + $40,000.00 (%) = $175,000.00 (payable monthly and calculated annually)

Negotiating an artificial break point versus a natural break point

The break point is the level of sales a tenant must reach before percentage rent is due to the landlord. Say a tenant's natural breakpoint is $967,000 in annual sales, and their percentage rent is 6 percent. For every $100 in sales above $967,000, the tenant must pay the landlord $6.00. If the tenant can negotiate for percentage rent to kick in at an artificial breakpoint of $1.2 million in sales, they only have to pay the 6 percent on sales over *that* figure.

Of course, if you can also negotiate your percentage down from 6 to 4 percent, you can save even more rent money. Jeff and Dale often negotiate to ensure that percentage rent is calculated on net sales versus gross sales. If you take merchandise returns, coupons, and so forth, you won't want to pay rent on those sales, so calculate and report your sales accordingly. This may require an adjustment to the wording of the percentage rent clause in the lease.

Insider secrets that can lower your percentage rent

Here are two things you may never learn on your own or think of when it comes to lowering your percentage rent:

✔ **Decrease the level percentage rent downward as sales go upward.** So, 6 percent applies, for example, to sales between $1.2 million and $1.4 million. Then the percentage is reduces to 3 percent for sales from $1.4 million to $1.6 million. And so on.

✔ **Eliminate certain goods from being applicable to percentage rent, such as online sales or drastically discounted items.** One jewelry store tenant we worked with said his mark-up on large diamond rings was quite low (compared to other rings). By negotiating to have all diamond rings over $4,998 dollars exempt from calculation in the percentage rent total, he dramatically decreased the rent he had to pay.

Identifying Other Rents

Space isn't the only thing your landlord may charge you to rent. You may also be charged for signage, parking, a marketing fund, or even extra storage. Not all lease agreements disclose that there's an additional charge for these items, so don't assume that you can get these things for free, or even at all.

Discuss all rent items in this section individually with the landlord before signing the lease.

Renting signage space

A landlord typically sees signage as an extra rental income stream. By creating a pylon sign that has fewer panels than tenants in the building, the landlord assures that demand is greater than supply, allowing them to charge a substantial fee or monthly rent for these pylon signs.

When it comes to paying rent for signage, sometimes you're paying for both sides of the pylon sign. Sometimes the landlord may try to charge you for fascia signage on the front of the building or even electronic signage if your property has illuminated or electronic signage board.

If you're not sure whether you'll benefit from signage or how long you may want to be on the pylon sign, negotiate a right to terminate your signage rights and rent obligations associated with this. Make sure you understand whether the landlord has the right to increase signage rental rates or terminate your right to signage.

Parking lot rental

For many tenants, parking is free. But for some, monthly parking charges for their vehicles can range from $85 a month to several hundred dollars per month. In some downtown properties, parking can be $300–$400 per month. Even if you're prepared to pay for parking, don't assume it'll be available. When negotiating on parking, there are three considerations: negotiating the number of parking stalls, the location of those spaces, and the rental rate, if any.

Paying on the marketing fund

The marketing fund is a cost that may be apparent in your negotiations or may be buried on page 20 of the formal lease agreement. We've seen the fund stated as a set rate or left open-ended at the landlord's discretion. Some landlords have this marketing fund in place and expect all tenants to participate, but may not expect all tenants to participate at the same rate.

The marketing fund is a negotiable point that you may want to look at reducing or removing entirely if you don't see the value for your business. The key is to ask questions. Are all tenants paying the same rate? Are all tenants contributing to the fund? You don't want to find out only half of the tenants contribute or that you contribute more than most.

Chapter 10

Negotiating the Area (or Square Footage)

Choosing space means more than choosing the right location. Finding the right amount of square footage, in the right configuration, is also a big part of your decision-making process when it's time to set up your business. To know what works best for you, you need an understanding of how landlords measure space and what your space requirements are. This chapter explains how the industry measures space and how to determine and get the space you need.

Determining Your Space Requirements

When it comes to initially choosing the right amount of area to lease for your business, you need to consider several factors, including the following:

✔ Landlords traditionally lease space based on a per square footage basis. This is neither good nor bad, it's simply the industry standard. As a tenant, this means you can't always choose or control the exact amount of space you are able to lease, because landlords create individual commercial retail units (CRUs) that are preset in size.

✔ The amount of area you need now could change in a few years. Many tenants outgrow their current location as they expand; this happens less with franchise tenants because they work from a predetermined cookie-cutter formula that determines their space.

Not being able to customize your space to fit your needs can be a disadvantage when choosing a site. If each side by side CRU in a plaza is 1,200 square feet, and you need 1,700 square feet, your need may limit or impede your leasing opportunity in that building. Sort of like when you find a great pair of jeans in a store, but they're not your size. This is not to say that individual CRUs can't be *demised* (cut down in size or expanded), but you must consider factors such as preexisting electrical panels, firewalls, HVAC systems, and ducting, just to name a few common obstacles.

This section walks you through the decision-making process of choosing a space that will work for you both now and in the years to come.

Looking down the road

A space that isn't exactly the right size for your needs can become an issue both now and down the road as your business grows or shrinks or as you add more employees and need someplace to put them. Over the years, we've negotiated lease renewals for many tenants who were either downsizing or expanding — often because they were adding or subtracting various lines of merchandise. At The Lease Coach, we picked up some office space for ourselves that was twice the size we needed at the time, but within two years we had grown to the point that every office was filled and storage space was running short.

Because the tenant is paying rent for every square foot (and operating costs) the size of your space can make quite a difference in your monthly rent check. Although you must consider a number of factors when looking at space needs, one that's often overlooked is that the landlord's leasing or real estate agent can be paid a higher commission if they can get you to lease a larger location or more area. It's easy for a tenant to be pushed toward leasing a larger unit or a multiple of contiguous CRUs just because that's the existing inventory of space for lease or because the real estate agent can earn a larger commission.

The truth is most business owners don't know how much space they really need to lease for a 5-year term, let alone for 10 years or longer, especially for a startup business. Experienced business owners may have a better idea of what they need. So when a tenant leases space, it's no wonder they often miscalculate, and end up with one that's too large in the beginning and too small at the end of the term when the business has grown and matured. We've seen tenants with two washrooms convert one of them to storage because they outgrew their current location. Frequently Jeff and Dale see healthcare tenants who design waiting rooms and restrooms far larger than necessary — and then are forever stuck with the wasted space. One of The Lease Coach's clients for whom Dale was negotiating a lease renewal previously installed a shower in their small office. Now they are ripping it out to make way for storage.

Depending on the type of business you operate, there are often loose industry guidelines for sizes of waiting areas in medical offices, seating areas for food service tenants, or sales floor space for retailers, just to name a few. Look to your competition to get a rough idea of how much space you might need.

Where office tenants often go astray is in using the same office space left by the previous tenant. That's fine if you have the same type of business and use the offices for the same purposes, but that's often not the case. Some offices might be too large for your purposes, and others too small. Just because the last tenant had eight employees and you do too doesn't mean you need the same amount or configuration of space.

We've all dined in restaurants with too much or not enough seating. Unfortunately, there are too many industries and leasing variables to make determining the perfect-sized space a science. You have to balance the area you need with the rent per square foot — and stick to your budget.

As a former shopping mall manager, Dale spent a lot of time shoulder to shoulder with some very powerful landlords who measured their tenant's success not by their volume of sales but by their sales per square foot. As an example, to the landlord, a 5,000 square foot store doing $3 million dollars in annual sales wasn't more successful than the 2,000 square foot tenant with $2 million dollars in annual sales, because the smaller store produced more revenue per square foot. In shopping malls, they refer to the tenant's *average annual sales per square foot*. The higher the sales per square foot, the better the tenant is doing, business-wise.

Conventional office tenants or light industrial tenants don't have to consider the retail factor. An office tenant may face some of the same challenges trying to pick the right size space, but it generally doesn't matter if he ends up on the 6th floor or the 11th floor of an office building. From a business stand-point, they do the same volume of business no matter what floor they're on. It's often easier for an office tenant to find exactly the size they need than it is for a retail tenant.

Adjusting your business plan to the circumstances

Sometimes a site seems perfect, but obstacles are working against you. In these cases, you may need to roll with the circumstances and get creative to use the space — or negotiate with the landlord to change it to suit you.

Dale remembers negotiating a new lease for a major submarine sandwich franchisee right beside a major coffee shop chain. This was a new development with several outparcels and pad site tenants. But the rent per square foot was a bit high for the franchise tenant, who needed 1,300–1,500 square feet according to their franchisor. By leasing just 1,100 square feet, the tenant was able to afford the higher rent per square foot commanded for this premium location adjacent to a very strong neighbor.

Of course, this meant the franchise tenant needed to make some compromises on how their quick service restaurant (QSR) was designed. More offsite storage would be required, but based on the rental savings (base rent and operating costs) coupled with being an ideal location, it was worth it to the franchisee to store paper cups and condiments in his garage.

Another client in Salt Lake City called Dale to explain that there was a prime 2,400 square foot unit available for lease that he really wanted. Dale reminded the tenant that he only needed 1,200 square feet for his concept, to which he protested that the leasing agent said the landlord wouldn't demise down the size of the premises. Dale looked at the site plan and knew the space could be demised into two smaller units. When he told the listing agent that they were walking away unless the landlord agreed to demise the space down, miraculously the demise request became possible, and the tenant could now lease the 1,200 square feet they required.

Understanding why the physical shape of the space matters

For retail tenants considering the perfect space, the magic word is *frontage*. Most retail tenants want as much frontage as they can get. *Frontage* is the exposed area of fascia and windows that prospective customers walking or driving by can see from the parking lot or the road.

Some CRUs are irregular in shape, but most lease spaces are generally rectangles. If a plaza is 100 feet in depth, and the tenant wants only 1,000 square feet of space, this means that the tenant has just 10 lineal feet of frontage (not nearly enough to make shoppers comfortable). Sure, the space is a rectangle, but it's more like a bowling lane. As customers, we often don't want to walk to the back of long, narrow shops and stores. Not to mention the merchandizing challenge that the retail tenant has.

A perfectly square box isn't necessarily ideal for all tenants, but you can certainly have plenty of frontage, as well as more parking spaces directly in front of your store if your building is configured that way.

Planning the layout of the space

Tenants who utilize a professional space planner run less risk of leasing the wrong amount of area. A space planner knows from experience how many people can fit into a certain area and whether the HVAC can handle it. We've seen some poorly laid-out offices with narrow hallways, interior offices with no windows, doors that don't lock, and insufficient or poorly placed electrical and communication outlets.

A good space planner can be worth their weight in gold; you can find substantial cost savings with respect to placement of the washrooms, doorways, and hallways if they're well thought out. Often a space planner can help factor in columns and irregular corners or protrusions to maximize functional use of the space available. In Dale's new corner office, he tried a couple different layouts, but only one worked efficiently due to the presence of a support column that of course could not be moved.

 One quick and dirty way to measure rooms or a space — counting ceiling tiles — requires few tools and little effort. Although counting ceiling tiles is unscientific and imprecise, it can help you get a feel for the size of various rooms, areas, and offices. Though not all ceiling tiles are 2 feet by 4 feet, get your tape measure out to double-check and you can develop an eye for sizes. Another good idea is taping off the floor where you think walls should be built. This is an extremely useful exercise. Once you've taped off the individual rooms to the sizes you require, you can determine whether the space is adequate for your needs.

Getting the Space You Pay For

Space measurement is one of our favorite topics, and it's amazing how often it's done incorrectly. When an area isn't measured correctly, you can end up with *phantom space*, or space that really isn't there even though you're being charged rent for it. We include a couple case studies dealing with phantom space later in this chapter. It's absolutely shocking how much space is mismeasured. It's not always a lot, but why should any tenant overpay on the rent if they don't have to?

Eliminating phantom space

So why does phantom space exist? First of all, at least half of the space or measurement discrepancies we uncover are accidental, perhaps negligent, but certainly not fraudulent. If three side-by-side units are 1,400 square feet each, they total 4,200 square feet. Then the landlord decides to change the units to a 1,300 square foot unit and a 2,900 square foot unit, so he hires a contractor to put up the demising wall between them.

If the wall is built slightly off line or crooked, that can affect the area in each unit; one might end up with a little more space, and the other will have phantom space. Back in the 1980s and 90s, when Dale did a lot of work for landlords, they rarely had a space measured or certified after the wall was built or the work was done; it was assumed that the contractor followed instructions and built the wall where they were supposed to.

Phantom space or measurement discrepancies are more likely to occur where the space is irregular in shape, such as if a room is partially round. The lease line can also affect your space. A *lease line* is the point in the property from which your rentable space is measured. Depending on your type of building, some lease lines may be calculated to various points such as the outside of the interior wall that faces a hallway, to the exterior wall surface, to the midpoints of the demising wall shared by two tenants, or even to the outer edge of an overhang on the building. If the person measuring the premises is unaware of the measurement standard and lease lines, they make measurement mistakes or over-measure your space, mistaking where the lease line should really be.

The bottom line is: No landlord should be collecting rent on 107 percent of a building just because the property wasn't measured properly. Check the measurements yourself to make sure you're not paying for phantom space.

Checking the measurement clause in the lease agreement

Although commercial lease agreements come in all shapes and lengths, most contain at least a few paragraphs defining the measurement standard that the landlord and tenant agree to abide by (this is a good thing). This doesn't mean the space has been accurately measured — it simply provides a guideline or set of rules. The measurement clause might look something like this:

Measurement of Premises

Landlord may, from time to time, at its option, have the rentable area of the premises measured by an expert in accordance with the Measurement Standards and deliver a certificate of measurement to Tenant, and, if necessary as a result of such measurement, the annual Basic Rent and the calculations of Additional Rent shall be adjusted by Landlord. The effective date of any such adjustment shall be:

1. In the case of any measurement made prior to or within six months of the Commencement Date, the date Tenant is allowed possession of the Premises under this Lease; and

2. In all other cases, the date of the determination of the measurement.

Any such measurement by an Expert shall be final and binding on Landlord and Tenant. Neither Landlord nor Tenant may claim any adjustment to the annual Basic Rent or to the calculation of Additional Rent based on the Rentable Area of the Premises except in accordance with a measurement by an Expert made pursuant to this Section and, for greater certainty, neither Landlord nor Tenant may claim any adjustment to the annual Basic Rent or to the calculation of the Additional Rent based on such measurement for the period prior to the effective date of such adjustment as set out above.

"Measurement Standards" means the Building Owners and Managers Association ("BOMA") 1996 standard provided that notwithstanding the foregoing or anything else contained in this Lease, Landlord may, at its option from time to time, choose to measure the area of the Premises or any space included in the Building in accordance with the BOMA standard method of measurement then in effect from time to time.

Alternatively, the clause may define the measurement specifications in detail rather than indicating a guide or standard you must research.

"Measurement Standards" mean the Premises area shall be measured to the exterior of any outside walls and to the midpoint of any demising walls seperating the Premises from other leasable space in the Shopping Center.

Rectifying measurement discrepancies

If you discover that your area has been mis-measured or miscalculated, you need to take action. Although many landlords may agree to correct an obvious measurement discrepancy for the future, they can be resistant about paying the tenant back for past years of rent overcharges.

Using a measurement company

When landlords have space measured, they typically use a surveyor, architect, space planner, or professional space-measurement company. A few companies do specialize in space measurement, and their number one customer is the commercial landlord. These measurement companies can work for tenants too, but usually the landlord hires them.

The fee for measurement services can range from a few hundred dollars on a simple measurement to over a thousand dollars for more complicated or larger units. The price can vary if you want the partition (inside) walls shown on a floor plan. Measurement companies use CAD drawing software that automatically calculates the area when the measurement numbers are entered. The measurement person visits a location and within an hour or two, using a laser measurement device, gets the info they need.

In the old days, these measurements and calculations were done with a regular tape measure and a calculator, but not so much anymore. Once the measurement and optional floor plan drawing is finished, the company usually stamps it or certifies the measurement, so everyone can see who did the work and who stands behind it.

Many long-term tenants are left high and dry if the property they occupy is sold. The new landlord may correct the discrepancy for the future, but will not want to refund for the past. The clearer the landlord's fingerprints are on the original measurement, the greater your chance of recovering overpayments. Even if the measurement company the landlord hired made a mistake years ago, and no one has ever re-measured the property — we've seen this happen — ultimately the landlord is responsible.

Other parts of the lease agreement are tied to the area or square footage: the operating costs, the deposit, the tenant allowance paid to the tenant, and so on. So, the issues — the extra expenses to the tenant — may multiply themselves.

Area discrepancies are a matter of fact, not opinion. If two different parties measure the same space and come up with different totals, at least one of them is wrong. The landlord can't charge you for space you don't have if the space is incorrectly represented and you are overcharged.

You may think that a landlord with a proven area discrepancy may just roll over and play fair. But that's often not the case. A landlord may point to the words in the lease agreement like *approximately 2,300 square feet*. The intention of the word *approximately* is to prevent the tenant from voiding the lease contractually because they have less or more area. Many landlords learn their lesson and include language in the formal lease agreement that creates a statute of limitations — so their exposure is only limited to one year back from the date the discrepancy was discovered.

You can see the importance of understanding the measurement standards and confirming the measurements in a new lease. Discovering this partway through a lease term or when renewing can create a much more difficult situation to resolve. As we mentioned, landlords may correct the discrepancy for the future but resist providing a refund for past overcharges.

In the event a discrepancy is found partway through a lease term where the landlord is resisting a refund, the tenant has a couple options:

- ✔ **Factor the recovery in as part of the lease-renewal negotiation.** This only benefits the tenant if you plan to stay in the property and the lease expires soon. Some landlords can be reasonable to deal with, but others not so much.

- ✔ **Take legal action or explore arbitration.** This can be an expensive path for the tenant and, depending on the wording of your lease agreement or the size of the potential recovery, not necessarily the best route.

  Give Dale or Jeff a call first and get some free inside advice on how best to proceed. They've done plenty of these projects, as you will read about later in this chapter.

Understanding Measurement Standards

Every industry follows standard rules and norms, and the commercial real estate industry is no exception. It never makes sense to a tenant to pay rent on 2,900 square feet of rentable area when there is only 2,650 square feet of usable area. And why should the tenant pay a grossed-up square footage for the hallways and public washrooms? But that's the nature of this industry. It seems ridiculous to a tenant that when their space is measured it includes the width of the wall, but that's the way it is. And because most landlords play by the same set of rules and guidelines, tenants are unlikely to find a different set of rules across the street.

Industry standard measurement guidelines

Building Owners and Managers Association International (BOMA) has a set standard of measurement that many landlords follow, especially for office space. There are other standards that are used regionally. The landlord can create their own measurement standard if they so desire, and the tenant may never know that the industry standard measurement wasn't used.

Typically, the landlord stipulates that the space is measured to the outside of all exterior walls and windows and to the middle of a wall that you share with another tenant. So the thickness of walls can add up in the measurement process.

When it comes to mezzanine space — often a partial floor created above the main floor with access by stairs — a true standard rulebook doesn't seem to apply. Some landlords measure the mezzanine using the same formula as the main floor, and charge rent on mezzanine space, too. The rent per square foot may be less than for the main floor, but don't assume it is or isn't being included — ask.

You must understand the measurement standard (if any) being used, because it varies from landlord to landlord and from office to retail to industrial space. Ideally, the lease may contain a detailed description of the measurement calculations, but at a minimum it should contain the measurement standard being used so you can research and understand it to avoid disagreements down the line.

If a landlord claims to have had the space measured and certified, then they should be able to provide the tenant with documentation or a space plan to prove it — ask.

Understanding measurement terminology

Knowing the difference between the industry terms and what types of buildings these terms apply to is essential to understanding how space measurements are calculated. This section covers a few key terms:

Retail space

✔ **Gross leasable area (GLA)** is a term used when calculating the size of retail space in shopping centers and strip plazas. This area is the total enclosed space intended for the exclusive use of the tenant and is the number used when determining the rent you pay.

✔ **Lease line** is the term that refers to the measurement point for determining the gross leasable area for a retail tenant. This is typically the exterior face of any outside walls or walls separating the tenant space from a common area and to the center point of any walls shared by another tenant.

✔ **Common area** is an area in the building not intended to be rented but used by all tenants; a shared lobby or hallway is a good example.

Office space

✔ **The usable area** for an office space is typically measured or calculated from the dominant interior finish of any exterior walls, often the glass windows, the interior finish of any walls between common areas, and the midpoints of any walls shared with other tenants.

✔ **Load factor or gross-up (rentable/usable factor)** is used to account for common areas and building amenities such as shared washrooms and hallways that are outside the tenant's actual premises in which they conduct business. In simple terms, the *load factor* is how much your usable square footage will increase to determine your rentable square footage.

Load factor

The calculation to determine the load factor can vary with different industry standards and is a complex calculation that goes beyond the scope of this book. What we want you to take away from this is to understand the basic idea of what a gross-up or load factor is and how it impacts the size of your space and the rent you pay.

A *gross-up* or *load factor* can vary between buildings, but typically runs between 8–12 percent. Jeff worked with a dentist a few years ago who was looking at a two-story office building with a nice but large common area on each floor. What this meant was that, although the rental rate per square foot was similar to other buildings in the area, the gross-up was a lot higher than average, at 19 percent, making his total rent higher than other buildings with smaller gross-ups.

A common question we get from tenants is whether or not elevators, stairwells, or washrooms are something they pay rent on. Washrooms, common areas, electrical rooms, janitorial closets, and so on are included as part of the gross-up factor but elevators and stairwells shouldn't be.

A gross-up or load factor typically applies to office buildings, but some landlords of retail units may apply a gross-up factor to account for a common utility room.

The rentable area for each tenant is your usable area multiplied by the load factor or gross-up. For example, if your usable space is 3,000 square feet, and there is a load factor of 10 percent, then the amount of space you actually pay your rent and operating expenses on is 3,300 square feet.

Negotiating Rights of First Refusal on More Space

Not all tenants need or want to add a clause that allows them to increase their area, but it's a smart move for some tenants. After all, if you've signed or committed to a 5-year term but outgrow the space before the end of the lease, landlords frown upon your just walking away from the lease. But if the adjacent tenant is thinking of moving or not renewing their lease and you can snatch up their space, you can get the space you need without having to move.

One downside to annexing more space is that you often can't get just a portion of your neighbor's space. You will probably have to take it all or none of it, although some landlords may be flexible, provided you leave them with enough space to be attractive to another tenant. If there's any expectation whatsoever that you may need to expand your business in the future, you can negotiate for a right of first refusal to lease either a portion of the space adjacent to you or all of it at the time of lease signing.

However, that requires the neighboring tenant to move or close out, before you can benefit with the option to expand. It won't help you much to have this clause in your lease if you desperately need to expand but your neighbors aren't budging.

Measure — it's worth the trouble

Dale was having dinner one evening with the COO of a major franchise chain. She was saying how much the company was enjoying their new office space and corporate headquarters. With 160 plus stores across the country, they had outgrown their old office a long time ago. Now, she said, they all had individual offices, not cubicles, and it was a great space. When Dale asked her if she'd measured the space for accuracy, she said no. The lease agreement said they had 4,400 square feet, and there was plenty of room, so why be concerned?

It took about three weeks for Dale to convince her that he should measure the space for her. What was supposed to be 4,400 square feet turned out to be only 3,600 square feet. They had been paying for 800 square feet of phantom space for many months. The office building had recently been purchased by a lawyer who had simply taken for granted that the previous landlord's space measurements were correct.

After some skillful negotiating, Dale not only got the tenant a refund for what they had overpaid, but in this case (and more importantly) he corrected the error for the future. The tenant saved over $52,000 in rent from this measurement, in just the first 5-year term. They stayed another five years and benefitted again. It was no wonder that almost every tenant in the building then hired The Lease Coach to measure their space too.

Another example: We have the most wonderful accountant. He has not only used The Lease Coach for his lease renewals negotiations several times, but we use his firm to do our corporate bookkeeping and tax filing. During our first lease renewal project for his office, we recommended a space measurement. He agreed but really did not have any expectations we would find anything. Turns out, there was a small discrepancy in the area, and he was short 32 square feet. Because he had leased the space for many years, we negotiated with the landlord and got him a $3,200 refund and fixed the error, lowering his rent payments for the future. As an accountant, he truly could appreciate the $3,200 refund as an incredible, unexpected gift.

In some deals, we negotiate for the right to terminate the tenant's lease agreement if the tenant needs to expand and the landlord cannot provide additional space. In most cases, you'd want the space to be contiguous to your original unit, but occasionally a tenant may move to a new location within the same plaza or building in order to expand. So why would a landlord agree to this? Well, every landlord wants to retain successful tenants, and if you're expanding because business is so good, then it may be seen as a natural progression. On the other hand, a landlord may be skeptical about your ability to expand and want to discourage this plan, thinking the tenant will be in over their head rent-wise.

Many tenants who think they have a right of first refusal clause don't have the proper wording in the lease agreement to provide them with what they actually want — the ability to expand. If the option to lease more space is based on your matching another tenant's offer to lease, then the wording of this clause must require the landlord to give you sufficient notice and to provide you with a copy of the other parties' offer or proposal. Don't accept casual wording. Be precise if you want certainty.

Chapter 11

Choosing your Commencement Date and Dealing with Construction

. . . .

In This Chapter

▶ Picking the right date to start your business

▶ Organizing the leasing process to avoid costly problems

▶ Working with landlords on new construction

▶ Dealing with removal of conditions

▶ Avoiding paying rent before you open your business

. . . .

*Y*ou may think that understanding which day a lease begins (the *commencement* date) and ends (the *expiration or termination* date) is fairly simple, but you're wrong. Sometimes tenants and landlords agree on a *desired or* target opening day for the business, but then come the delays (and they will come). The commencement date of a lease agreement marks the official start date of the lease term. It's *not* necessarily the date you open or plan to open your business, which may be some months down the road. This is why disagreements between tenants and landlords arise.

This chapter helps you figure out how to determine a commencement date that benefits your type of business and navigate the construction process leading up to the day your business opens its doors.

Selecting the Best Commencement Date for Your Business

Most landlords deem that the commencement date stated in the lease agreement is the tenant's anticipated day of opening for business. But a few landlords may state that the commencement date is the day you sign the lease agreement, or shortly thereafter. This is a critical distinction to make. This section generally pertains to the first example, where the commencement date is the tenant's anticipated opening day.

Landlords and their leasing agents often push a tenant to open sooner than the tenant may feel is feasible or desirable. When it comes to picking the best lease commencement date for your company, do what's best for you — and don't be swayed by other parties.

If you're in an industry that has seasonal ups and downs, it's typically best to open your business going into your busy season. For a retailer going into a shopping mall, this could be in September or October, just before the busy Christmas retail season. Even if you're an office tenant, there may be times of the year that are more desirable to launch or relocate the business. If your winter climate is bitterly cold, make your commencement date in the warmer summer months. If your family traditionally travels for Christmas holidays, don't let your lease expire around the Christmas season. We have many accountant clients who have some very busy months around tax time — needless to say, April is not a good time for them to move or negotiate a lease renewal.

Anticipate in advance setting the commencement date, how many months you need to build out and fixture your premises. Too often, tenants pick an unrealistic commencement date and open their business late. If you pick the right commencement date but can't open on time, you may be losing valuable sales. Plan for Murphy's Law: "Anything that can go wrong will go wrong," and at the worst possible time.

This section explains how to avoid the dilemma of a retail store franchisee we know. His franchisor advised opening and commencing business in October, going into the shopping mall's busy retail season, because he would do almost 50 percent of the year's sales volumes in the few months leading up to Christmas. Even though the commencement date was scheduled for October 1, the tenant actually opened for business on December 21, missing valuable sales and killing his bottom line for that year.

Starting your lease term going into your busy season

Assuming that the commencement date is the intended day for opening your business, set it so you open going right into your busy season. If you're one of those few business owners who thinks you should have a really casual and soft grand opening to work out all the kinks in your business, then open a few weeks before the busy season rush — but not a few months before. There's absolutely no reason to open a business during the slow season. Cash flow is critical, and you want as many customers coming in your front door as possible as soon as you open it.

Some concepts require several months of pre-marketing in order to have a successful business launch. If yours fits this description, allow yourself the time to build interest and a market for your product, service, or concept several weeks in advance of your busy season. If you're relocating your business, you have the additional complication of having to factor in the expiry date of your current lease at your existing location.

If your current lease expires at the wrong time of year, it might be better to move sooner or later so you can get positioned in your new location for the busy time of year.

Having your lease term expire going into your slow season

If you open your business going into your busy season, and you signed a standard 5-year lease term, then unfortunately your lease will expire going into your busy season, too. Obviously, that's exactly what you don't want to happen. It puts you at a disadvantage:

- ✔ Competitors in your industry may want to take over your location if you're moving out of it. The more generic your *use* (the kind of products you sell), the less reason a past customer has for changing their shopping habits. Some businesses need to be more sensitive to this than others. For example, if a liquor store closes, and another liquor store opens in the same space, most customers will keep shopping there. On the other hand, if a pediatrician relocates his practice, most of the patients will follow along to the new location, even if another pediatrician opens up in the old location. In the former case, it's better to have your lease agreement expire going into your slow season to reduce the attraction of the location to a competitor.

- ✔ Different use tenants who aren't direct competitors to your company may also be a threat. Say that your lease term is about to expire and you're negotiating the lease renewal with the landlord. Another tenant may have made a leasing inquiry to the same landlord on the same property, and now that tenant has eyes on your space. Or it could be that the landlord or their real estate agent who shops your space to new prospective tenants. The desirability of your leased premises fluctuates throughout the year.

- ✔ Delays and unexpected temporary closures of your business during a relocation are better dealt with during your slow season than in the middle of your busy season. If you plan not to renew your lease and simply close your business, you're also better closing down going into your slow season rather than limping to the finish of your lease.

The time to deal with all these potential hazards is when you first agree to lease terms. Although it's customary for a commercial lease term to be stated in yearly increments (such as three, five, or ten years), the length of the lease term is fully negotiable. But it's to most tenants' advantage to enter into a lease calculated not in years but in months. Then the commencement date can be going into the busy season and the expiry date can be going into the slow season.

For example, most shopping center tenants who open in a major enclosed mall in September or October, just prior to the busy Christmas retail season, should take a 64- or 65-month lease term to maximize their tenancy to position them better for their lease-renewal negotiations. By negotiating and signing a 64-month lease instead of a standard 60-month/5-year term, they not only get one extra Christmas season out of their lease term, but their lease expires when the landlord has no other tenants interested in leasing the space.

Avoiding Problems with the Commencement Date

For a typical business to pick a specific commencement date that's best for them isn't so difficult. The problem lies in the coordination or timing involved to bring all the ducks into a row. Many moving pieces and parts need to be brought together, coordinated, and completed in a specific sequence to keep the project on schedule. It's not uncommon for the tenant to miss their target opening date, not just by weeks but by months. If you can anticipate what might go wrong or what issues are outstanding, you'll have a better chance of opening on the target commencement date.

Anticipating delays in opening your business

Some delays prior to your business opening are common and predictable. They may be caused by you, the landlord, or outside factors such as contractors or permit processes with the city. They can include the following:

- The landlord may fail to execute the formal lease agreement and deliver it back to you in a timely manner. Without an executed agreement and access to the space, your contractor could have difficulty completing the work on schedule.

- Delays can happen if the landlord does not approve the tenant's design drawings, which therefore delays your ability to start the build-out of your space as planned.

✔ The landlord may not complete landlord work in a timely manner before turning over the space to you — such as taking months instead of weeks to create demising walls or install HVAC systems.

✔ If you lease a space currently occupied by another tenant who doesn't move out on time, your ability to enter into the premises may be thwarted. In one case, a tenant was able to hold the landlord and their new tenant at bay by filing a court injunction and appealing an eviction process by the landlord. It took the landlord five months to successfully evict the tenant so the new tenant could move in. This forced the new tenant to open for business going into their slow period rather than opening months sooner.

✔ Zoning approval and building permits can slow a tenant down to a crawl for many weeks.

✔ There can be delays in delivery of products or fixtures to be installed within the leased premises. This can include floor covering, cabinetry, signage, or trade fixtures. You may not be able to prevent these delays, but planning for a little extra time and accounting for some of these situations in the lease language may help you limit their impact.

If you anticipate the landlord causing delays, consider adding language that imposes financial penalties on the landlord, such as reduced or free rent for each day of delay, or adjustments to the dates in the lease, which may lessen the impact on you. If the landlord faces a financial penalty, they may put in extra time or effort to keep things on track.

Establishing the fixturing period

The *fixturing period* is terminology used by most but not all landlords. The fixturing period typically precedes the commencement date, representing the period of time the tenant uses to get building permits, create space plans and designs, build out, and stock their business so that opening occurs on the target commencement date. Most tenants want the fixturing period to be as long as possible. Most landlords want the fixturing period to be a short as possible — so the rent can start sooner. Standard office space can typically be built out within 60 days, a large restaurant or dental office may take 3 to 5 months to build out. A lot depends on the designers, suppliers, and contractors.

The fixturing period should be clearly stated in the offer to lease, letter of intent (LOI), and the formal lease agreement. You must state the length of the fixturing, whether any rent is to be paid during that period, and when the fixturing period begins. You may sign the lease agreement in January, and the landlord finishes constructing the building a few months later, but no one knows the exact date. By creating another time marker, the *vacant possession date*, you can avoid having the timelines overlap. Here's how you want to set that up:

- ✔ If the tenant's possession date isn't predetermined, the tenant shall receive 20 days' notice from the landlord prior to receiving vacant possession of the leased premises.

- ✔ The fixturing period shall be free of all rents and begin on the date that the tenant receives vacant possession of the premises.

- ✔ The commencement date shall immediately follow the last day of the fixturing period.

Removing conditions

During the lease-negotiating process, it's customary for the landlord and the tenant to come to a *conditional agreement*, which means that the agreement is subject to certain conditions being met:

- ✔ The tenant's conditions may be items such as obtaining suitable financing, proper zoning and building permits, the cost of construction, or even getting franchisor approval of the location.

- ✔ The landlord's conditions may include reviewing the tenant's background and approving the tenant financially.

It's premature to start designing or building out the space before all the conditions are met. Occasionally, conditions can't be removed within the time period allotted (often ten days or more). The party who can't meet the conditions can then request an extension of time, but this request must be approved or accepted by the other party, who may not want to wait any longer.

Condition clauses are normally phrased so that the deal dies or becomes void if the parties don't actively remove their conditions. Some landlords phrase condition clauses the opposite way, stating that the deal goes forward if the tenant doesn't enforce their condition, in writing. Be sure to read the fine print carefully.

Executing lease documents

Many landlords are quite slow when it comes to generating and executing formal lease documents. The landlord typically creates the documents, which the tenant most often signs first. If the tenant doesn't stipulate an acceptance period, they could be waiting quite some time for the landlord to sign the lease document and return an original to the tenant.

Typically, the tenant doesn't want to or may not be able to start the construction process until receiving a landlord-executed original lease agreement.

Therefore, the fixturing period shouldn't start prior to all documents being executed and returned to their respective parties. You should anticipate this delay, because it can put a kink into your entire timeline for opening the business.

Although most landlords handle formal lease documentation in-house, some busy landlords farm it out, which can either slow down or speed up the process, depending on how busy the landlord's lawyer is.

Getting design and space plan approval

Most lease agreements state that the tenant's design plans need pre-approval by the landlord prior to any construction in the premises. This is customary and reasonable, because it's the landlord's building and the landlord is entitled to know what the tenant is doing within that building.

The problem that often arises is that the landlord or the landlord's architect or construction supervisor takes so long to approve or make recommendations on the space plan that the entire project gets behind schedule. In some cases, it's the tenant's own fault because the tenant's designer took too long to get the preliminary plans done. The wait for design approval generally slows down the process.

Pulling building permits

In some cities, it can take six weeks or more to get a building permit. If you're at the beginning of your fixturing period, and you're just now applying for your building permits, there will be a long delay before your construction can begin. This is such a common problem that tenants need to be more proactive in communicating with their designer and contractor to anticipate these delays. You don't want your entire fixturing period eaten up waiting for the city to approve your building permits.

 If you're delegating the process of acquiring building permits to your contractor, make sure the contractor is on top of it. Many tenants wait weeks for the contractor to even apply for permits because the contractor is backed up. Don't assume your contractor is working expeditiously on your behalf.

Zeroing in on zoning issues

If the type of business you want to open in a particular building doesn't comply with the current zoning code, you're not necessarily up the creek without a paddle. It's common for the city to grant a special use zoning permit for a tenant in a particular building (they don't change the zoning). However, it may be the waiting period or six-week delay that once again steals your fixturing period and puts your project behind schedule.

Don't take for granted that your particular type of business will be automatically approved from a zoning perspective. Just because a similar type tenant occupies space in the same property doesn't mean you can too; it may simply mean that they had to go through that special permit process years ago for their business.

Carving out time for contractor delays

When it comes time to build out your leased premises, delays with the contractor are commonplace. A smart tenant builds in a cushion, or extra time to allow for a contractor to be slow. Some common contractor issues may include a labor force shortage in sub-trades (not enough electricians, for example), or even a simple delay in the availability of building materials or products for installation at the premises.

For the last office that we designed and built for The Lease Coach, we picked a wonderful floor covering that everyone loved. However, we were informed that it would be at least six weeks before the carpet could even be delivered from the factory. That was unacceptable. It would have put us way behind schedule on the build-out because various sub-trades have to work in sequence or in conjunction to finish their portion of the project.

To mitigate this delay, we simply went to a local carpet wholesaler and picked from in-stock inventory carpet that could be delivered in 48 hours. Problem solved. The point is, product delivery timelines should represent part of your decision-making process when picking tile, carpet, and even window coverings.

Don't assume building permits are included in your contractor's quote or that the contractor will get down to city hall and get those permits in a timely manner. Controlling sub traders and managing buildout times are critical to getting your business open on time.

Avoiding Paying Rent Before You Open

Most lease agreements state that the rent becomes due and payable on the commencement date or the day the tenant opens for business, whichever is sooner. The rent is paid in advance on the first day of each month.

A major franchise tenant at the end of his lease term came to The Lease Coach for help negotiating his lease renewal. When we inquired about the initial lease term and how that leasing process went for him, he was quite disgruntled with the franchisor's in-house real estate representative who was supposed to help him. Everything that could go wrong did go wrong on his first lease (Murphy's Law strikes again). His monthly rent was $15,000, and he opened the business three months late. That's a tough way to start a business. He flushed all that money down the toilet simply because he wasn't prepared and hadn't planned well.

If this can happen to a franchise tenant who supposedly has the help and support of a franchise organization, then it can more easily happen to an independent tenant.

It's possible to sometimes negotiate for a clause stating that rent isn't due or doesn't begin to accrue until either the tenant opens for business or the commencement date arrives, *whichever is later*. This ideally protects you from having to pay rent before you're open to the public.

Examining the landlord's expectations

The landlord expects you to start paying rent on the date specified in the lease agreement as the commencement date, unless otherwise stated. The landlord won't normally take responsibility for delays in your construction or any other delays you may experience. The only time you should reasonably expect to get help or sympathy from a landlord is if the landlord caused the delays.

Landlords sometimes try to throw the tenant a bone with a few months of free rent that they say the tenant can use for building out the premises and doing their construction and fixturing. This does not really qualify as free rent, because most tenants aren't expected to pay rent during the fixturing period. Try to ensure that free rent applies immediately upon the commencement date, once the tenant is open for business.

Communication with the property manager and the landlord is critical when situations arise. Sometimes landlords overload their employees with too many projects and tenants, and that's why things take so long or are not getting done.

This doesn't mean you don't have alternatives; make yourself heard in a professional way, show up in person, and bring your issues to the landlord or property manager's attention. It's easy for the landlord or property manager to focus their attention on another tenant or property if they don't see your issue as pressing.

Interpreting what the lease agreement says

The answers to most tenants' questions are in the various lease clauses themselves, if you know how to decipher them. The lease agreements created by landlords are strategically and deliberately worded to take into consideration or to anticipate common problems with commencement dates and the many delays a tenant can experience when opening.

Dale and Jeff spend many hours on the phone with tenants each week interpreting and explaining lease clauses. Understanding is the first step to changing or negotiating these points effectively.

If you need help interpreting these clauses and understanding what they mean in your specific circumstances, seek help from a professional lease consultant rather than just blindly assuming it will all work out for the best in the end. Unless you know exactly what you're agreeing to, it probably won't, at least not to your benefit.

Dealing with a Building Under Construction

Pre-leasing activity on new properties and buildings under construction is quite common. Even though the landlord may have a projected turnover date for completion of the property, delays can occur. If you're an existing business planning to move into a new building under construction, it's critical that you time-manage both your current lease agreement and your new one.

If the landlord is delayed in completing the new building, you may have to overhold in your current location for a few extra months. *Overholding* or *holding over* is when the tenant's lease term expires and they continue to occupy the premises month to month. This can get complicated, so you need to know as far in advance as possible if the landlord's construction time lines change.

Language in the lease agreement gives the landlord plenty of flexibility if they're delivering the property to the tenant late, but what protects the tenant? Lease language may need to be included right up front giving the tenant the opportunity to potentially renegotiate for compensation due to overholding rents, penalties, or loss of business. Don't be afraid to approach the landlord if their problem is becoming your problem. This section will help you work through this potential problem.

Leasing different types of undeveloped space

A doctor using The Lease Coach to negotiate on the purchase of a business condo thought she was safe by allowing an eight-month overlap on her current lease and the new condo project. Delays in the landlord's construction work resulted in the doctor having to overhold in her leased premises for several months until she could take possession of the condo.

Spaces that need construction before they're fit to move into fall under several different categories, each with its own potential for delays or setbacks.

- **Raw or undeveloped space:** Typically, a brand new construction property isn't fully developed or ready for you to move into. The space is essentially raw in nature, especially if the landlord has agreed to create a smaller unit within a larger space (called *demising* down the space). The landlord has to create demising walls or perhaps install a new HVAC system.

- **Grey box:** A grey box unit has all four walls, but no concrete slab. The commercial real estate industry created the *grey box* term to describe the condition the space is in, but there are often misunderstandings and different interpretations of this definition across the country. If the landlord or their real estate agent is using the term *grey box*, have them define it further on paper so that you know exactly what you're getting.

- **Partially finished space (vanilla box/shell):** One step up from the grey box is the *vanilla box*. Typically the concrete slab is poured; walls are built but not necessarily taped or sanded. Some plumbing or electrical may be in place, but once again, you need to have the term *vanilla box* defined in the lease agreement to avoid costly surprises. On a new construction project, vanilla box is the condition most tenants receive their space in. From this state the tenant can design and build out the space.

- **Developed space:** When we moved The Lease Coach office into a very nice downtown high-rise office building, we took over a unit that was no longer needed by an architecture firm. The space was fully developed and required minimal changes. The design was fresh and bright, and nothing was left to the imagination — what we could see is what we would get. The move took only a few weeks. The fewer moving parts, the more predictable you can be with the commencement date of the lease term.

- **"As is":** The term *as is* in a commercial lease agreement means exactly that. You're accepting the space as it is — good, bad, or otherwise. That's why it's so important to do a thorough check of the premises. If it turns out you need to do additional work to the premises to ready it for use, that may mean commencement date delays and more expenses. One of our clients reported that a space they were looking at leasing had fresh paint near all the hand sinks. Upon closer inspection, they discovered that either the previous tenant or the landlord had painted over moldy walls in an attempt to conceal that problem from the next tenant.

Approach space inspection with a *buyer beware* attitude. We like to go into units, flush the toilets, open doors to see if the property has shifted, test the locks, look for broken glass, water leaks (water stains on carpet, tiles, or walls), and so on. It's also perfectly acceptable to bring in an independent inspector or a specialist to check the HVAC system and any other parts of the property.

Anticipating delays when the landlord is constructing a new property

The landlord's work, by definition, is work done by the landlord to any part of the property or within the tenant's leased premises. Sometimes landlord's work is at the landlord's expense, but in some lease agreements the landlord may plan to charge some of this work or infrastructure back to the tenant.

Many of the lease deals we negotiate for tenants require a certain amount of landlord's work. This could be demolition of the last tenant's space or removal of the previous tenant's old floor coverings, partition walls, or ceilings. It could also include bathroom installation or pouring a concrete slab. It's smart to expect delays in landlord's work and negotiate for the fixturing period and commencement date to adjust accordingly if the landlord doesn't complete his work on time. And make sure you stipulate who will pay for the landlord's work — don't automatically assume it's the landlord.

The landlord should be willing to provide you with a 90/60/30-day countdown to your receiving vacant possession of the tenant's individual unit or premises. The landlord should report any potential delays to you immediately so that both you and the landlord can adjust your tenancy dates. This is not a time for you to be bashful; staying in contact with the construction superintendent, property manager, or the landlord is critical if you want to know sooner rather than later that there are construction delays.

Another type of construction delay is quite different. Most landlords require a certain amount of pre-leased deals before building the project. We've completed many pre-lease deals for tenants when there was no building yet at all, just bare ground that hadn't even been broken. We often negotiate on a specific unit based on preliminary space plans and CAD drawings that the architect had put together for the landlord.

If you're one of the first tenants to sign a new lease on a future project, you need to be wary in case the leasing program stalls out and the building is never erected. If the landlord is unsuccessful in signing up enough new tenants, they may not qualify for the construction loan or mortgage from the bank. A lease agreement may state if the landlord doesn't actually construct the building, there are no ramifications for the landlord — all they have to do is return your deposit. If the landlord can keep you on the hook for a year or more and hasn't constructed the building, that's unacceptable.

You need to negotiate for the right to terminate the lease agreement by a specific date if the landlord isn't committing to moving forward with timely construction of the plaza or new building.

Determining what remedies to take

Open communication with the landlord is important if construction plans aren't going as expected or if you sense the landlord's pre-leasing program for a new property has stalled out. First, refer to your rights in the lease agreement. Second, get an appointment to talk to with the property manager and start discussing the matter. Potentially, you can negotiate to terminate the lease agreement, but they may want to keep your deposit. That's why you avoid paying all your deposit too far in advance on new construction projects.

Your best opportunity to build in rights for termination or compensation is up front when you negotiate the lease agreement. Landlords who fully intend to complete and launch the project want to keep you happy. A negative or uncooperative attitude on the part of the landlord may be a sign that things will get worse before they get better, or will just get worse.

Negotiating unexpected changes

It's not uncommon for a landlord developing a new commercial site to move tenants around, shift outparcel buildings, or adjust a tenant's square footage. The lease agreement often gives the landlord sole discretion to make these unexpected changes to the property or your unit. Changing roadways, entrances, or the location of pylon signage can all have negative effects on your long-term tenancy.

You need to make yourself heard. The landlord's actions may be pure in intent and for the good of the overall complex, but if your storefront is suddenly hidden or blocked, your entranceway is changed, or your area is decreased by 12 percent, then you need to get in to the landlord's office and make your complaints known. Twenty-five percent of getting what you want in a lease deal is being heard by the right people, with the balance coming from actually working out and negotiating these terms into an agreement.

Dodging Penalties and Fines for Not Opening by the Commencement Date

Some landlords who develop prime retail properties hope and plan to have a grand opening launch for the center. This may involve all the tenants opening simultaneously and on time. If that's the type of location and lease agreement you're entering into, watch for a penalty clause where the landlord can fine the tenant several hundred dollars per day for every day the tenant isn't open for business.

Delays in opening your business may not be your fault if your contractor lets you down or you encounter unforeseen circumstances. Negotiate on the penalties and fines for late opening up front and have them deleted if possible. The last thing you want is to be in default of your lease agreement before you open your doors.

We try to add a clause saying that the fines or penalties only apply if the tenant is more than four weeks late in opening or if the tenant isn't diligently making reasonable efforts to complete their build-out. If you sign a lease and run out of money or have a health-related issue that delays opening, the landlord may or may not have mercy on you.

Landlords don't have to actually charge tenants with fines and penalties; they're meant more as a deterrent to late openings than as revenue. Sometimes you can beg off these fines through good communication between yourself and the property manager. It costs you nothing to ask for a break, at any rate, if you're hitting a snag that you know will delay your opening.

Getting Everything in Writing

Misunderstandings and lease misrepresentations can victimize a tenant's dreams and aspirations. We've said this several times throughout the book and it bears repeating here.

Everything needs to be written down in the lease agreement. Landlords sell buildings, property managers get replaced, and banks foreclose on commercial properties. When these things happen, tenants are often the victims of verbal or handshake agreements because the agreement was not recorded for perpetuity. The commencement date of your lease term and when you open for business are too important to take casually. Be purposeful and thorough and protect yourself at every turn in the negotiating process. The time you spend thinking things through and anticipating problems will never be wasted.

Chapter 12

Dealing with Deposits

. . . .

In This Chapter

▶ Understanding and negotiating security deposits

▶ Getting your deposit back

▶ Transferring deposit money

▶ Handling lease renewal deposits

. . . .

*A*lthough landlords often ask for security deposits on commercial leases, such deposits aren't legally required. In fact, you can often negotiate them. Unfortunately, too many business owners don't know that and willingly pay the deposit, without negotiating the amount or the terms. Your goal as a tenant is to pay as little deposit as possible — no deposit at all is better. Deposit money, which generally doesn't earn a penny in interest, can better serve as working capital for your business than as security for your landlord.

In this chapter, we look at the process of negotiating security deposits and getting them returned when your lease ends.

Defining the Security Deposit

A *security deposit* is just that — financial security for the landlord in the event you don't pay the rent or in some way damage the property. Many lease agreements don't use the word *security*; they simply contain a *deposit clause*. You can use the wording in this clause to begin your negotiations. For example, many proven and successful business owners aren't a security risk at all. If that description fits you, you can justify negotiating for no security deposit on that basis.

The following sections explain why landlords want a security deposit and how this knowledge can help you negotiate an appropriate deposit, if you pay one. You also need to understand how the deposit clause wording affects your ability to get the deposit back at some point.

Realizing why landlords try to collect security deposits

From your standpoint as a tenant, paying a security deposit confers no advantage or benefit. It ties up your money — money that many landlords try hard not to give back to you if you don't renew your lease. From a landlord's perspective, a security deposit makes perfect sense; it gives them a chance to recoup some of the money spent on bringing in a new tenant.

Acquiring a tenant can be an expensive proposition for a landlord for several reasons. Any deposits they can collect offset the following leasing costs:

- ✔ The commercial space may have sat vacant for some time, bringing in no income for the landlord.

- ✔ The landlord may have to offer monetary inducements, such as a tenant allowance or free rent to lease their space.

- ✔ Landlord's work may be required to make the space suitable for showing and leasing.

- ✔ The landlord has to pay real estate commissions, in most cases. These fees can cost a pretty penny — typically a percentage of the total base rent (between 5 and 6 percent). But the landlord's commission costs are not your responsibility.

Regardless of how the landlord and their agent handle the incoming tenant deposit, a credit to the tenant remains on the landlord's books. This credit should be clearly documented in your lease agreement, because it's the record of your deposit. If the landlord sells the building, you may receive an estoppel certificate confirming the basic terms of your lease and any outstanding obligations, including the amount of the security deposit currently being held by the landlord. An *estoppel certificate* is a document verifying information as true and correct; it's commonly used to verify facts and information for a third party.

Landlords typically want to hold the deposit until the lease agreement terminates and the tenant vacates the premises. This happens for several reasons. If the tenant causes damages to the premises, the landlord can deduct those repairs from the deposit. If the tenant doesn't remove their leasehold improvements, the landlord may pay a contractor to do so and deduct the cost from the deposit. If base rent is owing or if the landlord has underbudgeted or overspent on the operating costs, a CAM reconciliation balance can be outstanding, which the landlord may deduct from the deposit. If the tenant doesn't hand in their keys to the premises or clean the premises, it can result in a deduction from the deposit — all depending on the wording of the deposit clause.

More than 20 years ago, when Dale was a shopping mall manager, a real estate agent brought in an offer to lease from a tenant without a deposit. Dale's boss, the landlord, demanded there be a deposit or the agent would not be paid a commission.

Even though landlords and real estate agents may tell you that the purpose of the security deposit is to provide the landlord with protection in the event that you default on the lease agreement, the real reason is to offset the commission being paid out to the real estate agents.

Covering yourself with proper wording in the deposit clause

The deposit clause in your lease agreement can either contain specific wording dealing with every detail of the deposit or it can be loose and simple. Keeping the wording simple isn't a good idea. You want to cover every detail about the deposit, especially when you will get it back, to prevent arguments down the road. Simply stating that the deposit is "$X amount of dollars or two month's rent to be held for the term" isn't nearly enough information.

Ask the following questions of your landlord, and make sure the lease contains the following information:

- **How much is the deposit?** Most landlords request one to two months' rent as a deposit. In most of the lease deals The Lease Coach negotiates for tenants, there's no deposit at all, so remember: it's negotiable. We've seen many landlords request more deposit — up to four months' rent. Your financial strength or experience as a tenant sometimes determines the amount of the deposit. The landlord may look to a number of factors in determining your financial strength, which can include the following:

    - Corporate and personal income tax returns

    - Profit and loss statements

    - Personal net worth statements

    - Credit scores

    Your experience, whether you're a first-time business owner or have operated your business for a number of years — or if you're a multi-location owner — also comes into play for the landlord determining the deposit they expect.

- **Where is the deposit applied?** In most cases, the deposit isn't applied to a specific month but is returned to the tenant at the end of the lease term after the premises are vacated. You can negotiate to apply the deposit to the first and last months' rent or any of the months in between. We've seen instances where landlord defines your "last month" of rent as the last month you occupy the space, meaning renewal terms as well, (not necessarily the last month of your initial lease term). No tenant wants to have their deposit in place renewal term after renewal term. You can avoid this by indicating the deposit will be applied to month 60 of a five-year lease, for example, rather than the last month. The Lease Coach sometimes includes language that says *the deposit shall be refunded at the end of the initial term if the tenant renews the lease or continues leasing the premises.* The longer you occupy a property (and the more rent you pay over time), the less financial risk to the landlord.

✔ **Is it fully refundable?** Not all deposits are fully refundable. The fine print of the lease agreement may state that the landlord can apply the deposit to rent arrears or to any damage you, as the tenant, create to the premises. *Rent arrears* are any rental obligations within the lease, which you are behind in payment or which remain unpaid.

✔ **When will the deposit be returned?** Having the deposit applied to a specific month is better, even if it's the 60th month. However, in most cases, the landlord returns it to you between 15 and 45 days after you vacate the premises, provided you've completed their entire term and not defaulted.

✔ **When would the deposit *not* be returned?** If you default, go out of business, or damage the property, you can't expect to get back your deposit. But the landlord's definition of *damage* and yours may not match. The section of the lease agreement pertaining to surrendering the space at the end of the lease term outlines your requirements as a tenant when you leave the space. This section delineates what you can remove, what you can't remove, and what damage must be repaired upon your moving out of the space.

This section is also negotiable because some tenants prefer to demolish the space and take it back to the condition in which it was delivered to them; others simply want to remove all their trade fixtures and personal belongings and leave the space as is, subject to reasonable wear and tear, such as carpet wear. The more detail that's included in this section on what can and can't be removed and the condition the space is left in, the less chance a disagreement may happen when you leave the property.

Landlords are notorious for deducting money from the deposit. As a tenant, you don't have much hope of recovering money that the landlord decides to hold on to if the deposit clause was loosely worded or deliberately vague.

Negotiating the Deposit Terms

Everything is negotiable when it comes to deposit terms. Don't assume that you have to accept the landlord's terms without trying to turn them to your advantage rather than theirs. Most landlords naturally prefer that you pay a large deposit as soon as possible and that you get as little as possible of it back as late as possible. That's why you have to negotiate for the best deposit terms possible so that you can keep more of your money. This section explains ways to arrive at a dollar amount, figuring out the best time to give the deposit, and understanding how to avoid paying more deposit when you renew your lease.

Agreeing to the dollar value of the deposit

Although one to two month's rent is an industry standard deposit amount for commercial properties, the actual amount can vary dramatically. Sometimes landlords ask for two months' *base rent*; sometimes they ask for *gross rent*. *Base rent* is the minimum amount of rent you pay if you have a rental agreement. *Gross rent* is a combination of the base rent and the operating costs that the landlord charges. If the deposit is designated as the first and last months' rent, the last month's rent is often higher than the first month amount.

How you negotiate the amount of deposit may depend on a number of factors:

- ✔ **Your financial strength:** The stronger you are financially, the better argument you have for a smaller deposit.

- ✔ **Existence of a personal guaranty:** If you've given a personal guaranty, then isn't a deposit redundant? That is your argument for no deposit or a smaller deposit.

- ✔ **The size of landlord inducements:** If the landlord is providing a substantial tenant allowance, they may expect a larger deposit.

- ✔ **Competing offers from other landlords:** The more offers you have in hand, the better position you're in to play one landlord against another, as you negotiate on the deposit amount, with each property.

- ✔ **The strength of the landlord's position:** The longer the space has been vacant, or the more vacancies there are in the property, the better the chance that you can obtain the terms you're looking for if you stand firm or back away from the negotiating table.

Dale remembers one client in Washington, D.C. relocating from one office building to another office complex on the same property owned by the same landlord. Because the tenant substantially increased the square footage she was renting, the landlord demanded a bigger security deposit, even though the tenant had regularly paid rent on time for many years prior. Dale flew to the tenant's city, met with the landlord, leasing agent, and property manager, and negotiated the deposit from $60,000 to $14,000 — which shows that the deposit amount is clearly negotiable.

Knowing when to pay the deposit

Many tenants who agree to pay a deposit inadvertently write a check at the wrong time in the negotiating process. Rather than submit a deposit when you sign the offer to lease, negotiate to pay the deposit three days after the landlord has accepted and executed the offer to lease. Better yet, make the deposit due and payable three days after you and the landlord remove the conditions and executed the formal lease agreement.

These conditions may include the tenant's obtaining financing, the tenant's satisfaction with the formal lease agreement, approval of board members, and the landlord's review of the tenant's financials, just to name a few.

If you pay the deposit too soon, the landlord may dig in his heels and lose any further motivation for negotiating with you or giving you concessions. If the deal falls apart, and the landlord drags his feet in returning your deposit, not having that money may make it more difficult for you to move on and deal quickly on another property.

Postponing or delaying payment of any deposit in any amount for as long as possible is important, just in case things don't work out; some examples are:

✔ Getting it back later if the deal falls through can be difficult and even risky.

✔ Although the deposit may be refundable, you may not have the money to simultaneously pay multiple deposits on multiple properties.

✔ You may want to pay just a portion of the deposit up front and the rest later if construction of the property hasn't been finished because it may be many months before you get vacant possession of the space.

✔ From the landlord's point of view, when a tenant makes a deposit, it demonstrates both emotionally and physically that the tenant is committed to doing this lease deal and concessions to the tenant may cease.

Having the deposit applied to future rent

Most lease agreements state that you can get your deposit back at the end of the lease term. But they often don't state how quickly the deposit will be returned — you could wait 7 days, 60 days, or anything in between, unless your agreement specifically mentions a time frame. And then again, more commonly than you may think, you may wait in vain forever for the return of your deposit. Tenants lose their deposits for a variety of reasons, but you can prevent it from happening to you.

One way to avoid losing your deposit is to put it on the lease that your deposit be applied toward your last month's rent. If you do this, you don't have to worry about trying to collect your money or begging for the deposit back from the landlord when it's time to move on.

Landlords, unlike diamonds, aren't forever: The landlord you have today may not be the landlord you have when your lease expires. To avoid the complications that can occur if your building changes hands before your lease ends, ask to have your deposit applied to the first *accruing* rents (the first rent payable); that way, your deposit can be used early on and won't unfortunately disappear.

Avoiding security deposit pitfalls when renewing your lease

You can hit some potential pitfalls with your security deposits when renewing your lease. Be prepared to fight against all these potential traps when negotiating your renewal lease:

- ✔ Even if you pay no deposit up front when you sign your initial lease, the landlord may try to add a deposit clause to your lease renewal.

- ✔ If you do pay a security deposit, the landlord may try to keep the deposit for a longer period as part of your renewal.

- ✔ If your rent increases or goes up with the lease renewal, the landlord may also ask for an additional deposit, arguing that your deposit was based on *monthly rent,* which has now increased, so the deposit should increase too.

If you encounter any of these situations, be prepared with your response or arguments that the landlord not require a deposit or increase to your deposit. The strongest argument for you during a renewal is to demonstrate that you're a proven, low-risk, rent-paying tenant. If you can point out that you've never missed a rent payment and are of little risk to the landlord, they have little justification to increase or require a deposit during a renewal.

In fact, the landlord should return any deposit in place. In some cases, while negotiating renewals for our clients, we've shown the landlord proposals from other landlords courting the same tenant and that were asking no deposit on a new lease term. This can be a strong bargaining tool. If another landlord on a new lease term doesn't expect a deposit from you, neither should the landlord who already knows your track record.

Getting the deposit back at renewal

A restaurant/bar owner came to us for help in negotiating his lease renewals. Upon reviewing his lease agreement, we saw that he had a $40,000 deposit with the landlord, which seemed excessive. When questioned, the restaurateur stated that he bought the business a few years ago, and the landlord wanted extra security money before he would consent to the lease assignment. Even though the previous owner had a very low deposit, the landlord used the renewal as an opportunity to leverage his position and increase his security. The Lease Coach went to work on this project and got all the $40,000 back on the lease renewal.

Even if you're considered a security risk for the first 5, 7, or 10 years of the lease, and you regularly paid the rent all those years, you're certainly no risk to the landlord for the renewal term. Use this point as a negotiating plus.

Avoiding paying any deposit

Of course, you'd prefer not to pay any security deposit at all. That's quite possible. You can use the following arguments as ammunition when negotiating to avoid paying a security deposit:

- ✔ **Showing you're not a risk:** Your credit score, the depth of your financial resources, and so on may show that you aren't a risk to the landlord. An established tenant with a proven track record who is relocating to another property or even opening his second, third, or fourth location typically isn't a security risk because he has a proven track record. A startup business by a first-time tenant and business owner may be more susceptible to a security deposit.

- ✔ **Using your improvements as leverage**: If you take a vacant shell of a space and invest several hundreds of thousands of dollars building it out, fixturing it, and stocking it for business, but then go out of business, you're leaving the landlord with re-useable improvements far exceeding the risk the landlord took in leasing you the space initially. The landlord would have no difficulty re-leasing their premises at a higher rental rate with your improvements.

- ✔ **If no real estate agent is involved, and you know there's no commission being paid, use this as leverage with the landlord.** Because landlords often use the security deposit to offset commissions to agents, the lack of a commission can strengthen your argument to avoid a deposit.

✔ **Explain that the deposit depletes startup capital that you need to achieve your business goals.** Be careful with this argument; if you appear to be spending every nickel you have on starting up your business, the landlord may consider you a high risk — and therefore require a higher security deposit or back away from the deal because you lack sufficient startup and working capital.

Getting Back Your Deposit

Before your lease expires, talk to your landlord about getting back your entire deposit as soon as you vacate the premises. You may be afraid to bring the subject up for fear your landlord may have some excuse for not giving the deposit back to you, which may be true. But you can't determine if there is a problem (and then start to solve the problem) if you don't ask before you move out.

When The Lease Coach is helping an existing tenant relocate, we also like to work with our client on their exit strategy from the current location. This can mean discussing the deposit with the property manager during the last month of the term, arranging for a walk-through on the last day, and even invoicing the landlord for the deposit. Some landlords are so large that if you don't invoice them in writing, they take no initiative until you come calling for it.

Over the years, one landlord may sell the property to another, and the new landlord may claim they don't have your deposit at all. Communication is the key. Don't rely on casual letters or e-mails. Be proactive with a phone call, too — discuss the deposit verbally with your current landlord or property manager to confirm the credit on your account and the terms for getting it back — all of it!

This section explains how to ask for your deposit to be returned to you and identifies some possible roadblocks you may encounter (and how to get past them).

Asking for your deposit

Most landlords don't mark their calendar with a date to return your deposit. In fact, most would be quite happy if you never brought up the subject again. Business owners often contact us months after moving out and ask why their landlord hasn't refunded their deposit. We usually start with asking, "Have you asked for the money back yet?" They usually say, "No." So we begin with the basics: You have to ask to receive.

We recommend that you ask your property manager about the landlord's process for refunding deposits three to four months before your lease expires. Ask these questions:

✔ Does the landlord require a letter or an invoice?

✔ On the last day of the lease, will there be an exit viewing and walk-through of the premises to ensure no damage?

✔ What should I do to get my full deposit back? Have the carpets cleaned, surrender keys?

Receiving your refund: Obstacles you may face

Landlords have many reasons why they can't or won't return your security deposit, including any of the following:

✔ You damaged the premises.

✔ You didn't remove your leasehold improvements.

✔ You removed leasehold improvements the landlord wanted you to leave behind.

✔ You owe CAM charges from that year.

✔ You did not pay penalties or interest for late rent charges.

✔ You did leasehold improvements to the premises without landlord consent or knowledge.

✔ You sublet or assigned the lease agreement without landlord consent.

✔ You didn't remove your signage from the building and do repairs.

✔ The landlord may have whittled away at your deposit over the years for small rental incidentals or items that they invoiced you for that you didn't pay.

✔ If your building has been sold since you first leased, the new landlord may claim he doesn't have it because the previous landlord never passed it on.

✔ If your original landlord lost the building into receivership or had it taken over by the mortgage holder, your new landlord won't have the deposit because he bought the property from the bank, and your deposit was long gone.

If the landlord acknowledges that he has your deposit, check your lease agreement. It may state the amount of time the landlord has to refund your deposit. If not, ask for a refund within ten days of your invoice to the landlord.

The landlord may issue the deposit refund to the tenant company. If you've gone out business and closed your bank account, you can have a problem cashing that check. The landlord may personally issue the check to you, but you have to let him know that's what you need.

Getting your deposit back in difficult circumstances

After you invoice the landlord in writing, call the landlord's accounting department to ask how it plans to handle the return of your deposit. It may respond in one of several ways:

- ✔ By telling you that the deposit was applied to one of the points we just talked about and that you'll receive a statement of account (meaning you may owe the landlord money)

- ✔ By indicating that the landlord has a cash flow problem and can't return your deposit yet (yes, this does happen — the landlord is broke)

After you know the reason for the delay, you have options on how to get your deposit back from the landlord. You can do one of the following:

- ✔ If the landlord is holding back your deposit to cover damages, you have to wait until repairs are completed so the landlord can determine the total cost. After the repairs are finished, you may receive a statement of account and any monies due at that time — if any money is left.

- ✔ If the landlord's reason is cash flow, you may want to obtain a legally enforceable payment plan in writing from the landlord. Getting your money over a period of time is better than getting back no money at all.

- ✔ Lawyer up. This process could be long, drawn-out, and expensive if it eventually goes to court.

- ✔ File a small claim action against the landlord (depending on jurisdiction).

- ✔ Call the authors of this book; Dale or Jeff will be happy to hear you out and lend some guidance.

Transferring the deposit if buying or selling the business

If you're buying or selling a business and have a lease deposit with the land-lord, you need to include this asset (or this deposit) in the purchase agree-ment for your business. When you sell your business, you and your seller may not discuss how to handle the deposit in the purchase agreement. The landlord likely has a preferred way of handling it, which will guide your actions.

Landlords can do one of two things when you sell or buy a business:

- ✔ The landlord can retain their tenant's deposit and apply it to the account for the new tenant.
- ✔ The landlord can pay you your deposit back and collect a new deposit from the new tenant when the lease is assigned.

Most landlords have a policy regarding these transfer situations. You prob-ably won't be in a position to dictate to the landlord which of the two ways just mentioned they'll handle it, but if you have a preference, there's no harm in asking when you make the lease assignment application.

The best way to handle this situation is to ask the landlord in advance which way they'd handle a deposit and then accordingly structure your purchase agreement. If you can't do that, make your purchase agreement flexible enough to cover whichever way the landlord wants to apply or refund the deposit.

Part III

Reviewing the Formal Lease Agreement and Dealing with the Landlord

The 5th Wave — By Rich Tennant

"When we go in to negotiate our lease renewal, try not to be so defensive."

In this part . . .

With the basic business terms established in the offer, it's now time to tackle the formal lease agreement. This document will contain dozens to potentially hundreds of terms. The chapters in this part can help you interpret and understand how to negotiate what's important to you, the tenant. We also describe the different types of landlords you may encounter so you can learn to think like your opponent and outwit, outlast, and outplay in the negotiating process.

Chapter 13

Understanding and Negotiating the Rest of the Lease

*E*very commercial lease agreement contains primary business terms that are essential to the deal (as discussed in Chapter 8). The rest of the lease agreement contains hundreds of secondary or ancillary clauses that may or may not be financial in nature. In fact, much of a commercial lease agreement is dedicated to landlord rights and the enforcement of the business terms.

In this chapter, we explore the secondary lease clauses, what to focus your negotiations on, and which clauses simply require understanding so you can play by the landlord/tenant rules that govern most tenancies.

Factoring in Visibility and Accessibility

If your business depends on customers being able to find you and physically walk into your store or place of business, then you need to examine how visible and accessible your location is to the public. Taking your parking and signage for granted is sure to end in disappointment. Even if you don't depend on drop-in customers because your business is mostly appointment oriented like a health spa, massage clinic, or even a veterinarian clinic, your customers and employees need access to adequate parking. If you want and need good signage to pull in customers, make sure your lease agreement factors in the clauses covered in this section.

Understanding the significance of signage

It's much easier for customers to discover or find your new business if you have a prominent sign with your company's name on it out front. The bigger, the better — and the more attractive, the better, too.

Don't assume that your landlord shares your vision of a large sign on or in front of his property. It may not have occurred to you, but the landlord may want to restrict all tenant signage on the property. Tenant requests for more or larger signage are often rejected by landlords.

Landlords impose signage criteria and restrictions mainly because whatever they allow one tenant to do signage-wise, the other tenants will also want to do. Most landlords prefer an uncluttered property without extra signage, simply because it looks more attractive. If your landlord does allow you to place a sign on the property, creating and maintaining it is your responsibility. The advantages of your signage include the following:

- ✔ It makes your business easier to find for customers who are specifically looking for you. Obviously, if you're in an area with a sea of shopping plazas, a sign with your name on it makes it easier to pick you out of the crowd.

- ✔ It can bring in foot traffic. Shoppers who don't know you are there may be drawn in by your sign as they drive by.

- ✔ Local residents who see your sign as they drive to work and back each day are eventually more likely to do business with you when the time comes.

Your landlord may allow some types of signage and not others; typically the landlord usually requires graphic drawings of your sign for written approval or provides you with a signage criteria package you must follow as part of your lease agreement. The following are the most common types of signage and signage issues:

- ✔ **Building signage:** You may want office building signage on the exterior of the property, in the lobby, and on the floor where your office is located. Some landlords may even allow directory signage that includes your company logo instead of your name in plain letters. Ask what's included or available to tenants.

- ✔ **Fascia signage:** *Fascia* or *bulkhead* signage is typically located right on the front of the retail tenant's store above the entrance. Although most landlords don't charge tenants for placement of this signage on the building, some do. The rental charge is calculated typically by linear foot. One tenant put up his sign without getting landlord approval and then discovered it was too long. The landlord made him take it down. If your lease agreement states that you're entitled to fascia signage, determine exactly what you can put up.

As part of lease-renewal deals, some landlords are starting to spring new rent charges on signage that was previously free, so make sure your signage clause specifies *no charge*.

- **Monument signage:** A *monument sign* is often like a tombstone coming out of the ground — smaller than a pylon sign and close to the ground, it advertises just one or a few select tenants. Monument signs aren't that common, but can make your business look more substantial if you can get one. Tenants typically pay rent for monument signage. One of the tenants whose lease renewal and expansion The Lease Coach negotiated included a right to construct a monument sign. Because the tenant paid to build and install the monument sign, Dale negotiated for no rental charge — all he had to pay for was the utility bill to illuminate the sign. A monument sign like this is powerful advertising and can be worth every penny to your business.

- **Naming rights** for a building can be attractive to extremely large corporations, but they don't come cheap unless they're included in a multi-floor package lease to attract a major tenant by the landlord. Jeff recently negotiated a lease agreement for an office client for the top floor and a portion of the floor below in a 20-floor office building. As part of this agreement, he negotiated to have the exclusive exterior signage on the upper edge of the building. This can provide significant prestige and exposure for your company when everyone starts calling it the [Your Company] Building.

- **Pylon signage:** The tall sign by the roadway that tells passers-by what tenants are in the plaza is called the *pylon sign*. A property may have several pylon signs, which display the name of the plaza at the top of the sign. Tenants typically pay rent to advertise on the pylon signs, so don't assume you get a panel automatically. There are often more tenants than panels, so make this part of your offer to lease or LOI. Ideally, try to pick your actual panel (front and back), because a panel higher up on the pylon is usually more visible and read first. Keep an eye on this section of the agreement for not only what the landlord is currently charging for pylon signage, but also for any provisions for increases or to terminate your signage rights. For situations where there's no current pylon signage available, Jeff negotiated for a tenant to get the first right of refusal for any signage panel that may become available in the future.

- **Sandwich board signage and banners:** Sidewalk sandwich boards and banners can be extremely useful for tenants trying to attract business or offer specials, but landlords may say no. Once again, negotiate for this in advance. Because landlords like to resist or restrict these signs, Jeff often negotiates predetermined times in which the tenant can use these signs, for example 4–6 weeks in advance of registration periods for learning center and dance studio tenants. Landlords may be more comfortable in knowing these signs will not be out all year, which may create in their minds, signage clutter.

- **Temporary pull-away signage:** Temporary pull-away signs are those approximately 6×8-foot signs on wheels covered with images or letters (the ones where local kids mess with the letters to create inappropriate messages). Most landlords hate these signs and the problems they create. Don't assume that for your grand opening or special events you may be able to have temporary pull-away signage. Landlords think they clutter or obstruct the property and may only allow limited numbers of signs to be used and shared by many tenants throughout the year. For a flower shop, for example, this signage can significantly increase sales during special times of the year such as Valentine's Day. Negotiate pull-away signage rights up front, because the landlord doesn't have to let you put these signs up if they are not included in the lease agreement.

Paying attention to parking rights

Landlords typically address parking rights in one of two ways. Their lease agreement either totally ignores parking altogether or lays out a very detailed parking plan and list of regulations. Parking rights are too important to leave to chance; parking can make or break your business if you depend on walk-in traffic. Downtown properties that provide parking to the tenant generally do so for a monthly fee.

Although parking is important for customers, it's also important for you and your employees. Consider all the parking options when negotiating on space, include the following:

- ✔ **Customer parking:** One of the first things we look at when visiting a prospective site for our tenant clients is the customer parking. Most properties offer what's called *rush parking,* meaning first come, first get. If you're a first-time tenant or opening a business in a successful property or densely populated area, realize that insufficient parking can cost a tenant tens of thousands of dollars in lost revenue each year.

- ✔ **Staff parking:** You and your staff need a place to park when you come to work. A larger, more global problem occurs when staff park in the prime customer stalls. Determine whether the landlord has a designated area for staff to park and whether there's a parking policy that the property manager polices or regulates. Smart landlords require tenants and staff to provide their vehicle license plate numbers to the property manager for this exact purpose.

- ✔ **Designated parking stalls:** It's nice to be able to pull into the same parking spot each day or to have the spaces right in front of your storefront designated for your customers. Of course, people abuse these designated stalls, and the landlord doesn't want to be the one responsible for policing the tenant's parking. Nonetheless, you don't want to skim over this opportunity and find out that the neighboring tenants have parking rights and designated stalls but you don't.

Don't take your parking for granted. We've seen landlords convert free parking lots to paid parking lots. We've also seen landlords give away or designate parking stalls right in front of one business to another tenant, especially if that's what it takes to sign up the other tenant on a lease deal. If there aren't enough parking spaces for your customers during the times of day that you need them, your business can suffer accordingly.

If the landlord or real estate agent tells you that all parking is first come, first get, you may want to include a clause in the lease agreement stating that if (in the future) the landlord gives special parking rights or privileges to other tenants, that they will have to give those same privileges to you. Parking is often used as an incentive by a landlord trying to attract new tenants, and landlords have been known to unfairly divvy up the parking to suit their own needs.

Dealing with Default Clauses

Every lease agreement has a standard *default clause*, which is there to protect the landlord. This default clause allows the landlord to sue or evict you and to basically enforce the lease agreement if you don't pay your rent or otherwise disregard the lease deal. No business owner or tenant would expect otherwise. But landlords and their property managers deal with default notices differently. Some fire out nasty default letters to tenants without so much as a courtesy call to find out from the tenant what the problem is. Others may have a friendlier approach, but at the end of the day, they all want to collect the rent.

Occasionally, landlords default on a lease agreement too — but tenants rarely think to add any language to protect themselves in those cases. Read default clauses carefully to understand your rights and how the landlord plans to deal with defaults if they occur.

Differentiating between default types

Default clauses fall into two general categories: material defaults and non-material defaults. Material clauses generally deal with money, whereas non-material clauses deal with other actions that go against the lease terms:

✔ **Material defaults:** A *material default* by a tenant involves nonpayment of rent or some other issue having to do with money. Maybe you're late with payments, or your rent checks bounced. Sometimes tenants object to rising operating costs and year-end reconciliation statements and refuse to pay them out of protest. Landlords can evict for default, but what they really want is the money you owe them.

✔ **Non-material default clauses:** Parking issues are a good example of a *non-material* or non-monetary default. Perhaps your staff is parking in an area of the parking lot that's designated for customers. Or you haven't fixed a broken plate glass window, or you're not open for business on Sundays and the landlord expects you to be open seven days per week. In these cases, eviction isn't usually on the landlord's mind. The lease agreement may state that they can fine you or penalize you in some way for violating these clauses.

Defeating default clauses

The time to defeat potentially dangerous default clauses is in the formal lease agreement. Many of the clauses that can come back to bite you can be modified or removed if you negotiate for them. In the following, we list some of the most common default clauses and how to defeat them:

✔ **No advance notice of default from the landlord:** Many lease agreements state that the tenant is automatically considered in default when the default action or event takes place — in other words, the landlord isn't required to notify the tenant (and the tenant may not be aware that they defaulted). The solution is to make sure your lease clause states that the landlord must give the tenant 5 to 10 days' advance notice to cure the problem before the tenant is actually in default.

✔ **Loss of rights such as renewal options and use exclusivities:** Some leases state that if the tenant defaults they lose important rights. The solution is to either delete this clause or include language that reinstates these tenant rights once you've cured the default. Don't assume that these tenant rights are automatically reinstated just because you cure the default; the lease clause should allow for reinstatement.

✔ **Penalties and fines or interest:** The solution is to negotiate for lower penalties, or a *three strikes clause,* meaning the landlord can only penalize you if the same default occurs three times.

✔ **Future rent immediately due and payable:** When a tenant defaults, the landlord wants to be able to sue for more than the immediate rent arrears — they want to hit you harder. Removal of this clause or modification to a lesser amount, such as three months of rent becoming due, is advisable.

✔ **The landlord goes directly to the personal guarantor without any due course or dialogue:** The landlord should exhaust efforts with the tenant first before going to the personal guarantor and should also notify the guarantor of all default notices. These requirements need to be negotiated into the lease agreement if possible.

Modifying Relocation and Termination Clauses

Most landlords include a unilateral right to relocate or terminate a tenant for various reasons. Unanticipated relocation or termination for reasons that aren't your fault occur only occasionally in actual reality, but can cause a major disruption in your business when they do. We dealt recently with a group of 13 tenants in a mall that were evicted because the landlord wanted to renovate and replace the mostly local tenants with major name brand chains and franchises.

In some cases, you may be the one wanting to insert a termination clause, because circumstances in your life can also change.

Getting moved to another location

The landlord may decide to relocate you within the same property because they want to redevelop or remodel the property. Or perhaps a larger next-door tenant wants to expand, and moving your business makes more sense than moving theirs. Whatever the reason, relocation clauses do appear in lease agreements to give the landlord this option. It's up to you to protect yourself against them.

You may not be able to eliminate a relocation clause altogether, but you can minimize its impact. Just having enough notice that the relocation is coming makes a huge difference to the tenant, but your lease may state that the landlord only has to give 30 days' notice. Negotiate for a longer time period.

The relocation clause may also state that the landlord only has to cover undepreciated leasehold improvements costs, meaning the move will cost you money. If the landlord is the beneficiary of the relocation, it only makes sense that they should foot the bill. If the new space is larger, you may be expected to pay more rent, and of course that's not fair. Including a sentence that says your base rent and CAM cannot go up if the landlord relocates you would be helpful.

Termination clauses imposed on tenants

Your landlord can terminate your lease for several reasons having nothing to do with your defaulting on rent or other typical reasons for eviction. You can be terminated because you refuse to relocate. Or the landlord can have a right of demolition, meaning that if they're redeveloping the property, all lease bets are off.

One tenant who came to The Lease Coach for help had absolutely no rights in the lease agreement to protect them when their landlord was renovating the buildings on one property. Fortunately, we were able to negotiate a package deal for the tenant where the landlord moved him to another building that was just finishing its renovation (all those tenants were evicted). This may have been a very sorry ending to a long tenancy if level heads had not prevailed.

If your lease agreement does include a landlord's right to terminate, there should be plenty of notice and compensation for the tenant built in to the clause.

Including your own early termination clause

We frequently negotiate for early termination rights for tenants under specific conditions. For example, one older medical doctor we worked with needed a lease renewal but also wanted to add the right to close his practice if his health took a turn for the worse or if he wanted to retire. When we explained to the landlord that an early termination right was not to move to a competitor's property but to actually close the practice, it was acceptable to him.

You can also negotiate for early termination rights if you don't achieve or maintain projected sales levels. If the landlord (or their agent) is promising you that your business will do well in their property, then the ability to terminate under those circumstances, say after two years, is not necessarily unreasonable.

Operating Costs and Additional Rent Clauses

Operating costs are charges levied by the landlord over and above your base rent and include all costs associated with maintaining and operating the building, such as lawn maintenance, snow removal, sweeping parking lots, property management salaries, building insurance, property taxes, and almost any other cost you can imagine, plus some you can't.

Tenants are rarely happy with their operating costs; at best, they're ambivalent to them and at worst, they're upset with them. The two issues that most upset tenants are ever-increasing operating costs and the landlord's lack of attention to properly maintaining the property. Save yourself some aggravation down the road by addressing these operating cost issues and others in the formal lease-agreement clauses.

You can, of course, request a cap or limit on the amount operating costs can be increased each year, but landlords resist this because these are supposedly true costs passed onto the tenant and not normally a profit center for the landlord. But you should also watch out for other issues buried within operating cost clauses that can cost you dearly in the future, including the following:

- ✔ **Administration fees:** If tenants are paying the property manager's salary through operating costs, but the landlord also adds a 15 percent administration fee to CAM costs, this can be considered *double-dipping* (double billing for essentially the same service). If the landlord levies administration fees on property taxes and insurance, this can also be considered overreaching, because there's very little administrative work involved in these.

- ✔ **Following industry guidelines:** The commercial real estate industry has clear guidelines that a landlord may or may not choose to follow. Adding wording to the operating cost clause that requires the landlord to follow industry guidelines may help ensure the landlord isn't inventing their own self-serving rules.

- ✔ **Landlord operating cost reports to tenants:** Many landlords provide only superficial operating cost information to tenants. Sometimes these reports are not only insufficient for the tenant but also much too late or not sent in a timely manner; these are issues you can address in the formal lease clauses.

- ✔ **Occupancy levels and operating costs:** A lease agreement may state that operating costs are charged back to tenants assuming the property is 95 or 100 percent leased and occupied. This means that if the property is only 70 percent occupied, those tenants carry 100 percent of the operating costs. Change this to state that the landlord must pay or assume the operating cost charges for vacant space.

- ✔ **Proportionate share misallocations:** If you're located on the main floor, should you have to pay a proportionate share of elevator or escalator maintenance? Just because a tenant occupies a certain percentage of the building doesn't mean they're equally responsible for all operating costs either.

- ✔ **Reconciliation billing:** The industry norm is for landlords to budget future operating costs and then reconcile once per year. Tenants often get walloped with unexpected reconciliation statements from landlords with only 15 days to pay or be found in default. Negotiate so that you are allowed to repay these overages over time, perhaps six months.

✓ **Tenant audit rights:** The landlord has a fiduciary responsibility for accountability to the tenants for the money they collect from and spend on behalf of the tenants. The lease should include tenant audit rights, which allow you to examine the landlord's books.

✓ **Underestimated budgets on new properties:** If you're leasing space in a new building, don't be surprised if the operating costs jump 25 to 50 percent or more after the first or second year. Landlords have been known to under budget operating costs on new properties to help their pre-leasing program.

✓ **Utilities:** Electricity, natural gas, and water may be provided by the landlord or separately metered for each tenant. In some cases, the landlord may have one main meter on the property and a check meter on each tenant's unit to measure consumption. If you're paying your own utilities to the utility company, you'll have your own meter. In many cases, the landlord bills back utilities to tenants in operating costs. Make sure you know in advance what the lease agreement calls for so you don't pay twice.

Troubleshooting Miscellaneous Lease Clauses

Every formal lease agreement includes a variety of *boring* clauses that you may be tempted to gloss over while concentrating on what seems more important, such as the amount of your base rent. If you ignore the lesser clauses, you almost certainly can pay later in one way or another. As dry and dull as it is, read every word of the lease agreement and take the time to remove or change any troublesome clauses.

Some lease clauses don't fit into neat categories but can nonetheless affect your bottom line. Look carefully at the common lease clauses described in this section, because they can all affect your future money outlay:

✓ **Condition of premises when lease expires:** Most commercial lease agreements, whether for retail or office tenants, describe how the landlord expects you to leave the property. This includes what to remove and what to leave behind for the next tenant. A landlord may require the tenant to remove interior partition walls and floor covering, but to leave the ceiling and lighting intact. Most tenants want to remove their trade fixtures but leave the premises in what's called *broom-swept* condition.

The exception to this is when a tenant wants to discourage a competitor from taking over his location and setting up a competing business with very little capital investment. It can cost a fair bit of money to demolish an entire store or office at the end of your tenancy, so know what you'll have to do ahead of time.

✔ **Days and hours of operation:** Most lease agreements state that the tenant must follow the days and hours of operation as set by the landlord for the plaza or property. Many tenants may want to set their own days and hours of operation, so pay attention to this clause and negotiate it accordingly. Office tenants may find it difficult or impossible to see clients during off-hours if the office tower is shut down.

✔ **Design construction issues:** Landlords want to know what improvements you will make to the leased premises. Will you be installing one unisex washroom or multiple washrooms (and will they be handicap accessible?). Will you be deep-frying foods and installing a grease trap? Will you need to penetrate the roof for venting to the exterior or for cable or satellite TV installation? Most lease agreements contain a detailed protocol for the landlord to review and inspect tenant leasehold improvement designs. The landlord may levy a fee for this work, which may be negotiable depending how much or how little work the tenant plans to do.

✔ **Determining who does the space buildout work:** A good lease document lists in detail the landlord's work involved in preparing the space for the tenant as well as what the tenant is responsible for. In many cases, The Lease Coach negotiates for a partial or full turnkey build-out by the landlord. In some deals, we use the landlord's construction team to complete the tenant's work. If the landlord's work and tenant's work are clearly spelled out in the early negotiation stages, try to sweeten your deal by moving some of your work into the landlord's work column. Toilet installations are a perfect example of work you can move to the landlord's column, because after you leave the property, the next tenant can use them. This can also apply to HVAC systems, lighting, and ceilings.

✔ **Holdover periods and penalties:** A typical lease agreement anticipates that a tenant might hold over after their lease term expires. *Holdover* occurs when the tenant continues to stay in the property beyond the expiry of their lease agreement on a month-to-month basis. The penalty is often a 150 to 300 percent rent increase. This is normally negotiable when you're signing the formal lease agreement.

✔ **HVAC:** A shopping mall or office tower may have one central HVAC system, but not all tenants are so lucky. Strip plaza tenants, freestanding properties, and light industrial tenants often don't understand who's responsible for installation, maintenance, and replacement of the HVAC system. Don't take this clause lightly because the HVAC system is expensive. Yes, it can last 20 years, but you don't want to be the one to have to pay to replace it. Some landlords require tenants to have their own maintenance contract on the HVAC unit serving their leased premises. Other landlords service all the tenant's HVAC units and charge the expense back into operating costs. Make sure you understand what you're responsible for.

✔ **Insurance:** Every tenant needs to carry a variety of insurance, including liability, fire, theft, and in some cases even business-interruption insurance. Negotiating the insurance clause is not so much trying to remove it but to shape it. The landlord may request $5 million dollars of coverage, but you only want $3 million. Don't be concerned if the lease agreement states that the landlord is to be named co-insured on your policy. This is perfectly fine. It allows the landlord to collect the insurance and make repairs if you don't file an insurance claim.

✔ **Property purchase options:** Only a few tenants are given the chance to buy the premises they're leasing. If you're locating in a business condo or small property, you may want to negotiate in advance to have the first right to purchase the condo unit or the entire building.

✔ **Radius restrictions:** The lease may contain a provision restricting you from opening another location or business within a certain radius from the current location. Landlords do this to help ensure your other locations will not cannibalize your sales, especially if they're collecting percentage rent and their profit goes down if your sales go down. However, every industry differs in how close one location can be to another without having an impact; consider some coffee shop chains, where you may see the same name brand almost directly across the street. Both benefit from the heavy directional traffic. If you don't pay percentage rent (see Chapter 13 for percentage rent advice), you have greater negotiating power to remove the radius clause or decrease it to a distance that's acceptable to you. Reducing a 5-mile radius clause to a half mile for most tenants would be perfectly acceptable.

✔ **Vacancy protection:** If you're attracted to leasing space in a particular property or plaza because of its anchor tenants, don't automatically assume that the anchor tenancy is permanent. Movie theatres close, big box stores relocate, and major department stores and grocery stores change locations. Negotiate for *vacancy protection*. After all, the rental rate you're agreeing to pay is presumably based on a fully leased property, which includes the current anchors. Negotiate to have your rent automatically reduced or for the right to terminate your lease agreement if certain anchor tenants disappear.

Chapter 14

Finalizing the Formal Lease Agreement

In This Chapter

▶ Negotiating the formal lease agreement

▶ Getting some professional help

▶ Making changes to the formal lease agreement

▶ Communicating and negotiating with the landlord

▶ Signing and finalizing the lease deal

*O*nce you completed the offer to lease or letter of intent (LOI), it's time to take the final step: signing the formal lease agreement. An offer to lease is sometimes called the *short form lease document*, with the formal lease agreement called the *long form lease document*. In a few cases, the landlord may create only one lease agreement.

As tedious as it may seem, read everything in the lease, even if the clause title seems very straightforward. Landlords have been known to go off-topic in various clauses and include unrelated points you may never realize you were signing off on unless you read the entire clause. This is why many lease agreements state that the headings or title of the clause is not part of the actual agreement — the heading is simply for ease of information access. About half of all lease agreements include a table of contents page at the beginning, which is helpful.

In this chapter, we help you take the lease agreement apart and scrutinize it carefully, so you don't end up with any surprises.

Getting Your First Look at the Formal Lease

You have two choices when negotiating an offer to lease or LOI. You can review the offer to lease and the formal lease agreement simultaneously or leave the formal document until you and the landlord have signed the offer to lease. Some landlords and their real estate agents attach or send you a fill-in-the-blank version of the formal lease agreement when they send out the offer to lease. The hope and intention of sending both at the same time is to potentially speed up the process but also to box you in to a short conditional period. If the blank formal lease agreement accompanies the offer to lease, the offer may include a 10-day condition period where, if you don't object to the formal lease document, you're essentially accepting it as is with the terms of the offer to lease to be filled in without changes for your signature.

It's not always a good idea to start reviewing the formal agreement before signing the offer to lease. The more time you invest in the deal-making process, the more likely you are to move forward, and the landlord knows this. If he can prompt you to start making comments on the formal lease agreement before the offer to lease is finalized, this sends a very strong buying signal to the landlord — which can work against you in the offer to lease negotiations.

Making the offer conditional on the formal lease agreement

It's standard practice to make your offer to lease conditional upon tenant's acceptance of the landlord's formal lease document, so *make sure* it says just that. The formal lease agreement may contain deal-breaking clauses that need revisions, deletions, or additions. Once you come to an agreement on the final terms, and you're satisfied with the revised version of the formal lease agreement, you can then remove this condition in writing to the landlord.

If you and the landlord can't reach an agreement during the typical 10-day condition period, you can request (in writing) a 10-day extension. This is actually common and customary as long as things are going well between you and the landlord and they don't think it's a stalling tactic on your behalf. Some landlords may extend the condition period with a simple e-mail or may send you a more formal one-page agreement. If you're 8 days into your 10-day condition period, and you know you're going to need more time, don't wait until the last day. Request the extension now.

Asking for a copy of the formal lease agreement

If you're in the middle of negotiating the offer to lease and ask for a copy of the formal lease agreement, the landlord will probably send you one. It usually is a fill-in-the-blank boilerplate agreement to give you a feel for what their standard lease looks like, but these blank documents are often not up to date. When the deal comes closer to completion, the formal lease document they send you with all the business terms included could actually be slightly different.

We've often seen new clauses added and existing clauses updated or tweaked in the landlord's favor in the final version. As sick as you are of reading these documents after several go-arounds, you *must* be diligent when reviewing documents to ensure there are no changes or updates that they're essentially trying to sneak in there.

Doing a preliminary review of the formal lease agreement

If you're going to review or have the formal lease agreement reviewed by a professional in advance, you don't have to tell the landlord that you're going to this trouble or expense. You don't want to signal the landlord or tip your hand that you intend to move forward while you're still in the offer to lease negotiation stage. Landlords love it when the tenant is running up a bill with a lawyer because it means the tenant's more likely to commit to the deal.

That being said, if you do see their formal lease agreement in advance, you may be able to pick up on clauses that weren't mentioned in the offer to lease that the landlord plans to spring on you later. But a word of caution: Don't start negotiating bits and pieces of the formal lease agreement until the offer to lease is finalized because, again, you're giving the landlord a buying signal.

For example, default clause language and insurance fine print don't always appear in the offer to lease but may be stated in the formal lease agreement. If you're still negotiating the offer to lease or LOI and you notice these points in the formal lease agreement, just leave them alone for now. Landlords and their agents know that an objection is actually a buying signal in disguise.

Understanding the Significance of Signing an Offer to Lease or LOI

The reason so many tenants loosely sign a letter of intent is that right there at the bottom, the agent has very clearly specified that the deal isn't binding on either party. So you may think that signing an LOI seems almost harmless. You've got to start somewhere, so why not run the flag up the flagpole and see what happens? The next sections give you a better understanding of why you take signing the offer to lease or LOI seriously.

Getting stuck with what's in the offer to lease

Tenants often don't understand that the information in the LOI is carried forward to the more formal lease agreements. Say that the real estate agent types in your personal name as tenant and you sign it. Later you realize that you want to form a corporation or you already have a corporation that you want to be the tenant. You're now changing the deal, and this makes you look like an amateur. The landlord may accuse you of negotiating in bad faith because you signed the LOI and now you're making changes. What if you go back and now want seven months of free rent instead of three? The same scenario applies; you look bad.

To avoid disappointment when you reach the formal lease stage, be very specific in an offer or LOI, especially when there are choices. The LOI says the tenant gets five parking stalls. But which five stalls? Is there a charge? Are they designated and close to your business? If you're in a cold climate, are the stalls energized so you can plug in your vehicle during the winter months? Whether you get stuck with a bad formal lease can hinge on how detailed you are in the offer or LOI.

If tenant and landlord sign an offer to lease, it's usually binding, subject to conditions both parties have placed on the agreement. At this stage, the land-lord may want to see financials for both the corporate tenant entity and you. The landlord may also ask for your business plan (if the landlord is conduct-ing their due diligence). You also have items to take care of: finalizing your financing, preliminary design or construction costs, and of course review-ing the formal lease agreement. The offer or LOI may have a stipulated time period such as 10, 15, or 30 days for both parties to do the required research and remove their conditions.

After you sign the LOI or offer to lease, you set in motion the next steps in the deal-making process. The landlord may ask for a deposit and start putting pressure on you to move more quickly. If all you were doing when the agent convinced you to sign the LOI was test-driving the deal, you may hurt your chances to complete the deal at a later date when you're more fully ready.

Keeping details from falling through the cracks

After the LOI or offer to lease is signed by both parties, delays can occur if you don't stay on top of the agent or property manager. Whatever you do, don't sit back and patiently wait for the puzzle pieces to fall into place. This may be the only lease deal you're working on, but landlords and their people are up to their eyeballs in lease deals all day long with many tenants. The more time-sensitive a point or detail is, the more you need to stay on top of it. It never hurts to ask the landlord or agent for definitive dates, answers, and guidance.

The landlord may be waiting on you to provide financials while you're waiting on the landlord to ask you for those financials. All the while you're losing precious time Landlords often assume the tenant knows how the leasing process works, and tenants often wait to be told what to do. E-mails are great for settling issues quickly, but don't hesitate to make phone calls too if you need clarification that requires some give and take that's more easily done in an actual conversation.

Providing financial information to the landlord

Most offers to lease and LOIs loosely state that the tenant is to provide financial information. That's unsatisfactory wording, in our opinion, because it leaves a lot unsaid. You should know, ask or determine in advance exactly what the landlord expects to see for financials. If you think all they want from you is last year's personal tax return or a profit and loss statement, but what they really want is three years of audited financial statements from your company, a personal net worth statement, and verification of where the cash funds are coming from to actually build out the space, you may not be able to provide this quickly, if at all.

The offer to lease or LOI should say exactly what financial information the landlord expects to receive from you, your partners, your spouse, or your company (and when they expect to see it). How far you're willing to undress financially — and at what stage of the courtship — is negotiable.

We rarely send tenant financial information through the landlord's real estate agent, but opt to send it directly to the landlord in a hard copy format, making it less likely to be forwarded to other people by e-mail.

Many sophisticated or larger landlords may provide an application or credit forms right up front for you to fill in and return. Once you sign these, it often gives the landlord the right to check your credit score and financial history. The agent or landlord may ask you to do this up front or even to include your financial information or application with the LOI or offer to lease. We don't recommend providing that information up front. Remember, it's just a form, and not all the blanks have to be filled in if they're not relevant. Some tenants avoid these forms altogether by having their own financial paperwork ready. Your financials may alter the way they negotiate with you, because now they can see that you're rich, poor, or a potentially risky lessee.

Rather than provide your financial information off the bat, it's better to let the landlord make that one of their conditions. Let the deal be negotiated with the impression that you're in great shape financially. If the landlord checks out your financials in advance and thinks you're a risky tenant, they may up the rent to offset the risk (much like mortgage lenders do when assessing what interest rate you may pay on your home loan).

When the offer to lease terms are finalized, then the landlord can check your financials, and if they don't like what they see, let them renegotiate with you at that point. If a landlord has other prospective tenants interested in the same space, you don't want potentially weak financials to push the landlord toward the other guy.

Watching the calendar for timelines

Get your financial information ready in advance so that you're not scrambling at the last minute (which we see tenants do far too often). You don't want to lose a lease deal because your accountant is out of town or your personal tax returns are boxed away in storage and you can't find the key to the storage unit.

Other timelines are also critically important. Most often, any condition stated on the offer to lease may be for a finite period of time, such as ten days. If you know up front that you need more time to get your bank financing in order to finalize a franchise agreement, or to have your contractor look the space over, ask for more days in advance. Better to have a 20-day condition period than keep extending 5-day condition periods.

One major oversight that many tenants face during this formal lease review and negotiation process is when they realize the commencement date they agreed to is approaching too rapidly and may arrive before they can actually be open for business. Or, because of various delays, the lease commencement date is already past, but the tenant just keeps pushing the deal forward. You must be realistic about timelines and be prepared to renegotiate important dates for receiving vacant possession of the premises, for your fixturing period and for the lease-commencement date.

Reviewing the Formal Lease Agreement

Formal lease agreements can be overwhelming and confusing. You might be an expert or leader in your field, but rarely do entrepreneurs have experience with commercial lease documents. The first thing to remember about formal lease agreements is that they're created or designed in favor of the landlord.

There's no such thing as a lease agreement that's fair to everyone, because *fair* is subjective. You may get hung up on a few particular lease clauses, but if those same clauses appear in virtually all lease agreements for all commercial properties, then the goal is not to remove the clause but to minimize the damage it inflicts on you. This section shows you what to look for so you don't miss something vital.

Taking a first look

Ideally, what you want to receive from the landlord is a formal lease agreement that's completely filled in, with no blank spaces. If the landlord sends you an incomplete or fill-in-the-blank template version of the lease agreement, you'll have to go through it twice — once now and once more when the agreed-upon business terms from the offer to lease or LOI are filled in or transferred to the formal lease document — to ensure there's no added wording or clauses (and this does happen frequently).

If the landlord insists that you review the fill-in-the-blank template version first, a good argument is to say that you're hiring a professional to review the lease document for you, and you don't want to hire them to do it twice. This argument or strategy usually works. Dale estimates that nine out of ten formal lease documents are prepared in-house by the landlord, with no real preparation cost, legal or otherwise, to the landlord — so don't let them fool you by saying it's too much work, money, or hassle to fill in the blanks. This is a reasonable request considering the scope of the transaction.

Part of reviewing a formal lease agreement includes cross-referencing it with the offer to lease or LOI that you've already both agreed to. Recently, Dale compared a client's offer to lease with the formal lease agreement, and he found that almost all the rental numbers were incorrect. Mistakes and omissions are common, because the landlord may delegate preparation of the formal lease agreement to an administrative assistant or property manager. The Lease Coach just received formal lease documents from a landlord who used his attorney to prepare them. We noticed that many details were missing. Additionally, the attorney had taken liberties to change the agreed-upon wording in favor of his client, the landlord. Dale had to point out that the offer to lease was signed and these changes were not acceptable.

Another client recently sent Dale their formal lease agreement along with the signed offer to lease to review, and the lawyer's legal secretary had made numerous clerical mistakes, including misstating the actual name of the tenant. Clerical errors and misinterpretations of clauses are common no matter who's preparing the documents. So double-check the documents for accuracy in wording and possible omissions and additional clauses.

Getting help from a lease consultant or lawyer

The way in which many lawyers review formal lease documents for tenants can leave a lot to be desired, based on comments we've heard from tenants who have used that process. Because there's no standard by which all lawyers review lease documents, we've seen reports to tenants that were less than one page in length and reports that were longer than the lease agreement itself. Tenants have told us they paid anywhere from $200 to over $20,000 just to have the lawyer handle the paperwork for them.

There are three distinct processes with regard to the formal lease agreement: first, cross-reference the agreed-upon business terms of the offer to lease with the formal lease agreement for accuracy and completeness. Second, review and determine what clauses need revisions. And third, negotiate with the landlord for those revisions. The negotiation part of the process needs to be verbal, but most lawyers try to make this into a letter-writing contest with the landlord, which is a mistake. Letter writing is not negotiating.

Most landlords don't want you or your lawyer to correct or change the wording of the formal lease document. If a lawyer goes to town making all kinds of redline changes to a 50-page lease document, it may actually offend or upset the landlord. Most landlords want the tenant to make thoughtful comments or arguments about why particular clauses should be deleted or reworded. You can do this verbally or by way of a side letter or an e-mail to the landlord. Dale and Jeff do both with summary bullet points in writing and verbal negotiations.

Better to have a discussion or negotiation, and when the landlord and tenant have agreed upon a change to the clause, the landlord wordsmiths those changes into a revised document. Tenants have told us that even when they had their lawyer give them written comments about a lease document, the lawyer provided no help for how to negotiate those changes. Pointing out that a clause is bad for the tenant is only a small part of the battle; fixing it is the ultimate goal.

Of course we're biased, but we feel that The Lease Coach method for reviewing a lease document for tenants is superior to anything we've seen or heard of. This is what we do, step by step for tenants through the lease review process.

1. **Step One:** Cross-reference the business terms of the offer to lease or LOI to the formal lease agreement for accuracy of terms.

2. **Step Two:** Conduct a 39-point lease document inspection or analysis using a detailed checklist. This is similar to the procedure a mechanic goes through when you wisely take a used car to them for a once-over before buying it. Using a checklist ensures that nothing is missed or overlooked.

3. **Step Three:** Write a concise report to the tenant that points out specific clauses that require amending. We also discuss which clauses are fine but warrant some explanation so the tenant understands them.

4. **Step Four:** Discuss each clause verbally with the tenant, not only warning and explaining which clauses need to be negotiated and amended but why. Most importantly, we explain how to negotiate each point and what to say as well as the landlords' reply and how to respond to their follow-up comments.

5. **Step Five:** At this stage, the tenant can decide whether they want to tackle this negotiation with the landlord themselves or delegate it to us. If we're doing the negotiating, we prepare a letter for the landlord outlining all the points of concern. We do that for a couple reasons: to avoid ambushing the landlord so they can thoughtfully prepare for the call, and to make sure nothing gets left off our wish list or missed, which can easily happen without a prepared list.

6. **Step Six:** Discussion and negotiation with the landlord, including offering *step-down* clauses (less severe or more reasonable ones) and wording that they might find acceptable. We're not necessarily trying to remove all the nasty clauses — more like make them fair and reasonable by adding additional wording that softens hard clauses.

7. **Step Seven:** Reviewing a revised version of the formal lease agreement provided by the landlord and then having the tenant execute the documents.

Responding and writing to the landlord or their real estate agent

After you've written your list of the clauses you object to or want to discuss with the landlord, the entire negotiation process can go much smoother. The landlord may agree to many of the points without much discussion at all. Keep in mind, most lease points fall into the financial or non-financial category; recognizing that in advance can be helpful so that you know how to approach that point.

Financial points such as parking charges and percentage rent are often much more important to the landlord because they affect his bottom line and are a source of revenue. Non-financial points, such as the wording contained in your renewal option clause or permitted hours of operation clause, may have virtually no impact on the landlord, financially or otherwise, but could have a significant impact on your business down the line.

It's fine to use actual letterhead correspondence, but you can also use e-mail for the initial correspondence, provided you keep the e-mail from looking too casual. Overuse of the written word as a negotiating tool is rampant, so go easy — use e-mail more to communicate than negotiate. This is still a business transaction.

Negotiating changes to the formal lease agreement

Once you've established the basic points, negotiation of the terms can be done by phone or in person, but not by e-mail. A good negotiator is like a juggler who can keep many balls in the air at once. Rather than focus on one point at a time, both parties need to be open to some give and take: you agree to this, and I'll agree to that.

If you hit a roadblock or impasse on a particular clause, don't get bogged down. Move on and finish discussing the rest of the clauses, and then come back to the problematic ones.

When raising a concern about a specific clause, don't launch right into your objection; instead, ask the landlord about it, including how important that clause is to them and why it exists. Perhaps they had problems with other tenants and this is the stopgap clause. Many times a landlord admits that they really aren't married to the wording of any particular clause. Some landlords are using leases that were prepared by lawyers, and removing or modifying a clause is perfectly okay. You won't know until you ask — just ask in the most positive way.

When you go through the lease, you may want to make the following changes:

✔ **Ensuring there are no "blanks":** In addition to ensuring that all the terms of the offer to lease or LOI are included in the lease agreement, you must ensure that all exhibits, schedules, or items to be further defined are included. The location of your parking stalls and the position of signage on the site or the sign itself should all be clearly defined. Schedules or exhibits with pictures or diagrams really help with this.

✔ **Adding to clauses:** By adding wording, you can soften a clause. If landlord consent is required for the tenant to put up new signage, or to change their business name, then adding the words *Landlord consent not to be unreasonably withheld* can make all the difference in the world.

✔ **Removing or deleting clauses:** If a lease agreement includes a percentage rent clause, and you're not required to pay percentage rent, then deleting the clause entirely makes sense.

✔ **Amending clauses:** An example of amending a clause is where the lease clause says the tenant has to give nine months' notice if they want to exercise their renewal option clause, and you change it to six months' notice. The clause remains intact.

✔ **Negotiating for lease step-down clauses:** You can replace an overbearing lease clause with a step-down clause that's essentially the same but less restrictive or punitive. Many sophisticated landlords have pre-prepared step-down clauses that they can use to replace other overbearing clauses — if the tenant objects or requests it.

Getting a Copy of the Revised Formal Lease Agreement

When the formal lease document is revised and ready for execution, it may either be sent to you by e-mail or printed and sent by courier from the landlord. Don't assume that even though the landlord verbally agreed with your requested changes on the phone that he actually changed them, or changed them correctly. You must thoroughly go back and re-review the formal lease document again, because mistakes *will* creep in. We've even seen landlords try to slip in brand new clauses that weren't even in the first lease agreement — so be careful and cover the bases mentioned in this section.

Negotiating a few more rounds

So now you're holding the revised version of the formal lease agreement in your hands. If you're still not happy with the changes or you want to negotiate a bit more on some items, there's nothing wrong with making minor handwritten amendments to the agreement, rather than keeping the landlord guessing on what language would satisfy you. This might simply mean crossing out a few words or adding in a few others as opposed to completely changing a clause or adding a whole new one.

Make sure you initial any changes you make on all the pages. When you return the lease documents fully executed to the landlord, point out the changes you made in a cover letter. Bring it to the landlord's attention and even put sticky notes on those pages where you made changes so that he can see you're not trying to pull a fast one on him.

Rescinding the deal

If you can't come to an agreement on the terms and conditions of the formal lease agreement, the deal may fall apart. This is rare, but does happen occasionally. There are rules to follow, and if you've already paid your deposit, you want to make sure you get that deposit back. Once the landlord sees that you're serious about walking away, they may actually come around to your line of thinking and give you what you want. Real estate agents who are holding your deposit in trust need to be talked to as well to ensure you're refunded any deposits already paid.

Removing tenant conditions

When it comes time to remove tenant conditions, you must do it in writing and/or according to any rules stated in the offer to lease or LOI. Remember to check the actual wording in the offer to lease or formal lease agreement. Pay special attention to the *condition* wording, which can be stated as an action you perform or don't perform within a time period. The condition clause may state that your conditions are automatically *removed*, and the deal goes forward, if the tenant does not state otherwise. Or it can state that the deal *automatically terminates or dies* if conditions aren't removed by tenant or landlord within a specified period of time. Make sure you have a receipt or some form of acknowledgment that the other party has received your notice. You can request a reply to your e-mail or copy the e-mail to other people at the landlord's office and to the real estate agent. Sending a fax or registered letter isn't uncommon either.

Executing the formal lease agreement

A formal lease agreement is a contract, so you can expect to jump through some hoops to get it signed, sealed, and delivered. Landlords typically have some formal procedure you must go through in order to complete the agreement. The landlord normally provides you with three, four, or five original documents for your signature. One copy comes back to you with the landlord's signature, one copy is sent to the local property manager, and the others are kept with the landlord.

Smart landlords not only include an instruction letter on where the tenant is to sign but also may use those "Sign Here" sticky notes to ensure pages aren't missed. You'll generally sign all originals and initial all pages in the bottom right-hand corner. Each page may actually contain boxes where tenant and landlord initial. This ensures that pages aren't missed or replaced later.

You also probably need a witness to sign the documents. A witness isn't required by law but is more evidentiary in nature. Or the landlord may stipulate that you sign the agreement in front of a notary public or commissioner of oaths. This typically costs about $25. Using a notary public or commissioner of oaths certifies that you or your official representative actually signed the agreement. In some cases, you may choose to use a corporate seal as well.

If a page is missing an initial or doesn't photocopy properly, the landlord may simply remove it, have you initial it, and then return it to the document.

Paying the deposit and/or signing the personal guaranty

If you agreed to a personal guaranty as part of the deal, this part of the contract is usually a stand-alone addendum or exhibit to the agreement that's either attached to the formal lease agreement or included within it. You may also need this addendum formally witnessed or executed. This should be completed at the same time you sign the formal lease documents

If you haven't already provided the deposit, it's customary to pay it either when you sign the formal lease documents or within a few days of receiving the lease back from the landlord, which normally completes the transaction. Including your deposit check with formal lease documents is common but not necessarily wise because it's not a done deal until the landlord signs the formal lease agreement and returns the original to you. You can always send the deposit a few days after receiving your original landlord/tenant executed formal lease agreement. Deposits are normally done by regular check and rarely certified.

Moving forward

Once you sign and return the formal lease documents to the landlord, there can still be a waiting period or delay. You can't assume the deal is done until you're holding a landlord/tenant-executed original agreement in your hands — and that can take weeks. In order to avoid delays in the construction process, you must stay on top of the landlord and get a landlord-executed agreement back to fully consummate the deal.

It's a good idea to make a few copies of the formal lease agreement, keeping one at your office, one at your home, and even sending one to your lease consultant. Many tenants have great difficulty finding their lease agreement 5 or 10 years later, so you may also want to scan it and keep an electronic version.

Chapter 15

Dealing with the Landlord

. . . .

In This Chapter

▶ Understanding the different types of landlords

▶ Preparing the right leasing strategy

▶ Communicating at the landlord's level

▶ Working on making your tenancy desirable to the landlord

. . . .

*T*enants need to understand that landlords and their property managers and real estate agents are professional business people. Their business is commercial real estate. Brand new tenants quickly come to realize what existing tenants already know. The landlord and their employees aren't there to assist the tenant with running their business. The landlord and their employees are running their own business in conjunction with the tenant.

A business owner leasing space in a commercial property should not view their landlord as a partner or ally nor as an enemy, but rather as another business owner with their own business goals and objectives.

Commercial real estate leasing is for all intents and purposes a zero sum game. If The Lease Coach gets 12 months of free rent for a tenant, then the landlord forgoes 12 months of income during those months. Dealing with landlords and their team of people can be challenging, even for a seasoned multi-unit tenant. For that reason it pays to know whom you're up against in the leasing process. This chapter shows you what you need to know.

Understanding Different Landlord Types

Most tenants don't realize that landlords fall into different categories, and these landlords have different motivations for owning the types of commercial real estate investments that they do. On the surface, to small business owners, being a landlord looks easy. They take care of the property, they collect the rent, life is good. However, landlords can become casualties of the economy and victims themselves when their tenants go out of business or can't afford to pay the rent.

A smart tenant, before climbing into the negotiating ring with a landlord, sizes up their opponent. What makes this process more interesting is that one tenant trying to open one business (while looking at different sites for lease) may have to negotiate with more than one type of landlord while looking for that one great location. Negotiating strategies and tactics that work with one landlord may not work with another.

We're not trying to make this sound more complicated than it is, but if you're unfamiliar with the workings of commercial real estate deals, chances are you'll always lack the experience. When you only negotiate a couple of leases in your entire lifetime, there isn't enough time to get good at this process. Nonetheless, do some homework. This section describes the different types of landlords and how to deal with each.

Professional landlords

A professional landlord isn't a person but a company that exists for the sole purpose of owning, developing, leasing, buying, and selling commercial, residential, and industrial property for profit. By definition, a truly professional landlord may not only own various real estate assets, but also manage those assets internally. In some cases, a professional landlord can set up a management company to create the appearance of an arm's length entity.

During certain business cycles in the economy, it's not always profitable to be a professional landlord, but it's always profitable to be the management company looking after the property for the professional management fees. Rent-paying tenants pay the property management fee; so as long as there are tenants, it's profitable to be in the property management business.

From a leasing perspective, you may be interested in one specific property owned by a professional landlord. When you get on their website and start to look around, you may find that they have 147 properties in 27 states, with 5 regional offices, and 1 headquarters. All of this information is relevant to the tenant who needs to grasp the depth, experience, and financial background of the landlord.

A professional landlord uses various commercial real estate formulas or specialized software to calculate and measure the rate of return on their properties. When you're negotiating a commercial lease, the leasing representative punches the numbers into the computer, giving the landlord a *net effective rental rate* and determines whether the deal is advantageous for the landlord or not.

Typically, a tenant may be dealing with a local in-house leasing representative who reports to a regional representative who is possibly reporting to a vice-president of leasing for the landlord's leasing department. Professional landlords have multiple layers of management, as does most of corporate America. Consequently, the tenant must realize that they're not negotiating with a stakeholder in the company or even someone with any authority to consummate a deal, but more so an employee.

Often the leasing process with a professional landlord can be painfully slow. One franchise tenant that Dale spoke with reported that she waited almost four weeks just to get lease documents because of the hierarchy set up by the professional landlord. The bigger the landlord, the more likelihood that the tenant has to move at the landlord's pace. Professional landlords generally need or want tenants with strong histories and backgrounds who are already successful in business. Most professional landlords lean toward national and franchise chain type tenants for their retail projects or Fortune 1,000 companies for their commercial office buildings.

Institutional landlords

A couple typical types of institutional landlords are banks and insurance companies. You may not have thought of your bank or insurance company as a commercial landlord, but most of them are indeed just that. One of the safest places for banks and institutional landlords to invest their profits and your deposits is in commercial real estate.

Frequently, these institutional landlords may delegate or hire professional property management companies to run their buildings for them, partly because banks and insurance companies aren't real estate management specialists. In addition, they also want a certain arm's length distance from their core customers and tenants.

An institutional landlord can generally afford to leave a property vacant rather than take a low rent deal from a tenant. To these institutional landlords, cash flow is important, but property value is paramount. In some cases, a bank may have started out as the mortgage holder for a commercial property, which eventually went into foreclosure. The bank's ownership of the property may be more by accident than desire.

Dale and Jeff are currently negotiating a lease renewal for a tanning salon tenant. The property went into foreclosure two years ago, and the bank is still looking for a buyer for the property. Interestingly enough, the bank retained the previous landlord as the property manager. The tenant has been dealing with the same people, but now the property is under the ownership of the bank. The bank decided not to renew any upcoming leases with the tenants, but prefers to wait until they find a buyer for the property. The buyer or purchaser will then deal with the tenants and their lease renewals.

In all likelihood, rental rates go down, and the bank doesn't want to devalue the property by signing long-term, low-rent lease agreements with any of the tenants. This kind of situation isn't tolerated by many business owners, and as a result, some of them may begin moving out.

 If you're dealing with an institution such as a bank, try to find out whether it's a landlord by design or by default. You may not have to go through so many levels of bureaucracy during the leasing process with an institution, but you can certainly find yourself playing a waiting game.

Investment fund landlords

Real estate investment trusts (REITs) are commonplace. Teachers, nurses, and other professional associations invest pension fund money to buy and hold commercial real estate. An investment fund almost never constructs a new building; it makes a purchase decision on a commercial property based on the existing and predicable rate of return. These investment fund landlords aren't gamblers or risk-takers. Their decision to purchase real estate hinges on security, predictability, and safety. This type of landlord is most likely to invest in large and stable shopping centers and downtown office high-rise complexes.

In most cases, an investment fund landlord may utilize professional management companies to maximize their investment. If you pursue one of their sites, you are dealing not so much with a personal landlord as much as a leasing committee that's responsible for approving all new leases and renewals.

Investment fund landlords want to own property that can produce a stable, consistent return for its portfolio. This type of landlord seeks national name brand franchises, corporate office tenants, and chains.

Developers and flippers

Commercial developers are individuals who pool their financial resources to purchase a parcel of land. They then create design specifications and property site plans to maximize their return on investment. It's very possible to underutilize a piece of land. Developers want to have the highest number of rentable square feet on their properties to maximize the return.

After completing the site plan, the developer, either on their own or using a commercial real estate brokerage, launches a pre-leasing program to attract new tenants. In a perfect world, their real estate agent may pre-lease the entire property and have signed lease deal commitments from reputable tenants before they even break ground. In many cases, developers can only break ground and begin the construction process once their construction mortgage has been approved.

The construction mortgage is typically predicated on a successful pre-leasing program achieving perhaps 50 percent lease up before the bank begins loaning money to the developer to start construction.

After the development and construction process, the developer and the bank convert the construction loan to a long-term mortgage. Some developments, because of their location, an attractive design, or the types of tenant that have located there, can be extremely profitable.

A developer can hold their investment for the long-term or flip it for a fast profit and move on to their next development. *Commercial flipper* isn't necessarily a derogatory term. From a tenant's perspective, it's important to distinguish whether the developer is a flipper. If so, you can bet your bottom dollar that within a year or so you'll have a new landlord who is more a long-term investor. A lot of hard work goes into finding land, designing good properties, pre-leasing, and finishing the projects. Many landlords don't want to go through this process; they'd rather purchase flipped properties.

The purchaser of the flipped property isn't likely to recognize handshake deals or unwritten side agreements between the developer and the tenant. Just because they're letting you use the back of a unit to store your inventory now, doesn't mean that arrangement will continue in perpetuity with the new landlord or at all.

On new properties, the operating costs (CAM or TMI) are often underbudgeted, to the detriment of the tenants. Every landlord must budget and collect each tenant's proportionate share of operating costs in advance monthly. As part of the pre-leasing program, some landlords have been known to underbudget projected operating costs. Many tenants of one property told us that when they built their new stores in the new property, operating costs were lowballed to make the total rent look more appealing to future tenants. A few years later, the operating costs were 40 percent higher than first estimated, and the tenants are now realizing they were taken advantage of.

A developer works hard and pays real estate agents high commissions to get quality, high-rent-paying tenants. The value of the property and the resale value of the property hinges on the rental stream of income. The more rent the developer is collecting each month, the higher the property appraises in value. Sometimes developers are willing to provide up-front incentives to induce tenants to sign high-rent deals. Once the free rent and tenant allowance are out of the picture, the buyer of that property only has to focus on the high rent coming in. From a developer's perspective, they put some of their own money into the deal-making process to maximize the resale value of the property later on.

Casual Landlords

A casual landlord typically has a few holdings. For example, we were negotiating a lease renewal for a tenant where the landlord was a large construction company. Road construction was their primary business function. Over the years, they bought a couple of properties as investments and as casual holdings. These casual landlords may or may not be managing their own properties. In this particular case with this tenant, the landlord was managing his own properties and was absolutely horrible to work with. They almost seemed ambivalent to whether the tenant renewed their lease or left the property.

A casual landlord may have a very casual attitude toward their investment and their tenants. They're often slow to respond and almost never proactive during the leasing process. Their properties outside and inside common areas are often poorly maintained or cleaned. The investment is simply not a priority to them, and as a result good tenants get neglected.

Mom and pop landlords

Commonly, mom and pop landlords are wealthy doctors, architects, or families that either have accumulated some real estate or have an accumulated wealth invested in real estate. Typically, they're hands-on with the property and often quite accessible to tenants on a personal basis. Some of the mom and pop landlords we know actually spend time cutting the grass and maintaining the property. One small landlord was a medical doctor in the plaza. In another case, a small group of lawyers owned their property and were tenants in the building as well. They used a professional property maintenance company to keep the building and grounds up, but did the leasing and rent collection themselves.

Most mom and pop landlords live in the same city as their properties. Some of them do their own lease negotiating, and others use commercial real estate brokerages.

Although all landlords want a maximum return on their investment, it's the mom and pop landlords who can be emotionally swayed either way. Mom and pop landlords typically want low-maintenance tenants who pay their rent on time and who don't call them at midnight with problems about the property. The longer they've owned the property, the more emotionally invested in the property they become. If you damage the property, it's the equivalent of kicking their dog, and of course that never ends well.

One of the greatest challenges in negotiating a commercial lease with a mom and pop landlord is that they're often unrealistic about what the rental rate should be and almost never understand that rental rates can go down or that their property can reduce in value. To get a better or lower rent deal from a mom and pop landlord, it's often necessary to show them comparative rental rates and deals for other properties in the area.

Communicating Effectively During and After the Lease Negotiating Process

It bears repeating: The larger the landlord, the more likely it is that you'll be dealing with the landlord's property manager or real estate agent. Therefore, everything you say gets filtered or accentuated on its way up the chain of command to the landlord or the landlord's decision-maker. This is why we like to communicate with *both* the verbal and written word. You can take 10 minutes explaining your position or making a point, and the person working for the landlord may condense that into 30 seconds or two sentences in their weekly report to the landlord.

Stating in writing what you've already said verbally makes it more likely that your e-mail gets forwarded to the decision-makers. When Dale was a commercial property manager, some of the conversations he had with tenants got recorded in their tenant file, and others didn't. However, every single e-mail or letter from a tenant was placed in their file and remained there. This can be extremely helpful to a tenant if the property is sold or the property manager is replaced, because the new landlord or new property manager won't be able to refer back to verbal conversations with the previous manager.

Tenants range in temperament just as landlords do. Some tenants are sharp business people, well educated, and professionals in their field. But other tenants are inarticulate, uneducated, and really not good business operators. Often women entrepreneurs and minorities with strong accents or poor language skills get walked over by landlords. Consider that the commercial real estate industry is dominated by males who want to be in the real estate game. And the real estate game is often defined as *make the sale, conquer the tenant, and move on.*

If the landlord is a bully, and the tenant is a bully, they usually get along just fine. But if a property manager is arrogant, and the tenant's retail store sells sewing machines to homemakers, there is a clash of personalities, and the tenant is easily offended by a busy property manager who doesn't show them the love.

Women are often less direct than men, and battles of the sexes to some degree happen between tenants and landlords.

When confrontations between a tenant and a property manager occur, the landlord virtually always backs up the property manager. If the tenant thinks they'll go over the property manager's head and get directly to the landlord, this typically serves to irritate the landlord (whether they admit it or not).

The landlord, for better or worse, hires and invests in their employees. Landlords don't normally buy into the old cliché' that the tenant is always right. If the landlord backs the tenant, the property manager may get ticked off and move to another company. The landlord understands that a tenant in the middle of a five-year lease term can't just walk away — but a ticked off property manager can quit, requiring the landlord to expend considerable efforts to replace and train a new property manager.

Landlords are people. They often make poor decisions and hire less-than-perfect people. A tenant's goal should be to have a solid and comprehensive lease agreement that acts as the rulebook for the conduct of both parties. The better the lease agreement, generally the fewer disagreements between tenant and landlord.

Standing in the Landlord's Shoes: Seeing Yourself as a Prospective Tenant

For the landlord, owning commercial property and leasing space is their primary goal. However, for the tenant, leasing space is not the primary goal. A tenant's primary goal is to run a profitable business, or provide a great service. The property is a place to attract customers or practice your trade or profession — it's not an end unto itself. Tenants don't *want* to lease space, it's simply a requirement if they want to see their goals and dreams come to fruition — a means to an end if you will.

For that reason landlords and tenants are not equal. The tail can't wag the dog. If the tenant is the tail, then the landlord is the dog. However, as we all know, dogs chase their tails. You also have to consider that a tenant typically has one landlord, whereas a landlord may have hundreds if not thousands of tenants. A tenant can easily feel like one small pea in a very large pod. The relationship between tenant and landlord is not like an equal marriage with common goals.

If the landlord sells the property, the independent tenants often feel abandoned. If the tenant sells their business, the smaller landlord often feels used. Feelings and emotions often find their way into business deals and lease transactions.

Tenants have business loans to pay, and landlords have mortgages to pay. Tenants bounce $5,000 rent checks, and some landlords bounce $50,000 checks. Their problems are not the same — they're sometimes similar, but on a different scale. Understanding where your landlord is coming from can help you turn yourself into a more valuable tenant in their eyes.

Getting off on the right foot with the landlord

It amazes us how, during the leasing process, many landlords avoid meeting their tenants — and most tenants don't even try to meet the landlord. When it comes to new lease deals, often there's a real estate agent (or two) brokering the deal between the parties. Rarely, in our experience, does the broker try to bring the landlord and the tenant together for an in-person meeting or even a phone call. Being busy is no excuse. If a tenant isn't creating a relationship with the landlord and making deposits to that relationship, how can they ever expect to make a withdrawal if they need a favor?

As a standard practice, Dale and Jeff always try to bring the landlord and tenant together for a personal meeting as soon as there's a reasonable likelihood that we can strike a deal. They coach their clients on what to say or not to say and prep them for questions the landlord is probably going to ask. If possible, Dale or Jeff actually attend that meeting with the landlord and tenant. There are some quirky landlords out there, and a sensible tenant should want to know who they're getting into a 5- or 10-year lease agreement with.

If you plan to open a fine chocolate shop or a gourmet cupcake store (or really any type of business) and you meet at the landlord's office, take not one basket of your goodies but two. Take one for the staff and another for the landlord to take home to his family. We're telling you, this goes a long way in the deal-making process. Even giving a gift certificate for your store can make you look good. If you're opening a retail clothing store with a special line of products, take the wholesale catalogue or samples of your merchandise.

Don't assume the landlord understands anything about your business concept. For example, we do a lot of work with dance and music schools. If the landlord has young children, he may be familiar with you or your competitors. But if the landlord is unmarried and living the single life, you may need to show him your industry magazine and explain that there are over 15,000 dance and music schools across the country with several million children and adults enrolled and taking classes.

Although you want to fully familiarize the landlord with your concept, you also need to play it cool to some degree. You don't want to look as if you're applying for the right to become the landlord's tenant. You shouldn't talk as if you've already decided to lease space at their property, because this can work against you in the negotiation process. Carry yourself in a manner that shows you fully intend to open a business, and part of your due diligence process is simply looking into various leasing opportunities. If you carry yourself right during the meeting and through the leasing process, you ideally create a scenario where the landlord is pursing you as a tenant — not where you're pursuing the landlord.

Grasping why your tenancy may be rejected

Landlords reject prospective tenants for many reasons. Often, a smart landlord is striving for a particular tenant mix. If the landlord is developing a retail plaza, then they may reject an orthodontic office. Rather than lease space to a low-end barber shop, they may prefer to hold out for a higher-end salon that attracts a more affluent customer.

Also, landlords sometimes reject tenants who have insufficient investment capital or bad credit scores. A mom and pop sandwich shop can get rejected if the landlord wants to attract a national sandwich shop chain. If the landlord has identified a specific 2,300 square-foot CRU for your industry, and you only want 1,500 square feet, they may reject your offer to lease and hold out for a similar tenant who can take all the space.

If you want to save yourself a lot of time kicking tires on different properties, find out what the landlord wants right up front. When The Lease Coach makes a leasing inquiry for a tenant client, they normally call the listing real estate agent. After standard introductions, we ask, "Do you think the landlord wants a (your industry) tenant for this property"? The real estate agent may say no or yes — but at least you'll know whether the landlord does or doesn't want your type of business in their property.

Dealing with Big Bad Landlords

A brand new, soon-to-be tenant may not be aware that all landlords have developed or earned reputations in the commercial real estate industry. Prior to 1993, Dale was employed by or worked on a freelance basis with about six different landlords. As a shopping mall manager and leasing rep on the side of the landlord, he was able to experience first-hand what it's like to work for many of the landlord types discussed in this chapter.

Know thy landlord

The Lease Coach is a magnet for tenants with problems. Dale recalls being contacted by one tenant who was behind in their rent and trying to decide what to do. Dale learned that they simply wanted to close their business, take their losses, and move on with their life. But they were paralyzed with fear about what the landlord would do to them if they simply moved out.

When they said what property they were in, Dale realized he had done several lease deals with that landlord. He informed the tenant that this particular landlord had a no-sue policy. If a tenant was in rent arrears, the landlord would try to collect the rent, but not a single tenant had ever been sued by this landlord — and many businesses had failed and closed out of this property. Dale told the tenant that, based on this landlord's historical reputation, no lawsuit or legal action would likely be taken against them if they simply closed. They decided to move out. Weeks went by, months went by, and they never heard from the landlord ever again. Keep in mind if you leave the premises in destroyed condition or fail to hand in your keys to the space, any landlord can be angered into action. If at all possible, close your business with communication and dignity. (All of that being said, don't try this on your own — get some guidance from a lease consultant, as this tenant did, so you're not acting blindly.)

Knowing something about the type of landlord you're dealing with can save you a great deal of grief.

In many cases, Dale was the landlord's frontline soldier doing their bidding. Much of what he said as part of the job description he's not proud of. Of course, collecting the rent was part of the job — but often Dale had to do seizures of tenants' goods. It was his job to change their locks and even attend tenant bankruptcy hearings to make sure the landlord was in line for whatever funds the trustee may shell out to the tenant's creditors.

Since then, Dale and Jeff have done more than 1,200 successful leasing projects working for tenants in all industries who leased space in all types of properties. They have since helped tenants avoid bankruptcy and secure lower or mid-term rent reductions that saved their business and possibly even their family.

It doesn't occur to new, soon-to-be tenants that landlords all have reputations for how they deal with tenants. Some landlords may be on a tenant's case within days of a late rent payment. This can happen in the form of an impersonal default letter, a reminder e-mail, or even a friendly — or not so friendly — phone call. Larger landlords often have layers of employees below them in the ranks. Some of these employees are compassionate and patient, but others can be ruthless and demanding.

A tenant should do their due diligence prior to signing a commercial lease with any landlord to try to ascertain just who they're getting in bed with, so to speak. In our part of the country, there are three or four landlords who are known for their extreme nastiness and are quick to generate legal default notices. But other landlords are known to allow tenants to be months in rental arrears and obviously care about the financial wellness of the tenant and their business. Whenever possible, we warn tenants of a landlord's reputation.

Part IV
Negotiating Your Lease Renewal

The 5th Wave   By Rich Tennant

Tell Her Highness we're almost out of time. If she's going to negotiate a lease renewal, she better do it now.

In this part . . .

The passage of time is a constant you can count on, and sooner or later, it's time to either renew your lease or move on to a new location. Negotiating the terms of your lease renewal can be every bit as complicated as negotiating a new lease, so in these chapters we look at the ways you can improve upon your previous lease terms and discuss why your landlord should give you more concessions as a renewing business.

Chapter 16

Starting the Lease-Renewal Process

• •

In This Chapter

▶ Positioning yourself to win the renewal negotiation

▶ Maximizing your negotiating leverage

▶ Dealing with the actual renewal document

▶ Getting a lease renewal rent reduction

▶ Negotiating for lease-renewal incentives

• •

*E*ach year in North America, approximately 2 million business owners, entrepreneurs, retailers, franchisees, and healthcare professionals negotiate a lease renewal for their location. Perhaps that's why negotiating lease renewals for tenants has become The Lease Coach's specialty. Many tenants make costly mistakes on their first lease agreement, and if they're not careful, may continue to pay the price for those mistakes in their lease-renewal term.

Having successfully negotiated hundreds of lease renewals for tenants, we can assure you that there is a tried and proven process worth learning and following. In this chapter, Dale and Jeff let you in on the secrets of successful lease-renewal negotiation.

Debunking Lease Renewal Myths

Each year Jeff and Dale speak with hundreds of tenants who attend The Lease Coach seminars or contact them directly for lease-renewal assistance. Considering that the average tenant only negotiates a couple leases in their lifetime, and sometimes with the same landlord, it's easy to understand how leasing myths can persist. Occasionally these myths are created and propagated by the landlord, but also by real estate professionals looking to serve their own interests. We review some of the most common in this section.

Myth #1: You must exercise your renewal option to extend your lease

You may mistakenly believe that the only way to renew your current lease agreement is through your renewal-option clause. This is one of the most common misconceptions tenants have and is the basis for much of the content covered in the coming sections.

Ninety-eight percent of the successful lease-renewal deals that The Lease Coach completes for tenants *don't* exercise the renewal-option clause. If they exercised the renewal-option clause, everything except the rental rate would have been off the table for negotiation.

Your renewal option, if you have one, must be viewed as a safety net or backup plan. All your negotiations on a renewal term should be done well in advance of your current lease term expiring. If the landlord is unwilling to negotiate with you or you're unable to achieve the terms you're looking for, that's when you consider exercising your renewal option. (We talk more about how to decide to exercise your renewal option in the upcoming section "Examining Whether to Use Your Renewal-Option Clause or Not.")

If you play your lease-renewal cards in the right order, you may be able to negotiate for all kinds of inducements and changes that you were not aware of when you signed your first lease agreement.

Myth #2: Rental rates can only go up

We hear this all the time from tenants: "The landlord wants a rent increase on my lease-renewal term." Of course the landlord wants a rent increase, but that doesn't necessarily mean they can get it. In fact, approximately 80 percent of the lease-renewal deals that The Lease Coach negotiates result in a *rent reduction* and big savings for the tenant.

Rental rates vary across the country and from property to property. In Michigan, we negotiated a lease renewal for a retail store that sold photography equipment. The rent was reduced approximately 45 percent, saving the tenant over $300,000 in rent over the next five years. In that particular case, the landlord initially wanted the rent to go up, but said they would settle to keep it at status quo. Obviously, when the dust settled, the tenant came out the victor.

One important factor to consider is the Consumer Price Index (CPI), or *inflation*. The inflation rate for various cities differs, and sometimes the economy is in a period of deflation or recession. It's unfortunate that so many tenants who negotiate their own lease renewal and avoid a rent increase think they've won the battle, when a rent decrease was achievable if they knew how to negotiate.

Myth #3: Landlords won't provide inducements on renewals

Typically, *inducements*, or leasing incentives, include free rent, tenant allowance, and landlord's work to the premises. We negotiate these common inducements for tenants on their initial lease agreements. Business owners are shocked in most cases to learn that these inducements are also potentially available on lease-renewal terms.

Dale was speaking at a business conference with about 300 business owners in the room. He was talking about how to negotiate for a tenant allowance and free rent when one person near the front threw up her hand and said, "Dale, what is a tenant allowance?" I went on to explain that a tenant allowance is money that a landlord pays to the tenant as an inducement to help the tenant build out their space. The tenant doesn't have to pay it back. If this particular business owner didn't know what a tenant allowance was, obviously she had not gotten one on her initial lease deal. Therefore, she couldn't know to negotiate for a tenant allowance on her lease renewal.

Although it's true that most landlords tend to take their existing tenants for granted, it can be argued that any inducements or incentives the landlord is prepared to pay to acquire a new tenant can also be offered and available to existing tenants on their renewals, because the existing tenant is the proven long-term customer of the landlord. Sure, a landlord can take a risk on a new tenant, but why wouldn't they provide incentives to keep their existing tenants, who already have a proven rent-paying track record? Of course, you have to know to ask for incentives to get them; the landlord won't offer them out of goodwill.

Myth #4: Next year will be better than last year

We don't know why, but business owners seem to think that next year is always going to be better than last year. It's a myth that just because you get a rent reduction on your lease-renewal term, business will get better. In many cases, your problem isn't that your rent is too high, but that sales are too low for your location.

If you don't change your location, your product, your staff, your marketing, your pricing, or whatever your real problem is, there's no reason to think that next year will simply be better than last year. This type of false optimism often wastes many years in the life of a business owner.

The franchise industry is a good case in point regarding the need to change locations. If a franchise system has 400 units, then some of those franchisees are at the top and some of them are at the bottom, sales volume-wise. The reason why the franchise industry makes a good example is that typically a franchise is the same brand, the same product, served the same way, at the same price, with the same service system. When you compare businesses in the same franchise system, the single most distinguishable *difference* is location. Therefore, if a tenant isn't willing to change location, business may probably be much the same next year as it was last year. So, don't have false optimism that it's all just going to get better on its own — in some cases, you must consider relocation over a renewal.

Knowing Who to Negotiate With

Before we start any tenant's lease-renewal project, we try to get to know a bit about the landlord and the people working for the landlord. The tenant needs to ask themselves who they are truly negotiating the lease renewal with; if you spend two months talking and going back and forth with a person who has limited or no authority to commit the landlord, you may very well be wasting your time. (Even though we use the word *landlord*, we're typically referring to the landlord's employees as the key personnel running and managing the property on a day-to-day basis.)

Studying the landlord's website

Not all landlords have websites, but many do. The larger professional landlords typically have websites listing all their properties in various states, and describing their history and company philosophy. With publically traded companies, sometimes you can see their financials and whether or not they made a profit. The point is to gather information before going into battle, and sometimes the landlord's website is a great place to start.

Here are some things to note when you visit a landlord's website:

- **Biographies of the landlord's team:** Often the website displays pictures and professional profiles of the people you may be dealing with and negotiating against. We like to see a picture of the person we're about to call and read about their history or see their credentials. Whether they have all kinds of degrees, are Certified Property Managers, have a real estate license, or if their last name is the same as the landlord's — all that gives us key information about who we're going to be dealing with.

- **Leasing updates for properties:** You may find information about spaces about to come up for lease or even the property your business is located in. Dale recently spoke with a lease rep for a large landlord. On the phone, Dale learned that the leasing rep is in charge of all lease renewal deals for more than 90 properties and was stretched very thin.

And although he had been to the property, he had never been in Dale's client's space, nor had he met the tenant personally (simply because he didn't have the time).

✔ **Growth in the future:** You may find out whether the landlord is acquiring new properties or building new developments; these things can be signs of a strong landlord.

✔ **Potential trouble:** Properties may have been recently sold or lost to foreclosure — that will give you a different signal.

Negotiating directly with the landlord

Jeff and Dale really enjoy negotiating face-to-face with landlords. Sometimes, because of a distance factor, we negotiate by telephone, but there's no one with more authority to make a decision on properties than the landlords themselves. Keep in mind that the landlord may be a group of investors, and you're speaking with only one of the investors/landlords who may have to report to a board of directors or another group of people. If you're negotiating directly with a landlord for a property, it's probably a smaller landlord who remains active in day-to-day operations. If the landlord built the property from the ground up, they may have an emotional attachment to the property.

Don't inadvertently slight or offend the landlord by making thoughtless comments about issues with the property management (there is a time to properly discuss that). For now, focus on relationships and the renewal terms.

If the landlord speaks with you but pushes you down to a subordinate for the deal-making process, you may have to respect that decision because after all that is the property manager's job. Don't copy the landlord on e-mails to the property manager because that's bothersome to the landlord. You can ask or request that the landlord weigh in from time to time. If you know that a landlord is going to be visiting or touring the property, it may be possible to set up an in-person meeting for when they come to town.

Facing off with the landlord's property manager

For many years, Dale was a commercial property manager working for landlords. One of his jobs was to negotiate lease renewals with existing tenants. Even though the landlord may have given a listing to a commercial real estate agent to find new tenants for the property, the landlord didn't want to pay commissions for renewing tenants he already had. Although sometimes as a property manager, Dale may get a small or token commission, it wasn't nearly as much as commercial real estate agents who brought in new tenants got.

Some property managers are personable, but others can be terrible to work with. The one advantage to negotiating with a property manager is that as a salaried employee of the landlord, they typically know what the landlord expects or needs, deal-wise. Typically, if you ask the property manager the right questions, you can also get better answers than you can from the real estate agent, because the property manager knows which tenants are moving in, moving out, what all the tenants are paying in rent, and who is and isn't current on rent. The property manager converses with the landlord weekly, if not daily, whereas a listing agent does not.

If you think you'll be negotiating your lease renewal with a property manager in the next few months, you may want to make a few deposits to that relationship now. If your relationship is tattered because of arguments over problems with the property or missed or late rent payments, you need to start repairing that relationship now so that you're on reasonable terms when it comes time to negotiate your lease renewal.

Though you may understand that you're the landlord's customer, sometimes the property manager doesn't have that same attitude. Note that landlords, rightly or wrongly, usually side with their employee rather than the tenant if they are butting heads with the property manager.

Dealing with the landlord's in-house real estate leasing rep

Larger landlords hire in-house leasing reps — real estate reps who only work for them. These are not real estate agents affiliated or associating with the big commercial real estate brokerages. In-house real estate leasing rep is a role that Dale played for many years. He was on salary and commission and handled both lease renewals and new leases for the landlord. This was typically because the landlord had a substantial set of holdings that the property management team had to focus on doing property management work, and leasing reps focused on leasing.

There's often a disconnect between the leasing team and the property management team. When we take on a new client to negotiate their lease renewal, we make a wish list and ask them about deficiencies that bother them about the property; this could be unfilled potholes, problematic neighbor tenants, broken glass that doesn't get replaced, street lamps that don't work, and more. If you bring these items up with the leasing rep, they're typically unaware of your dissatisfaction and concern with the state of the property.

We frequently incorporate the list of deficiency improvements that need to be done to the property in the renewal document for a tenant. Otherwise, the landlord may continue to ignore the problems, and it will drive the tenant crazy.

If you're dealing with landlord personnel who are not onsite or not familiar with the property you lease, you may want to send along a few digital pictures to show what you're concerned about. The in-house real estate rep has access to how much all the tenants are paying for rent, which tenants are moving in or out, and so on — just like the property manager. The leasing rep may not be aware of your rent payment history (good or bad), and therefore, going through them is to your advantage if you were late on rent payments or bounced a few rent checks.

In-house leasing reps tend to be a bit more social and often take the time to come and see you when they're at the property because they often work outside of the office. The longer the landlord has employed this person, the more likely the landlord is to take their advice. The in-house leasing rep may not have ultimate authority, but within reasonable parameters usually knows what deal the landlord may or may not accept.

Dealing with the landlord's listing real estate agent

Occasionally, The Lease Coach negotiates a lease renewal for a tenant and learns that the landlord has decided to delegate all lease renewals to a listing real estate agent (or brokerage). The primary role of the leasing agent may be to find new tenants for the property, but the landlord is also paying them a fee or commission to renew existing tenants. The agent may not be able to make as much commission from the renewal deal as they could from a new tenant moving in to the property.

If the property is fully leased with no vacancies, the agent may be thinking of finding tenants who could take your place. Hence, the real estate agent may shoot for unreasonable renewal rental rates from the existing tenants, knowing that if that aggressive proposal sends the tenant packing it opens another spot for the real estate agent to replace that tenant and earn a bigger commission. This seems to happen more often when the commercial real estate brokerage is both managing and filling all leasing roles for the property.

Although many real estate agents we know are skillful at their jobs, many more lack deal-closing business sense. That's why 20 percent of the real estate agents make 80 percent of the money. Some agents are extremely prompt and professional with callbacks, follow-ups, and e-mails, but others appear to be not that great at their jobs. This in turn affects your deal making.

The higher the rental rate and the longer the renewal term, the more commission the real estate agent typically earns. If you want to renew your lease for just three years instead of five, this may be okay with the landlord — but the real estate agent may push for five years to maximize the commission.

Examining Whether to Use Your Renewal-Option clause or Not

As we mention earlier, for 98 percent of the successful lease renewals we negotiate for tenants, we do *not* exercise the lease renewal-option clause. Is it good to have a renewal-option clause? Sure, but you should only need to use it in about 1 out of 50 cases.

Once in a while, if the renewal-option clause has expired, the landlord offers to backdate the agreement or still permit you to exercise your renewal-option clause as a means of locking you further in. This situation can be acceptable, provided you're on top of it. Ask yourself, why would the landlord want to do this? What do they know that I don't? Everyone has a motivation for what they do and why they do it that way. In this section, we help you make the renewal-option decision.

Reading what the renewal-option clause says or does not say

Having reviewed well over two thousand formal lease documents, we've pretty much seen it all. Some informal leases may dedicate only a few sentences to the renewal-option clause. Other formal lease documents may go on for a full page or two about it, stating not only that the tenant has a renewal-option right, but then elaborating on the conditions imposed by the landlord on that option (this is the catch).

In one lease agreement The Lease Coach reviewed for a tenant, the landlord had ten conditions attached to the tenant's renewal-option right. For example, the lease agreement said that if the tenant missed a rent payment, sold the business, or didn't achieve a certain threshold of sales volume — the renewal-option rights of the tenant are nullified. Why? Landlords who want tenants to pay percentage rent — rent above their normal base rent — may not want you for a tenant, especially if you're an independent and the landlord feels they could attract a national name tenant who could achieve percentage-rent sales.

So, it's not good enough for a tenant to have a renewal-option clause; it needs to be effective and reasonable as well.

Verifying that your renewal-option clause is assignable

If you only have 14 months or so left on your lease term and you want to sell your business, you may represent to the prospective buyer that they need not worry — you have a 5-year renewal-option clause. However, many leases are silent about whether this renewal-option clause is indeed assignable to the buyer of your business. Court cases abound over this issue because so many people have bought businesses, taken an assignment of the lease agreement, and then are told by the landlord that the renewal-option rights are personal to the original tenant and not assignable with the lease agreement. Effectively, the renewal-option rights die or evaporate when the business is sold.

Although some leases state that the renewal-option rights aren't transferable, most leases are simply silent on this matter. Different landlords may interpret this silence in their favor. The tenant cries out that the lease agreement doesn't say the renewal option is specific to them, and the landlord argues that it doesn't say it's transferrable, either. So, you see the disagreement that can arise when this point is not clarified.

Making sure your renewal-option clause is still valid

A franchise tenant coming to the end of their 10-year lease decided to hire The Lease Coach to negotiate their lease renewal. For various reasons, it was decided that exercising the renewal-option clause in this case was in the 2 percent range for which that would be wise. Upon contacting the landlord to inquire about doing so, we were informed by the landlord that the tenant had been late on their 17th rent payment about 7 years prior. Even though the tenant made up the rent payment in less than two weeks, they effectively defaulted. And because the renewal-option clause had a condition that voided the renewal-option clause in the event of a default, the landlord had the tenant dead to rights.

As years pass, it's easy to forget or disregard a past issue that may be held against you. Unfortunately, a casual e-mail or even a letter from a landlord or property manager stating that your renewal-option rights are intact can be overturned if inaccurate.

If you do want to exercise your renewal-option clause, the surest way to confirm that your right to do so is still valid is to get it in writing from the landlord. Once you do exercise the renewal-option clause, ask the landlord to reply in writing confirming that he has indeed accepted your letter and that the renewal option has been triggered, properly and on time.

Pulling the renewal-option clause trigger: Pros and cons

Sometimes we avoid taking certain medicines because of their side effects. Well, exercising your renewal option can produce or cause some touchy side effects that you may not have considered. Or try another metaphor: The decision to exercise the renewal-option clause is like coming to a fork in the road — the path you decide to take will lead you in very different directions. When you exercise the renewal-option clause, there's no turning back if you don't like where that decision or path is taking you. You can't rescind your renewal-option clause unilaterally, so you'd better make the right decision at this fork in the road.

When you should exercise your renewal option

You may want to become part of the 2 percent who should exercise renewal-option rights. See if any of the following is true for you:

- ✔ You have special exclusivity clauses that you want to protect because you know a competitor may infringe on your use. Exercising your renewal option usually protects those rights, but check the fine print. Many rights for exclusivity are for the initial lease term only.

- ✔ Your lease already states a renewal term rental rate lower than current market rents. Pulling the renewal option trigger can lock you in to that low, preferred rental rate. Most leases don't state a preset rental rate for the renewal term — its negotiated at the time of renewal.

- ✔ Exercising your renewal-option clause will prevent the landlord from taking the space back or giving your space to a neighbor tenant who wants to expand. These situations are rare but do exist in about 2 percent of all lease agreements.

- ✔ You think that the landlord may have demolition plans for the property or similar changes in mind. Exercising your renewal-option clause may protect you, depending on what the fine print says about the landlord's rights.

When you shouldn't exercise your renewal option

On the other hand, not exercising your right may make sense if any of the following circumstances apply to you:

✓ If your lease agreement states that if you exercise your renewal option, the base or minimum rent cannot go down — it can only go up. The rental increase may be a set amount or tied to the consumer price index increases. If you think the market rents are lower now than when you signed your lease agreement years ago, then obviously you must take this into consideration.

✓ You may be leaving free rent, tenant allowance, landlord work, parking, signage, and so forth on the negotiating table. These inducements and other points are back on the negotiating table again if you do not exercise your renewal-option clause. Although you may indeed renew your current lease, it becomes a new negotiation.

✓ By exercising your renewal option, you may lose flexibility and the potential of negotiating for a shorter renewal term (perhaps three years instead of the five years stated, for example). You also won't be able to negotiate to include additional renewal option(s) if you're down to your last option term.

✓ A lot of business owners sign a personal guaranty for their companies or enter into the lease agreement under their personal name, with spouses, or other partners. This guaranty may automatically renew when you exercise the option. These items can potentially be renegotiated at lease renewal time if you don't exercise your renewal option.

✓ Getting the deposit reduced, refunded, or applied to their rental account is something Dale and Jeff work hard at for tenant clients. Many lease agreements state that the deposit can be applied to the last month of the term (or renewal term) or simply refunded when the tenant's lease agreement expires and they move out. So, if you exercise your renewal option, you will probably not get your deposit back; the landlord will continue to hold it.

Doing Site Selection Even if You Don't Plan to Move

One of the most valuable exercises a tenant can go through prior to negotiating their lease renewal is site selection. Typically, many years have gone by since you last looked at the plazas or other commercial properties available for lease, and it's time to do that again. The reason so many tenants resist doing this homework is they say they don't have time, or there isn't any good space for lease near them, or they don't plan to move anyway, so why waste time looking at other locations?

Actually, the converse is true: The more you think you want to stay in your current location, the harder you have to look at what other space is out there available for lease — if you want to get a good lease renewal deal.

Checking out what the competition has done over the past five years

What if I told you two of your closest competitors were going to close out of business, move, expand, downsize, or were struggling to stay open? Would this information change or affect your lease-renewal plans? Of course it would.

What if you learned that a new competitor was coming into the neighborhood? This happened with several Christian bookstore tenants that Dale was negotiating lease renewals for. A large national competitor opened just down the street and took a substantial toll on their sales. If your rent is going up and your sales are going down, that affects your decision-making process about a lease renewal.

It might be difficult to know in advance if an independent business owner is planning to put down stakes near your business in the future, but predicting the growth of franchise systems is much easier. For example, if you're afraid of a particular franchise system coming into your community and competing with you, you can find out in advance by asking the corporate headquarters. Often franchisors know where they're planning to expand years in advance. General expansion plans typically become public knowledge, which you can often find out from the website or with a simple phone call. If you learn that they just sold the franchise territory for your city and plan to open eight outlets in the next three years, that may affect whether you want to renew your lease. Converting your location to join an expanding franchise system may have some merit if you face this scenario.

Kicking the tires on other locations for lease

It takes time, but its free: You can look at as much space for lease as you want to. The grass may be greener on the other side of the street but it still needs to be mowed, so don't get swept up too quickly. The more sites you look at and the more information you gather, the smarter you become and the wiser your decisions will be.

When making a leasing inquiry on a property, always call the listing agent who has their *For Lease* sign on the property rather than letting an outside agent introduce you to a property to avoid commission-splitting, which may work against you. Where The Lease Coach differentiates itself in the commercial real estate marketplace is that we only work for the tenant, who is paying our fee.

Getting lease proposals on other sites to increase your renewal leverage

Timing is critical when you request lease proposals from landlords and their listing agents. Ideally, you do all your site selection at once and receive multiple proposals all within a few days, including any renewal proposal from your landlord. This allows you to compare the deals on paper side by side.

Sometimes a landlord's real estate agent sends you a casual e-mail proposal, which is not as effective as a full proposal on their letterhead. If you want to show this competitor's lease proposal to your landlord to create stronger leverage for your renewal negotiations, it has more clout if it looks more official than a casual e-mail.

Don't assume that any of what you're doing is held confidential. The grapevine in commercial real estate is a thriving one, and if you want the real estate agent to keep the deal quiet, don't just tell them, ask them and get them to confirm that they will keep it confidential.

Talking with other tenants to gather valuable insights

A tenant hired The Lease Coach to negotiate her lease renewal. Dale flew in to visit and drove out to her location. On the first visit, he noticed that there was a vacancy directly adjacent to the tenant he was representing. About eight weeks later, he came back to see the client, and the space right next door to her was occupied. A tenant leased the space, moved in, and opened for business though he was still setting up displays and merchandising.

Without hesitation, Dale took out a business card, walked in, and introduced himself to the shop owner. After some small talk, Dale told him he was working with a neighboring tenant on their lease renewal — would he be willing to share some details of the lease agreement he must have just negotiated for his business? The shop owner paused and then said no, he was too busy to talk — but then he reached under the counter, pulled out his lease agreement, and handed it over, saying, "I'm too busy to talk, but look for yourself." He walked off to assist a customer.

Dale is not one to look a gift horse in the mouth. He walked to a quiet corner of the store and carefully read and wrote down all of the business terms. He could see his rental rate, tenant allowance, personal guarantee — everything. As you can imagine, this information helped Dale negotiate a much better lease-renewal deal for his client.

This advice about talking to other tenants applies to both your current property and any other properties in the area that interest you. Although some tenants don't want to speak with you or may even give you erroneous information, many tenants vent and pontificate and tell you rumors they're hearing about anchor tenants and so on, making it a worthwhile exercise.

Understanding How Far in Advance to Initiate the Renewal Process

Ideally, a tenant wants to start the lease-renewal process about 12 months in advance of their lease expiration date. More precisely, look at your renewal-option clause. If it says your cutoff date for exercising your lease-renewal option is 6 months before the lease expires, you would start the renewal process 6 months before that, or a total of 12 months in advance. If your renewal-option clause states that your cutoff date or last chance to exercise the renewal-option clause is 9 or 12 months before the lease expires, then start the lease-renewal process 15 or 18 months in advance.

Your strength or leverage may lessen the closer you get to the cutoff deadline, so the farther in advance you can find out what the landlord wants to do with your tenancy and rental rate, the more time you have to react. If you're going to get bad or disturbing news, you want that information sooner rather than later. Keep in mind, most landlords want and plan to have their tenants renew, so you're usually on the same page plan-wise anyway.

This also applies in cases where you don't have a renewal option and want to remain in your same location. The closer you get to the end of the term, the less relocation time you have, and it becomes clearer to the landlord that you cannot or don't intend to consider a relocation. There's also the peace-of-mind factor of putting the lease renewal to bed well in advance, if possible. You may want to plan renovations or, if you're a franchise tenant, you may need to also negotiate your franchise-renewal agreement or extension as well. This happened with one of our restaurant franchise tenant clients. Actually, his franchise agreement expired many months before the lease agreement was set to expire (because he signed the franchise agreement almost a year before he opened for business).

Ideally, the lease agreement and franchise agreement should run parallel, both expiring at the same time. We told the tenant it may be easier and more beneficial to get the franchisor to extend the franchise agreement for eight months or so, to align with lease agreement — which he did, and it worked out just fine.

Making first contact with the landlord's property manager

We recommend e-mail for first contact between a tenant and a property manager. What you're doing is using e-mail to book a telephone appointment to discuss your tenancy (not just your renewal term). Your e-mail attempts to establish that you're talking with the right person, whose job it is to handle lease renewals and so forth for this landlord.

You may have one landlord and one property manager — but they may have hundreds of tenants. Therefore, the importance or significance of the lease-renewal process may not be as acute for them as it is for you. We always prepare for these calls with the property manager by gathering some good things to say or reflect on. For example, if the landlord just got a new anchor tenant or finished painting the building, we mention this and get off on the right foot.

Depending on your past relationship, you may need to clear the air when you do get on the phone and reboot the relationship. If the property manager hasn't been to your location in a long time, inviting them out is a good idea. This is not the negotiation portion of the lease-renewal process, so it should all be positive. You goal is to get them to put a somewhat formal written proposal in front of you. Then you can get down to the negotiating process.

Knowing what to say and what not to say

Whatever you do, don't say, "I'm calling to renew my lease" when you get on the phone with the landlord. Everything you say and do at this stage is critical. When Dale was a commercial property manager working for landlords, he could read a tenant like a book. He could ask questions that when answered would reveal their desires and intentions, thereby giving Dale the upper hand, negotiation-wise. So, you've got to keep your cards close to your vest, as they say in Las Vegas.

What The Lease Coach does for tenant clients is the opposite of what most tenants do. We ask the property manager if he thinks the landlord wants or desires to retain our client's (the tenant's) tenancy for another term. Notice how we're not asking property managers if *they* want to retain the tenant. We're asking if they think the *landlord* wants to retain the tenant. This really opens the dialogue and gives the property manager some room to verbally run with.

This also turns the tables, making them state their intentions or position first. Ninety-eight percent of the time, the landlord or their property manager will say, "Of course we want the tenant to stay — they're not thinking of leaving, are they?" With this response in hand, we can now leverage the deal in the tenant's favor. Our response to the property manager is, "Well, what lease-renewal deal did you have in mind for them?" This is exactly where you want to be at this stage.

Inviting the landlord to send you a lease-renewal proposal

The goal is to receive a written lease-renewal proposal (or lease-renewal agreement) rather than make the first offer or renewal proposal to them. Once we have the property manager on record as stating the landlord wants to retain the tenant for a lease-renewal term, exercising the lease renewal-option clause almost always becomes unnecessary. Although more than half of all property managers respond positively to this request and comply with our suggestion for them to prepare a renewal proposal, some don't. Reasons why include the following:

- ✔ They think it's too soon, or that too much time remains on the lease agreement; they want to wait before starting negotiations. In some cases, you may have to patiently wait and follow up with the landlord or ask them when they're prepared to discuss a potential renewal. In some cases, we tell the landlord that this is their opportunity to retain this tenant well in advance of their lease expiring; as the term gets closer to the end, it's more likely that other landlords may pursue their tenant.

- ✔ They tell you, the tenant, to exercise your renewal option and that this is the only way to proceed. Of course it's not, but now the game really begins to get interesting. In some cases, with our clients, we strategically waive the option to renew so the landlord can't use this as a reason not to exercise well in advance of the expiration. Doing so allows us to negotiate all terms, not just the rent. Before you remove that safety net, though, you must be cautious here and ensure you're not a tenant that falls into that 2 percent who may have to exercise their renewal (see the earlier section "When you should exercise your renewal option" for more on that).

> ✔ They tell the tenant to make a proposal to the landlord. In some cases, you may have to initiate a proposal. This may be an instance when having other landlords actively competing for your tenancy may spur your landlord to provide a renewal proposal rather than risk losing you.

This is where a tenant may be inclined to blink or misread the situation. Lack of experience and sometimes fear or intimidation creep in, and the tenant caves to one of the preceding landlord reasons. Remember that you're the landlord's customer, reiterate your position, and wait them out. However, when we do this, we're not waiting without action. We're getting other lease proposals from other landlords and creating a situation more favorable to the tenant, which includes optional locations for lease elsewhere.

Reviewing the Physical Lease-Renewal Agreement

Various landlords across the country may call the renewal documentation by different names. The following document titles are synonymous:

> ✔ Lease-Renewal Agreement
>
> ✔ Lease-Amending Agreement
>
> ✔ Lease-Extension Agreement
>
> ✔ Lease Renewal and Amending Agreement

These renewal documents are typically one to three pages in length, depending on how many points you're negotiating to amend in the current formal lease agreement. All terms in the formal lease agreement remain in full force and effect, unless stated in an amending clause in the renewal document.

If the property is sold, the new landlord may want to introduce their standard long form of formal lease agreement instead of using a shorter lease-renewal agreement. This will essentially open a whole new can of worms for the tenant to negotiate and is generally not the best way to go for the tenant, but it's still a case-by-case decision-making process.

Negotiating to get your deposit back

When we talk with a property manager about the tenant's lease renewal, we ask them why they required a security deposit in the first place. They usually say that the tenant was unproven or that the landlord had contributed with financial inducements on the initial lease agreement. Well, now that the tenant has proven themselves worthy, has paid rent for almost five years or longer, and the landlord has recouped their investment — it's time to return the deposit to the tenant.

Landlord resistance to this suggestion or request will be that other tenants have deposits down or that keeping them is the norm. Nonetheless, we almost always succeed in getting the deposit back for the tenant or at least in getting it reduced substantially. If the tenant has a checkered history of late rent payments or other problems, the landlord may actually have some ground to stand on. But if you have a clean record, fight to get your deposit back.

Even if the landlord won't refund the deposit for this renewal term, negotiate now to have the deposit returned on the anniversary of your next lease-renewal term. You don't want to fight and lose this battle again five years from now. Get it in writing that the deposit is returned if you stay for an additional renewal term. You'll thank us for this advice five years from now.

Persuading the landlord to remove or reduce your personal guarantee

The reasons landlords want personal guarantees from tenants is almost the same reasons why they want deposits (or so they would say). The landlord wants security. But why does the landlord deserve this security anymore? Did anyone guarantee you that when you opened your business it would be successful?

Use some of the same advice from the previous section for getting your deposit back. Sometimes it's a victory just to get a partner or spouse removed from the guarantee, even if you have to remain liable.

One way we negotiate the personal guarantee on lease renewals is to limit and reduce it over time. Sometimes this is called *burning off the guarantee*, meaning that the guarantee is limited to a lesser dollar value — say, $50,000 for one year — and then reduced by $10,000 per year for the 5-year renewal term. If you do default or close the business, this caps the amount the landlord can personally sue you for.

If you're successful with verbally negotiating these changes, make sure to review the wording carefully. Sometimes the landlord may add a clause that says if the tenant (your company) gets behind in rent or defaults, the full personal guarantee is reinstated — which defeats the whole purpose of the negotiation and agreement that just came about.

Getting more renewal option terms added to your lease agreement

A lease renewal-option clause is for the benefit of the tenant only. It can help you secure a long-term tenancy and even help to sell your business. Seldom is a landlord surprised if you ask or negotiate for additional renewal-option term(s) as part of your negotiations. What they may do is try to limit your renewal options to the length of your current term. So, if you're renewing for 5 years and desire two 5-year renewal options, the landlord may resist and only give you one 5-year renewal term.

The more the location of your business contributes to the value of your business, the more important these extra renewal options can be. For an office tenant on the 4th floor of an office building, this is obviously less important because location is less important. The office tenant can move to almost any other office building with no effect to their sales volumes. But to a retailer, location may mean everything. One of our tenant clients sold his jewelry store within an enclosed shopping mall. Much of the value was connected to the physical location.

Cleaning up your assignment clause

The assignment clause is a vital organ in a living lease agreement. This is the clause that allows or disallows the tenant to assign their lease agreement for the purpose of selling their business. Occasionally, we see lease agreements with no assignment clause at all, but most often it's simply a poorly worded or one-sided agreement in the landlord's favor.

The key phrase you want in your assignment clause is: *Landlord shall not unreasonably withhold its consent to an assignment of the lease.*

Tackling changes in signage, parking, and various verbal agreements

Now is the time to negotiate with the landlord on signage, parking, storage, additions to your permitted use clause, and any other handshake agreements you have. Most landlords like to keep these lesser agreements verbal or off the lease-agreement radar, because if they sell the building they may want to terminate the unwritten handshake deals. In fact, many landlords facing a situation like this state that their agreement or permission to have extra parking, signage, or storage was only intended to bind them as long as they were the landlord. They feel no moral or legal responsibility to the tenant after the building is sold.

So, go to work and get all those loose ends in writing during the lease-renewal negotiation. The last thing you want is to be sideswiped by a new landlord taking away some extra items you thought were yours for good. Most formal lease agreements state what signage the tenant receives on the front of the building, but often there's no statement or reference to a rental amount. A few landlords have been observed buying properties and forcing tenants to pay a monthly rental charge for fascia signage or remove the signage from the building. As you can imagine, this would be a nasty surprise, so stipulate that signage is at no cost or at whatever charge you've already agreed to pay, to avoid future issues.

Dealing with outstanding tenancy issues now as part of the lease renewal

We often ask tenants to send pictures of the property they're leasing. We see dilapidated signage, broken windows, massive potholes, graffiti, and so on in those pictures. These all need to be dealt with as part of the lease-renewal negotiations if the landlord wants to secure your tenancy. If you're tired of calling the landlord because they won't replace burnt-out parking lot lights, clean the windows, cut the grass, or keep the property in good repair, then don't expect these things to cure themselves. This is when you're in the strongest position to rectify some of these issues. We often negotiate these outstanding issues into the renewal with a timeline for the landlord to correct them. In some cases, we even impose a penalty on the landlord should they not be corrected by a certain date.

Counteroffering the Landlord's Lease-Renewal Proposal

Your job isn't done once you receive the landlord's lease-renewal proposal — it's just beginning. Most tenants wouldn't make good boxers, because they would go down in the 2nd or 3rd round. Having the mental stamina, the will, and the desire to actually go back and forth with multiple counteroffers is very important. Many times, a landlord will win a negotiation over a tenant just because of greater endurance.

For the business owner, negotiating leases is a hassle — a necessary evil, one tenant called it — and often quite an undesirable activity. But landlords are different — they chose to invest in real estate. They employ property managers and other professionals who enjoy working in commercial real estate. For them, the fun is just beginning. For you, the fun ended when you realized you needed to buy this book and you start learning what we've been teaching tenants for more than 20 years.

Make sure you put your signed counteroffers in writing, with an expiry date within which time the counteroffer is open for acceptance. Normally, you would have had a prior verbal discussion with the landlord or their representative. It generally makes for a better deal-making process if you don't blindside them in the counteroffer. That means discussing your concerns with them in advance so that at least when they see your counteroffer, they aren't taken aback.

If one of your complaints is about the broken-down fence along the property line, start by asking them about it. If they say that the fence repairs are already scheduled for next month, then you don't have to ask for them to complete it. But you do have to stipulate that they not only plan to do it but *will* do it. Don't waste your negotiations on items they plan to take care of anyway — but still get them to verify it in writing.

Making your pitch for a rent reduction

We do a lot of lease renewal rent-reduction projects. Tenants struggling to keep their business open, pay their staff, and pay their rent don't know whether they should grab onto the tail or the head when they start negotiating for a rent reduction.

When a tenant comes to The Lease Coach, we look at whether their rent is too high relative to the marketplace and what they can reasonably afford to pay. Sometimes the landlord's asking rent (although negotiable) is not really out of line with the marketplace or what the tenant should be able to afford to pay. Sometimes it's that the tenant's sales are too low, not that the rent is too high.

So why are those sales low? Are there lots of other vacant units around you — did the anchor tenant move out of the property? Has an industry competitor opened nearby, or perhaps another landlord put up a brand new development a mile away that's drawing traffic away from your location?

A few years ago, Dale got a local dentist a rent reduction on his lease renewal when he was fully expecting and even prepared for his rent to go up. When Dale sat down with the landlord's leasing rep, he pulled out a map and showed him exactly where three other dentists had opened in nearby new developments. All of these new developments and competition happened in the last few years, right after the dentist renewed his lease on his own the last time. Dale wasn't blaming the landlord; he was simply presenting factual information about this tenant's new competition. The result, about a month later, after more negotiations, was a successful lease renewal with a rent reduction.

Tenants need to determine what the problem is and creatively show the landlord why it's in the landlord's best interest to give the tenant a rent reduction. Replacing a tenant can be terribly expensive for a landlord; it's easier (and often cheaper) to just lower the rent for an existing tenant to keep them for another five years.

Playing one landlord against another

Like an auctioneer trying to get the highest dollar from the bidders, we like to create a competition for a client's tenancy and make the buyers (the landlords) bid against each other. We won't say, "Don't try this at home, kids," but we will say that it's much easier if you have a professional coaching you through the process. Different types of landlords respond in different ways. Saying the *right thing* at the *wrong time* to a landlord can really mess things up.

You want your existing landlord to think or believe they may lose your tenancy to another property. It's better if your landlord thinks that listing agents for other properties are chasing and courting you for their property, rather than that you were shopping around. You don't like it when your customers are shopping around, but landlords can't blame you if they think it was simply another agent prospecting your tenancy.

Don't try to bluff your way through this. Landlords often know what spaces are for lease in their area and at what rental rates. When we start playing one landlord against another, hold a written lease proposal from their competition, and we even show it to the landlord (at the appropriate time) to drive home the point.

For example, if your existing landlord insists on a personal guarantee or on keeping your deposit for the renewal term, but another landlord doesn't care about getting that from you, then you've created leverage in your favor. If a new landlord is willing to give our client nine months of free rent, but the existing landlord is too stingy to provide an inducement package for his renewal tenants, then we've once again created leverage by creating competition for the tenant.

Tenants can create competition for their tenancy even if the properties are far apart or not equal in class or rental rate. Your existing landlord still inherits a vacancy, whether they lose you to a nicer building, an older one, or a more expensive property.

Walking away or waiting out a slow landlord

If you started working on your lease renewal well in advance, you have the time you need to play the waiting game with a slow landlord. If your lease deal is going too slow, don't hesitate to ask why. Maybe the landlord is thinking of listing the property for sale and doesn't want to renew your lease at a lower rate than you're paying now for fear it will devalue his property (and it will). Maybe the landlord is waiting to see if another key tenant is going to renew their lease or move out.

Generally, if a landlord is slow to respond or reluctant to engage in a lease-renewal process without a good reason, it means potential trouble for the tenant. The landlord may be thinking of demolishing the building to make way for a high-rise condo.

But there are situations like the one we're going through right now for a tenant. The landlord's in-house leasing rep has no discernible business skills, to put it nicely. She tells us one thing on the phone and puts something else in writing. She keeps breaking her promises to send a lease proposal and delays the process until we complain to her superior. You may be following the playbook, but if the person you're negotiating with is clueless, it becomes even more challenging.

Jeff and Dale encountered a similar situation with an in-house leasing representative recently. Knowing the renewal process was going to be delayed at the landlord's end, we resisted demanding a start date for the negotiations and instead asked him to tell us when we could begin the renewal process. We confirmed that date by e-mail and now at least we have a target date that the leasing rep set himself and will likely honor.

Putting your counteroffers in writing

It makes us cringe to hear of tenants making verbal counteroffers or sending unsigned casual e-mail counteroffers. Lack of attention to these protocols sends the landlord a message that you don't know what you're doing. Truthfully, some landlords don't know what they're doing either. Many landlords can misread and botch the negotiation process, by simply driving their tenant into the waiting arms of another landlord.

From experience, we can tell you that many of the sloppiest small-time landlords to deal with seem to be on the east coast. We've seen them put deals down on not much more than paper napkins. Sloppy and incomplete paperwork is dangerous for the tenant.

Executing the lease-renewal agreement

A deal is not a deal until both parties sign it and return the signed agreement back to the other party accepting and acknowledging that it's a done deal. Many tenants have hired us over the years with so many loose ends in their deal that they couldn't produce a final version of the lease-renewal agreement signed by both parties. There were strings of e-mails but nothing signed off.

The power of negotiation

After one of The Lease Coach Bootcamps, a tenant approached Dale to discuss his situation. The tenant took a lease assignment a few years prior when he purchased a business. He currently paid $25 per square foot plus operating costs. The landlord wanted to raise his rent to $28 per square foot. The tenant did not feel fully capable or experienced enough to negotiate his lease renewal and wanted help from The Lease Coach.

After exploring the tenant's situation, it was clear that he didn't want to relocate or move the business. It took Dale several attempts to convince him to pick a few alternative locations to use as competition against his current landlord. Even though he insisted he wasn't moving, he agreed and began looking for other properties for lease. Then Dale began to talk with other listing agents for these landlords and receive lease proposals on these other properties. This tenant was extremely desirable to other landlords but was taken for granted by his current landlord.

Once Dale had lease proposals from other landlords, he went in to see the current landlord. After several rounds of negotiating, Dale pulled out the proposals from the other landlords and used them as leverage to get this tenant a lease-renewal rent reduction. The tenant said he would be satisfied if he could just maintain status quo (keep his rental rate at $25 per square foot).

Using the strategies and tactics discussed in this chapter, Dale effectively negotiated his lease renewal for the next eight years down to less than $10 per square foot. In addition, Dale was able to get him a tenant allowance so he could replace the floor coverings in his premises. The rent reduction saved the tenant approximately $2,500 per month, and of course, he was ecstatic. He was also shocked that the landlord was that flexible. Since then, The Lease Coach has done several other leasing projects for this tenant and, we've become fast friends. Never underestimate the power of creating competition for your tenancy and using a professional lease consultant.

Make sure all lease documents are properly executed by the landlord and that you can find that lease document when you need it. About one out of ten tenants who hire The Lease Coach can't find their actual executed lease document or renewal agreement. A doctor recently sent Dale incorrect versions of his lease agreement, partially signed but not fully initialed where they had agreed on changes negotiated five years prior. It was confusing until Dale got the landlord to send the actual agreement from his files.

You've got to take the process seriously. The time to be cleaning up your loose-ended lease-renewal agreement is not when you're trying to sell your business. Scan the final document as a PDF and save it. And keep at least one paper copy at home and one at the place of business.

Chapter 17

Negotiating Renewal-Option Clauses and How to Best Exercise Them

The renewal-option clause in a lease is there for the sole benefit of the tenant. Essentially, its purpose is to ensure that you're allowed to lease your space for another term, as long as you meet the predetermined conditions listed in the lease agreement. Not all landlords automatically include renewal-option periods or terms in their offer to lease or formal lease agreement. It's your responsibility as a tenant to request, insist on, or negotiate for renewal-option rights. In some cases, there will actually be multiple renewal-option terms running consecutively.

But just because the lease-renewal clause is there for your benefit doesn't mean you have to exercise it. We recently spoke with a tenant who had been in the same location for over 25 years. He was mistakenly under the impression that if he wanted to renew his lease, he had to exercise the renewal-option clause. This is false in most cases. As we mentioned before, approximately 98 percent of the successful lease-renewal agreements that The Lease Coach negotiates for tenants *don't* include exercising the renewal-option clause at all. That's because 98 percent of landlords want to retain and keep their tenants in the property, paying rent. In this chapter, we look at the reasons for not exercising, plus the benefits and pitfalls of lease-renewal option clauses.

Including a Renewal-Option Clause in the Initial Offer to Lease or LOI

Even though you may never need to use your lease renewal-option clause or term, you may want to negotiate for it when you first sign your lease anyway. The main reasons a tenant wants a renewal-option clause/term(s) as part of their lease agreement include the following:

- **To keep the landlord from taking back your space:** In one case, our tenant client leased about 8,000 square feet, paying his rent on time, and had no landlord issues. The tenant assumed the landlord would automatically want him to stay and didn't bring The Lease Coach on board until only a couple months were left on the initial term. When we contacted the landlord, they were very apologetic, but they had committed that tenant's space to the neighboring 30,000 square foot tenant who needed to expand. The smaller tenant had to move.

- **To prevent being evicted without a chance to discuss it with your landlord:** For example, one tenant was paying his rent late, bouncing rent checks, and making the landlord's life miserable. If you have a lease-renewal option, you have a chance to explain why you can be a better tenant in the future.

- **To benefit a future potential buyer of your business:** If you're 4 years into a 5-year lease term and want to sell your business, you're probably selling a package deal (inventory, goodwill, leasehold improvements, fixtures, and so on). Of course, the buyer is also including or expecting to have the physical location or real estate lease included in the transaction. The buyer normally likes the comfort of knowing that once they buy your business, they can stay for an additional term.

Determining how many years your lease-renewal term should be

Most lease-renewal terms are the same length as the initial term. So if a tenant signs an initial 5-year lease term, it's common for the landlord to grant one 5-year renewal option term. Dale is currently coaching a healthcare tenant who plans to invest a tremendous amount of money in building out their practice to accommodate multiple doctors. They decided on an initial lease term of 12 years with one 8-year renewal option. Although there are no hard and fast rules, some landlords resist giving a renewal-option term that's longer than the initial term. The larger the financial investment you make in a location, the longer or more renewal-option terms you typically want or need.

A renewal-option term for the tenant doesn't give the landlord any particular benefit. From your perspective as the tenant, it may be better to have several short options terms, because longer may not be better. The renewal-option term in most lease agreements is for a set period of time, such as three or five years. You normally must make a full-term commitment if you do exercise the renewal option. Just because you have an initial 10-year lease term with a 10-year renewal option, this may not be ideal. What if you only want to renew for two years? You will have to forgo exercising the 10-year option and negotiate for just 2 more years.

If you can persuade the landlord to agree to a renewal-option term that's "*up to five years* as determined by the tenant," you can have maximum flexibility to exercise your renewal-option term, but potentially for a shorter period of time. Landlords typically resist this tactic because they want to retain as much control as possible. It costs you nothing to try for this *up to* clause, but it's not often that the landlord agrees.

Deciding what the rental rate should be for your renewal term

The majority of lease agreements don't preset the rental rate for the renewal-option term, for a couple reasons:

- ✔ Landlords want to be able to maximize the return on their real estate investment. No one has a crystal ball, so the landlord is simply keeping their options open for the maximum future rent increase possible.

- ✔ A landlord can constructively evict an undesirable tenant by simply dictating a much higher rental rate on the renewal term than is justified. So the tenant, thinking the landlord is crazy, relocates their business, and the landlord does a deal with a more desirable tenant.

Typically, if the landlord and tenant can't agree on a renewal-term rental rate, they use arbitration to settle the question. The goal of arbitration is to agree on the current market rent for the space.

A landlord might hedge their bets by including language in the renewal-option clause that states that under no circumstances (if the renewal-option clause is exercised) can the rental rate go down. If you've done your homework and determined that market rental rates have declined, then exercising the renewal-option clause can actually work against you.

Presetting the rental rate for the renewal-option term in advance

Less than 10 percent of lease agreements that The Lease Coach reviews for tenants include a preset rental rate for the renewal-option term. In most cases, if the landlord does agree to preset the renewal term rental rate, it's usually at an artificially high rate, which often makes it useless to the tenant. However, over a 10-year lease term, the country can undergo major positive economic changes, which could make a preset rate work in your favor. Annual increases can be determined in a few ways:

- **Preset annual increases** for the renewal term are often calculated as annual percentage increases — for example, 3, 4, or 5 percent. This means the rent is compounded by these annual percentage increases each year, regardless of what the market rental rate really is.

- **Consumer Price Index (CPI) annual increases** can also be used to calculate future rents. In some cases, a lease agreement states that the annual rental rate increase may be 5 percent or the rise in CPI, whichever is greater. So, if CPI goes down (or the economy enters a period of deflation), the tenant's rent goes up anyway — if they exercised their renewal-option clause.

- **Rental rates are a dollar figure** — some landlords set a one- or two-dollar-per-square-foot (for example) rent increase per year for the renewal term.

Getting the renewal-option clause wording right

Normally, the landlord constructs the actual wording of the lease renewal-option clause. Some sophisticated landlords do so with plenty of forethought and deliberation. Other, smaller landlords use boilerplate lease agreements provided by attorneys, who may or may not give careful consideration to the renewal-option clause. Landlords are accustomed to agreeing to renewal-option terms, often fully loaded with clauses with takeaway conditions. Protectionist wording may in fact dilute the clause's benefit to you completely.

For example, these typical clauses or conditions reveal what the landlord may add to the renewal-option clause for their benefit or protection — and why:

- Default (or uncured default) by the tenant, meaning nonpayment of rent or other non-material defaults, generally nullify the tenant's renewal-option rights. Even if a tenant corrects the default, it may be too late to salvage the renewal-option clause rights.

✔ If the tenant wants to sell the business, the sale of the business and assignment of the lease agreement often render the renewal-option clause void. This is where the landlord states that the renewal-option clause is personal to the tenant and for the sole benefit of the original tenant, not the person you sell the business to.

✔ Failure to hit certain sales volumes — especially if the landlord expects you to make percentage rent payments — can nullify the renewal-option clause. If the tenant is struggling, and their sales prove it, the landlord may want to replace you with a tenant who has a better chance of paying percentage rent (or simply staying in business).

✔ If the tenant company/entity has a substantial change in shareholders, this can render the renewal-option clause dead — because this may be interpreted as an assignment.

Timing is important; most lease agreements state that the tenant has a specific window of time prior to the lease-agreement expiration within which they can exercise the renewal-option clause. Typically, this is 6, 9, or 12 months (sometimes stated in days) prior to the lease expiration date.

At times you and the landlord may not agree on fair market value — even with arbitration. Binding arbitration may be used in some cases, but many leases state that the renewal option simply becomes null and void if the landlord and tenant can't agree on a rate. That doesn't provide a secure renewal option for the tenant if a landlord doesn't want to retain a tenant or wants to take advantage of a tenant with a large investment in the space and who is unlikely to move.

Brevity in a renewal-option clause doesn't necessarily benefit you. Just because a renewal-option clause doesn't state a specific condition or requirement doesn't necessarily play to your advantage. When we negotiate this clause for tenants, we add important sentences as well as take out harmful ones.

Additional Points to Negotiate if You Don't Exercise Your Renewal Option

Even if you agree to various points in your initial lease agreement, you don't have to carry those terms and conditions through into the renewal option term. Times change, tenants change, and even landlords change. Approach your lease renewal period as a fresh opportunity to negotiate anything and everything. We're not saying the landlord will welcome these ideas with open arms. Negotiating a commercial lease renewal can be a real battle at times, but it's a battle that needs to be fought thoughtfully and deliberately for the overall benefit of your business.

Getting the landlord to refund your lease deposit

We've never felt it makes sense for a landlord to keep the tenant's deposit forever. Tenants who renew their leases two or three times still have substantial amounts of money on deposit with the landlord for no apparent reason. If you agree to provide a deposit for your initial lease term, it doesn't mean you have to continue that deposit.

Lease deposits aren't legally mandatory — they're fully negotiable. It's quite possible to negotiate for no deposit or one that's credited back to the tenant early in the initial lease term. Dale and Jeff often successfully negotiate for tenants to have their deposits refunded, reduced, or applied to first accruing rents on their renewal-option term. Don't be silenced by landlords who claim that deposits are necessary or mandatory for all tenants — that myth is true only in the landlord's mind. (See Chapter 14 for more on deposits.)

Eliminating personal guaranties

The same philosophy and strategies that apply to the deposit also apply to personal guaranties. If you're willing to give a personal guarantee on the initial term and then exercise your renewal option, that personal guaranty typically carries forward to the renewal term. This is another reason to rethink exercising your renewal-option clause. If you negotiate your lease renewal-term from scratch, you can negotiate to eliminate or minimize personal guaranties as well.

Adding more renewal-option clauses

The average tenant signs a 5-year lease term with a 5-year lease-renewal option. If you exercise your renewal-option clause, you're out of renewal-option terms. Adding more renewal term options to a lease-renewal agreement is possible and desirable to some tenants, especially if you fix the wording in the clause that permits you to sell your business and have the purchaser inherit your renewal-option clause(s). That may also be important for a tenant preparing to do a large renovation or a tenant who wants several 1- or 2-year options to provide flexibility to relocate their business if they grow or shrink.

Deciding When Not to Exercise Your Lease Renewal-Option Clause

If the landlord truly wants to retain your tenancy, you can negotiate a lease-renewal agreement without exercising the renewal-option clause. Property managers and landlords may often tell you (incorrectly) that you *must* exercise the renewal-option clause. That's a trap because they know that if you fall for it and pull the renewal-option trigger, they don't have to risk losing you as a tenant and won't have to give you any of the incentives mentioned in this chapter. Some landlords try to trick tenants into exercising the renewal-option clause after the deadline by agreeing to accept or backdate the tenant's letter exercising their renewal option if time has lapsed. This too is a trap, for the same reasons.

It's critically important that you understand that once you exercise the renewal-option clause, you cannot rescind that agreement or change your mind. If the landlord plans or tries to double your rent, and you exercised the renewal-option clause, you're trapped. You cannot walk away, and you must renew the lease term.

If you want to stay in the premises but don't want to renew for the entire 5-year renewal-option period, don't pull the renewal-option trigger. This is just another reason for starting the lease-renewal process well in advance of the lease-expiration or termination date, and even well in advance of the renewal-option window.

If market rental rates have gone down — meaning you should get a rent decrease — be careful. If the renewal-option clause states that rental rates can't go down, then exercising your renewal-option clause can actually hurt you.

Lease renewal inducements to negotiate if you don't exercise the option

So, you haven't exercised your renewal option but you want to stay in your current location for an extended term. Most tenants don't realize that everything in the lease agreement is up for negotiation or re-negotiation, just the way it was when you negotiated your first lease deal. Although the details you negotiate may vary from those important to your neighbor, nearly everyone negotiates certain aspects of the renewal.

Renegotiating your base rental rate

Obviously, your focus should be on negotiating the lowest rental rate you can get on your lease renewal. Notice that we didn't say the goal was to negotiate a fair rent, or market rent, or a rental rate you can afford. When Dale negotiated a 70 percent rent reduction on one of his tenant client's lease renewals, the client was stupefied. Had he been overpaying his rent all along? Possibly. But the point is he'd still be paying an inflated amount if he hadn't negotiated the terms.

Tenant allowance

If you've been in business in a specific location for many years, the premises may need refreshing, perhaps a fresh coat of paint or new floor covering. Sometimes it makes sense to make internal changes with new partition walls or simply jazz up the waiting room. If you plan to make leasehold improvements or renovations to your premises, then it makes sense to negotiate for a tenant allowance from the landlord. After all, the landlord probably has to give a tenant allowance to a new tenant, so he might as well give it to you, a known entity.

The landlord typically pays a tenant allowance for money you've actually spent, if you put it where you promised to invest it. We explain to our clients that if we get them a $75,000 tenant allowance on their lease renewal, and they can't show actual receipts for those expenses, the landlord probably won't pay out all of the allowance. So, keep your receipts and don't look at a tenant allowance as a way to finance purchases outside your office or store such as furniture or fixtures.

Read the terms of negotiated allowances carefully. We've seen wording stating that the tenant must use the allowance within a certain number of months or lose it. Try to have the allowance terms written in such a way that you can use the allowance at any time throughout the renewal terms or have the option to convert the allowance to free rent.

Free rent

In addition to a large lease-renewal tenant allowance, we got one of our clients three months of free base rent. (He would continue to pay the operating costs). This tenant was planning to do a reasonably good renovation, meaning the business would be closed for some time — what better reason to also negotiate for free rent? Asking for free rent if you're going to be closed for renovations falls into the category of *you won't get it unless you ask.*

Creating your miscellaneous lease-renewal wish list

Do you need more signage, parking, or storage? Do you need the landlord to finally fill in the parking lot potholes? When one of our clients sent us pictures of his location, including the building exterior, we noticed graffiti all over the side of the building. We included graffiti removal as landlord work to be completed.

Reading this has probably opened your eyes to mistakes you made on your first lease deal. Now is your chance to have clauses modified and corrected to eliminate personal guarantees, get deposits refunded, and fix whatever else you missed when you signed your first lease.

Exercising the Renewal-Option Clause Properly

Tenants frequently make mistakes in exercising their renewal-option clauses, resulting in the landlord's not honoring or not legally recognizing them. First, a tenant must read the renewal-option clause to determine what conditions or prerequisites must be in place. One tenant told us that he made the mistake of verbally telling his landlord that he was exercising the renewal-option clause, instead of putting it in writing. Another tenant sent their renewal option letter to the landlord in writing, but the landlord claimed they didn't receive it, and the tenant had no way of proving it was sent or received. Both tenants were out of luck.

Another tenant e-mailed the landlord stating that they "wanted to exercise their renewal agreement" — which isn't the same thing as actually exercising it. If I want to give you $10, that's not the same thing as actually giving you $10. Most lease agreements state a process or required standard for how to exercise a renewal-option clause. Play by the rules when it comes to official notices to the landlord; don't be casual, because your tenancy may be the casualty.

Discussing the renewal option with the landlord first

When we say we talk with the landlord, often it's actually the landlord's property manager Dale or Jeff are talking to, and that's fine. If we handle a tenant's lease renewal, we call the property manager to discuss things verbally. And we certainly raise the renewal-option opportunity. We ask that the property manager confirm that the renewal-option clause is still in full force and effect.

If the tenant was in default years ago, the landlord may consider the renewal-option clause to be voided and we broach this subject. We confirm the lease termination date and other important information. Sometimes, the tenant has it right, and it's the landlord who's clueless. If the property was purchased, the new landlord's property manager doesn't sit down and read every lease — the tenant must look out for themselves.

Knowing how far in advance to pull the renewal-option trigger

Most lease agreements state a deadline for exercising the renewal-option clause, such as 6, 9, or 12 months before the lease term expires. But the lease agreement may also state that you can't exercise your renewal option too soon or prematurely; typically, there's a 6-month window where you can exercise your renewal option, but it can range from 6–12 months.

The landlord does this for one main reason: If you sign a 10-year lease term and exercise your renewal option immediately, you could turn out to be a very high-risk tenant (going into default, for example) over the next 10 years, and the landlord may not be able to void the renewal-option clause.

Often, due to misunderstandings, construction issues, and late openings, the landlord and tenant don't confirm the commencement date after the tenant opens for business. If you think your initial lease term expires in June, and your landlord thinks it expires in April, you may miss your renewal-option window. Make sure you get your lease expiration date in writing as you approach that stage of your tenancy.

If we're working with a tenant and we want to negotiate a lease-renewal several years in advance, the landlord may resist, saying that we're approaching them prematurely. They point to the 6-month window in the renewal-option clause. We normally talk to the landlord and feel them out. But ultimately, we may send them a letter rescinding the tenant's renewal-option rights/clause. This usually brings the landlord to the negotiating table, because there's no renewal-option clause/term to wait for.

Understanding the legal mechanics of exercising the option clause

Landlords aren't required to notify the tenant that their renewal-option window is approaching or closing. The tenant is solely responsible for keeping track of important dates.

Most landlords accept a letter or an e-mail saying that you're exercising your renewal-option clause, and some may even accept or insist that your verbal representation is enough to trigger the option (especially if you're now having second thoughts about staying). The key is to get written confirmation from the landlord or property manager that they recognize and accept your renewal-option letter. Silence is not acceptable.

Most lease agreements have a separate clause for how official notices must be sent and received by the tenant and the landlord. This often includes a specific mailing address for the landlord, which may differ from where you normally send your rent check. When we exercise a lease renewal-option clause for a tenant, we often do it in several ways simultaneously:

✔ Mail the letter to the landlord's official place of notice as a registered letter that produces a delivery receipt.

✔ E-mail or fax the same letter to the property manager or landlord.

✔ Mail the letter to the property manager by regular mail.

✔ Call the property manager or office secretary to make sure they received it, noting their name and title for follow-up or confirmation purposes.

Going to Arbitration with the Landlord

Many renewal-option clauses anticipate that the landlord and tenant may disagree on what the rental rate should be for the renewal-option term. Because of this, arbitration utilizing either one or three persons is a standard resolution mechanism. Arbitration generally takes place after a stalemate period of time. Either party can push the process to arbitration, with the other being forced to comply. This is normally binding arbitration, meaning that both parties agree in advance to abide by the arbitrators' decision, whether they agree with it or not.

Understanding the arbitration process

Professionally trained and licensed arbitrators can easily be found in pretty much any city. But just as most lawyers don't specialize or even work in the real estate industry, the same issue applies to arbitrators as well; don't assume every arbitrator goes through this process with a landlord and tenant. You must ask lots of questions about the process and the fee range before choosing an arbitrator.

Some lease agreements automatically set ground rules for the arbitration process, such as stipulating that the standard arbitration laws of that state apply. The landlord and tenant may represent themselves, each trying to convince the professional arbitrator that they're correct. The arbitration process is not fast or cheap, but it can be worth it if enough rental dollars are at stake.

Typically, the lease agreement states that whatever rental rate the arbitrator sets out will be retroactive to the lease-renewal date. The tenant, during the arbitration process either continues to pay the same rent as before or abides by whatever rate the lease states for the time being until the matter is resolved.

Doing your homework

Most of the tenant's homework is gathering comparable rental rates for comparable properties in that area. This is not as easy as it sounds, because similar buildings and cooperative tenants may be in short supply. But if it's an arbitration involving class A downtown office buildings, the properties in question are actually more alike than dissimilar. A property's amenity package or what a property has to offer can influence the value of the rental rate for that property.

If you're comparing two small high-rise properties, and the newer one has an elevator and the older one doesn't, that would factor into the rental rate; these properties would not be an apple-to-apple comparison.

Educate yourself more about the arbitration process as it applies to commercial real estate. Finding another tenant to share their experience of going through the process can also be helpful.

Inquire about inducement packages that skewed rental rates for other tenants. Did a tenant agree to pay a certain rental rate to get free rent and tenant allowance? If you don't get the same inducements, you can't be expected to pay the same rental rates as the tenant who did receive the incentives, which must be brought to the arbitrator's attention.

Involving other professionals to help you

An attorney may not be your best resource when going through arbitration. The rules of engagement are managed by the arbitrator, so what you need more than anything is professional real estate advice. The landlord knows, of course, what every tenant in their property is paying in rent and may have those cards to play potentially in their favor.

Typically, the landlord turns to real estate agents and brokers to do their homework. Unfortunately, a real estate broker or their agent may have a bias toward higher rents favoring the landlord, because brokers are typically employed by landlords and would consider it part of their job to get the landlord a higher rental rate for the space.

Estimating the costs and risks involved in arbitration

A lease agreement often states one of three ways for the parties to pay for the cost of arbitration:

- ✔ The loser of the arbitration process pays all expenses for both parties. This isn't realistic, though, because the arbitrator may pick a rental rate somewhere in between what the tenant and landlord thought the space was worth.

- ✔ The landlord and tenant split the cost of the arbitrator equally.

- ✔ If a three-arbitrator process is involved, each party pays for their own arbitrator or representative, and then they split the costs of the third, arm's-length decision-making arbitrator.

In our experience, arbitration cases are not that common, and have fees ranging between $7,000 and $12,000. One tenant told us his arbitration costs were over $50,000, but we suspect there were a lot of unnecessary legal expenses involved.

Understanding Month-to-Month Renewal Terms

If you decide to continue your tenancy agreement on a month-to-month basis, then all the rules and agreements within the existing formal lease agreement carry forward to apply to the month-to-month tenancy. Only if both sides agree to certain changes (such as a new rental rate) can the formal lease agreement be amended. You should get all of this in writing.

On one hand, if you decide to continue leasing the space month-to-month, there's a sense of freedom that comes from an ability to relocate if you find a more desirable location. Perhaps you're trying to decide whether to continue operating the business or close it down, and you're coming up on your industry's busy season. Staying in business month-to-month for a while longer could be more profitable for you and mean extended cash flow for the landlord.

However, both parties typically have equal rights. Sure, you can give the landlord a month's notice, but the landlord could find a replacement tenant and give you the same notice. Landlords reluctantly agree to month-to-month tenancies in order to maintain cash flow. Perhaps they don't know if they can get another tenant, so month-to-month cash flow is better than nothing.

Some lease agreements use the words *month to month* to mean a full calendar month. So, if you decide to give the landlord notice on December 10th to terminate the lease, the landlord expects you to vacant the property on January 31st (much like a residential apartment lease). However, if the lease agreement states that either party can give 30 days' notice to terminate, then the landlord could, for example, on June 3rd give the tenant 30 days' notice, and the tenant would have to vacate the premises literally within 30 days of the notice — by July 3rd. We recommend that you confirm this with the property manager to avoid being surprised.

Part V
The Part of Tens

The 5th Wave
By Rich Tennant

"What do you mean our ground lease is up?"

In this part . . .

We pare the essential info that will help you win the leasing contract battle down to a few succinct nuggets, including questions to ask the real estate agent that will uncover the information you really need to know, strategies for beating the landlord at their own game, and warning signs to watch out for.

Chapter 18

Ten Leasing Tips, Tactics, and Strategies for Tenants

· ·

In This Chapter

▶ Leasing strategies for tenants

▶ Tips that can save you money and time

▶ Insider advice worth heeding

· ·

We have to admit, the leasing wisdom Dale and Jeff have collected over the years has partially been the result of watching tenants make so many leasing mistakes. We've seen this happen while coaching tenants who failed to heed warning signs or advice. Every week we get emails and phone calls from tenants who don't pay attention to details or who don't think through their strategy. These tenants are shooting from the hip, as they say.

Hopefully the leasing tips in this chapter resonate and serve you well through the leasing process.

Negotiate to Win

Negotiating to win is be the goal of the tenant. Why? Because that's the goal of the landlord, the landlord's property manager, and their real estate agents. The landlord is not necessarily looking for a win-win lease deal. A typical landlord charges the tenants as much rent as possible, and who would expect anything less?

Tenants often mistakenly think that landlords set their rental rate based on what tenants can afford to pay. But landlords really set rental rates based on the cash flow they need to service their mortgage, manage the property, and make a profit.

The problem is that rather than negotiating to win, most tenants are simply negotiating not to lose. This happens for several reasons, including lack of experience, lack of knowledge, lack of time, fear of rejection, and a multitude of others.

Don't be naïve; if you're outgunned, get some professional help. Don't rely on the landlord to give you what you deserve. You've got to develop a strategy and negotiate for it.

Here are some of the items to consider when you negotiate to win:

- Lowest possible rental rate
- Biggest tenant allowance
- Longest free rent period
- Lowest deposit
- Most signage and parking
- Limited or no personal guaranty

We remember one tenant client earnestly cautioning us to *not* get them too much of a rent reduction on their lease renewal, or the landlord might not want to be friends anymore. We're all for having your landlord as a friend, but not at the sacrifice of your business.

Negotiate All Lease Terms at Once

Don't look at your lease as a list of individual points that must be negotiated separately. All those business terms are connected and must be negotiated collectively. For example, don't agree to the rental rate until you agree to the length of the lease term. And don't agree to a set tenant allowance until you know how much free rent you're getting and so on.

Let's say you're negotiating a new lease and agree to give a security deposit — and then a few weeks later the landlord insists you also give a personal guaranty. Well, why would both of these items be necessary? If the landlord needs a personal guaranty, and you give one, why should there also be a deposit? But try un-ringing that bell once you've agreed to it.

Don't Telegraph Your Intentions or Give Buying Signals

For years, Dale worked for landlords, leasing and managing their commercial real estate before switching to the tenant's side. During Dale's period with the landlords, a tenant would pour out information that they should have kept to themselves. Dale wanted to say to these tenants, "Why are you telling me all this — don't you realize the landlord will use that information against you?" On one level, we can understand how this happens, especially when tenants are dealing with friendly real estate agents who position and present themselves as the tenant's assistant buyer — there to help the tenant, it seems. But tenants need to be smarter with their vital information.

For example, if you're planning to open another location or relocate your business, and the landlord or his real estate agent asks what you can afford to pay for rent or asks what you're paying now in your current location, be aware that this is a loaded question. If you're paying $28 per square foot in your current location, and they were only going to ask $23 per square foot in the new location, they might jack that up to $28 per square foot as their asking price because they think you can afford to pay it. We've seen this happen especially with tenants who are doctors and in fact with all types of healthcare tenants.

If the tenant reveals somehow that emotionally or mentally he's already decided to renew his current lease — or if during a space showing, your partner is gushing over how nice it all is and how the space would be perfect for you — get ready to pay a higher rent. Check your emotions and mouth at the door when dealing in commercial real estate.

This may seem like common sense, but we remember a full floor office tenant making this mistake even after we warned them. Within five minutes of walking into the first location with the real estate agent, the office manager was gushing about how perfect the location was and whose office would be where. This was not information we wanted to share with the landlord's agent, and we had to guide the office manager out of earshot of the agent.

Assume Nothing and Get It in Writing

Tenants make all kinds of assumptions regarding their leases — sometimes blindly, sometimes because of prior discussions or negotiations with the landlord or their real estate agent. The last shopping center Dale managed (prior to switching sides and becoming a lease consultant exclusively working for tenants) had around 85 retail tenants and a ten-story office tower. Because most of the leasing for the property was done by outside real estate agents, tenants invariably signed a lease, opened for business, and then came to Dale, the property manager, with issues.

These issues were almost always linked to verbal representations and sometimes even written correspondence with the real estate agent about parking, signage, hours of operation, tenant allowance, or landlord's work. The landlord may have had no knowledge of these discussions. A common boilerplate clause landlords put into most lease agreements actually states that this signed lease agreement is the *only* agreement, and that there are no side agreements or other understandings between the parties.

When a tenant tells the real estate agent about some item they need or want or that's important to them, they often automatically assume that their wishes get conveyed to the landlord. Professional landlords and professional real estate agents know that during the lease deal-making process, many items are traded off, denied, accepted, and otherwise negotiated.

Unless a point appears in writing on the accepted lease document version, don't assume it's part of the deal:

- ✔ **Real-life example 1:** A new tenant is taking over space about to be vacated. The new tenant sees the old tenant's pylon signage by the road. The new tenant assumes they will automatically get that signage and mentions it — but doesn't get it in writing. The lease deal is signed, and the tenant moves in and finds out there was a waiting list of other tenants who wanted signage, and the new tenant gets shut out.

- ✔ **Real-life example 2:** A dentist uses a lawyer to facilitate a lease transaction. The dentist tells the lawyer that because this is new space, and the cement floor hasn't been poured yet, it will save the dentist money if the landlord doesn't pour the slab until the dentist is ready. The lawyer doesn't include this verbiage in the lease agreement, but the dentist assumes everyone understands about the work he needs to do first. The landlord pours the slab before the tenant is ready, seals the windows, and then mold begins to grow on the walls. By the time the tenant jackhammers out the concrete and replaces the gyprock walls, he's three months delayed in opening, yet is paying rent and lighter $25,000 extra out of pocket. All this was unnecessary, costly, and unfortunate. Bottom line? If it's not in writing, don't count on it happening.

Protect Yourself by Incorporating

There are a couple reasons to incorporate or form a limited liability company (LLC) if you're about to go into business and lease a commercial location.

Businesses fail all the time, often through no fault of the business owner. Incorporating protects you because

- ✔ If you allow the landlord to put your personal name on the lease agreement as the tenant (or even on the letter of intent or offer to lease), then you are personally responsible for rent payments and all other terms of the lease agreement. But if you make the tenant a corporation, then generally the tenant corporation is on the hook, not you personally.

- ✔ The majority of business owners are better off tax-wise running a corporation rather than being a sole proprietorship. Talk to your accountant about this.

Too many small or startup tenants want to preserve capital by only committing to forming a corporation once they're sure they're opening a business. They start dealing on a location and sign an LOI in their personal name, thinking they will simply form a corporation later and make the switch. "That ain't gonna happen," as landlords say in Texas. Even if they do let you assign the lease agreement from your personal name to your corporation, you will *still* be personally liable (like a co-signor on a loan). So don't get tricked into thinking it's that easy.

Keep Your Success Quiet

Back when Dale represented landlords, a main reason they raised the rent on a tenant's lease renewal wasn't because market rents had gone up — it was because of the tenant's apparent success. Five years ago the tenant was driving a Chevrolet and just getting started — now they drive a Mercedes to their three locations. Or the property manager found out from a Facebook page about a three-week European holiday the tenant had just taken.

Retail tenants and some restaurateurs may have agreed to report their monthly sales to the landlord during the lease negotiations — something you should try to avoid if you are not required to do so because you have a percentage rent clause. Don't be surprised if the landlord uses this information against you at lease renewal time to jack up your rent. If your sales are up 22 percent over last year, and the landlord knows it, you'd better buckle up for a bumpy lease renewal negotiation — the landlord wants a piece of the action.

Business owners don't fix what isn't broken, so why would a tenant want to relocate if business is booming? Yes, occasionally a tenant will need to expand with extra area, but often they will do so in the very building or plaza they now occupy, thereby solidifying the appearance that they can afford to pay more or higher rent.

Change the Day Your Rent Is Due

For many small business owners, the end of the month is not a pleasant time. Payroll is due, loan payments may need to be made, and of course the rent is due. Sometimes having even a few days' grace period to make the monthly rent payment can make a world of difference if your business has decent cash flow. By negotiating with the landlord to change the day your rent is due (to perhaps the 5th or 10th day of the month), you can breathe a little easier at month's end. The Lease Coach often negotiates this into the tenant's lease-renewal deal right up front if the tenant has been struggling.

Approaching and explaining this to your landlord or property manager is the first step. Many landlords understand your predicament and may grant your request even if you're in the middle of a lease term.

Resist the temptation to simply pay your rent late each month, even if the landlord tolerates it, as doing that can put you in a default position.

If you're successful getting the landlord to agree to this, make sure you get a proper one-page lease-amending agreement stating it — or at a minimum get an email acceptance. Keep in mind that when landlords give their permission for this type request, it's often stated that the landlord has the right to rescind their permission at any time. So if you get behind in rent or become uncooperative or in default (or if they sell the property), they can pull the plug on the agreement for later rent payments.

Creatively Build on Your Relationship with the Landlord

Making deposits to your landlord relationship can be invaluable. Many tenants in the property Dale used to manage for landlords were months behind in their rent. They would bring him wine and gifts and offer to talk with the landlord, and always returned his calls to keep communication lines open. So it makes sense to get in on good terms with the landlord and the property management team.

When you think about it, the landlord should be the one trying to initiate or sustain a good relationship with *you*, because the tenant is the landlord's customer. But because you may only have one landlord, and the landlord may have hundreds of tenants, it often falls to the tenant to build the relationships.

The Lease Coach has always leased office space for our business. We've found it extremely effective to make sure the caretaker gets a bottle of whiskey at Christmas time, a cold bottle of water on a hot day, and plenty of thanks and appreciation.

Ask the Property Manager or Landlord for a Favor

Have you ever agreed to do something you really didn't want to do, but you knew the other person would be beholden to you if you did it? We have, both personally, professionally, and even in commercial real estate. Simply asking someone for something in which there is no promise of return or benefit to the other party seldom seems to work. But if you ask for a favor and say those magic words, "I owe you one," or promise a specific future benefit, you're more likely to get your favor.

You can simply ingratiate yourself or acknowledge that the other party doesn't need to agree to this favor, but you'd appreciate it very much and be beholden to them you may get your way. In the commercial real estate industry, the players tend to have fairly healthy egos. Telling the property manager to do something is usually less effective than asking them to do it "pretty please."

 Remember to pause after you ask and let them respond. The tendency is to justify, over-explain, or run on verbally. Sometimes asking by email is fine, but doing it verbally gives you a chance to give more details if the property manager doesn't fully understand your request or initially turns your request down.

A simple example would be asking the property manager if, during November and December, you can store your extra Christmas inventory in one of the vacant units. Even if you're prepared to pay some token rent, ask for the favor and *then* offer to pay a small amount if that's required to close the deal. Consider giving the property manager's office and staff 20 percent off coupons or gift certificates for purchases.

Prepare for Murphy's Law

You know Murphy's Law, no doubt: Anything that can go wrong will go wrong — and at the worst possible time. But even good luck can have its downside. The baseball player with the most home runs is often the player with the most strikeouts as well. So you can focus on the home runs or the strikeouts; it's your life.

Emotionally and financially, it pays to plan ahead and try to envision what will go wrong. Say the contractor doesn't get your new space built out in time, and you're going to open for business five weeks late. Do you want to be paying rent while you're not open? Of course not. In that case, negotiate wording into your lease agreement so the rent doesn't start until the tenant actually opens.

One business owner we know was running a computer store. When thieves broke in and stole a quarter million dollars of merchandise, two things put him out of business: inadequate insurance and the rent that still needed to be paid even though he had no inventory left to sell. Some tenants carry business-interruption insurance to avoid these situations.

Get Professional Help with the Leasing Process

The Lease Coach does a lot of work with Christian book and gift store owners; Dale speaks at their conferences, writes articles for their magazines, and negotiates their store leases. These retailers need leasing help like anyone else. He received a call from a very nice lady who was planning to open a Christian bookstore and coffee shop in Minnesota. She had found the location and had read Dale's articles, prompting her to call him with questions and for some advice, which he happily provided.

When asked who would be advising her and negotiating her lease, she said that she was going to have her pastor do that. "Really?" Dale said. "You think your pastor isn't busy enough and that he is the best choice you can make for getting some help?" She said that he was very smart and knew a lot about business.

We've spoken with tenants who were using their brother, mother, residential real estate uncle, spouse, and so on to help them negotiate their lease. Although these people may know more than you do about leasing, they surely don't know enough. Getting the right help from a professional lease consultant who has a proven track record and earns their living serving tenants is a better choice. This is so important that it can be the deciding factor in whether your business succeeds. Read more about this in Chapter 6. (To arrange for a complimentary consultation with the authors of this book, visit www.TheLeaseCoach.com.)

Chapter 19

Ten Questions to Ask the Landlord's Real Estate Agent

In This Chapter

▶ Creating your question list

▶ Asking the right questions and when

▶ Uncovering the real facts

Asking the right questions when you need accurate answers about a property is essential. Most tenants face several challenges when asking questions: not knowing what to ask, not knowing who to ask, and not knowing how to sort truth from fiction in the answer.

The fear of rejection or looking stupid if you ask questions might also hold you back. You are the customer in this process, and asking smart or tough questions is a necessary part of the leasing process.

This chapter lists ten questions you need answers to before you sign on the dotted line. This chapter also gives you tips on how to ask them.

Getting the Answers to Your Questions

You need to know who to direct your questions to if you want to get honest answers. If you're looking at a new location, you can either speak with the landlord's real estate agent, your agent, the property manager, or the landlord. In many cases, the listing real estate agent who's handling the property is the proper person to ask, but the property manager has insight as well.

Dale and Jeff often ask the landlord, their agent, and even the property manager the same questions individually (even if we think we already know the answers) to see if they all give the same answer.

A licensed real estate agent generally won't lie to you, but their answers may not be complete or may be their opinion and not factual information. Sometimes landlords don't share important information with real estate brokers and agents — which means that the real estate agent may later protest that they told you the truth as far as they knew it.

You can ask questions in person if you'd rather watch the facial expressions and body language of the person you're asking. But asking in e-mails or on the phone are acceptable ways to ask the questions you need answered. The more important the answer is to you, though, the more critical it is that you get your answer in writing (e-mail counts) and then restated in the lease agreement. Misunderstandings occur.

For example, if the agent is representing that the budgeted operating costs for that year are $8.42 per square foot, they should have no problem putting this figure into the offer to lease or letter of intent — and, of course, in the formal lease agreement. If the agent actually said $18.42 per square foot, and you heard $8.42 per square foot, and this wasn't documented, you may get a nasty surprise on future rent payments.

Don't hesitate to ask the same question to more than one person or to ask the same question in different ways until you're sure you're getting a straight answer. It's not necessarily the landlord or their representative's job to fully inform you. It's *buyer beware*, and you must do a certain amount of due diligence work — which means asking lots of questions.

A real estate agent may answer you honestly, but also be honestly wrong, misinformed, or long gone by the time you open your business. Although the agent is the most appropriate and accessible person to answer your questions initially, the property manager or landlord are the best sources to verify answers to critical questions, especially if the information you're looking for isn't documented in the lease agreement.

No matter who you choose to ask or the method you use to keep in touch with them, try to gather detailed and honest answers to the ten questions in the next sections.

Who Really Is the Landlord?

All landlords, like all happy families, are not the same. It's essential that you know who you're dealing with — which might not be the person you're actually talking to. Find out who *really* owns the property. 'We've learned that the more you know about the landlord, the better equipped you are to negotiate the best deal possible. Some landlords are nationally known, and most are known at least in the region where they operate.

Use your favorite search engine to learn more about them. One landlord Dale used to work for in the early 1990's was losing a property every couple of months into receivership or selling off properties to stay afloat. Some landlords are entangled in court cases and litigation with tenants. A few landlords have such nasty reputations that becoming their tenant could be very risky, whereas other landlords are known for being cooperative and reasonable to deal with. The Internet — including social media — is a marvelous source for this type of information.

How Long Has the Landlord Owned the Property?

Generally, the longer a landlord owns a property, the better off the tenants will be in a tenant-landlord relationship. The landlord's knowledge of the building, its tenants, and the general area increases over time.

Commercial landlords generally fall into two camps. Some are developers; they find the land, design the building, and then begin the preleasing process. These developers often flip their properties within a few years to an investor (not that there's anything wrong with this — just don't count on having the same landlord forever). Investor landlords generally buy these properties from developers and hold them as long-term assets in their investment portfolios.

If a landlord develops or builds a property from the ground up, leases out the property, and holds it for many years as a long-term investment along with other buildings, it may be a sign that they are more careful about what they promise and overall how they manage a property and it's tenants to maintain good long-term relations with tenants.

Is There Local Property Management?

Although many large properties have local, onsite management, many properties do not. One property manager may look after several hundred tenants in as many as a dozen buildings. The ability of the property manager to respond to day-to-day issues — much less to lease renewal deals and new tenants —varies greatly. It pays to meet the property manager in person during the leasing process and after the lease deal closes.

Most property managers play an important role in negotiating *lease renewals*. Landlords typically don't use the listing agent or outside real estate agents for this, because they want to avoid paying commissions for tenants they already have in place. If the property manager is 30 miles away, one state over, or rarely onsite, they can lose touch with the tenants who can become disgruntled over time about how the property is being maintained, or over other issues. One of our clients doesn't even know his landlord but dislikes his property manager, and hates the landlord's caretaker even more — a feeling that appears to be mutual — which leaves the tenant wondering if he should move.

Management for fee companies, including some of the big brokerages, also manage properties for landlords. They typically take a percentage of the rent or operating costs as their fee. Although they tend to be more professional and organized, they're often less sensitive to the tenant-landlord relationship.

Mom and pop properties, where the son-in-law is doing the day-to-day management, can be a good thing or a bad thing. Again, try to meet the property manager and get a feel for what type of relationship you'll have before signing the lease.

What Is the Building's History?

When Dale and his wife built a home about 20 years ago, two strip plazas were also developed at that same time near the main intersections to the community. Over the years, it was interesting to watch as businesses opened and closed in these plazas, only to be replaced by other businesses. Sometimes a full five years (the standard lease term) would go by, but several opened and closed in less than a year.

A property may look perfectly normal to a prospective tenant or lessee, but each property has a history that can influence whether you locate your business there. A commercial retail unit (CRU) within a plaza that has been home to multiple businesses (especially restaurants) is sometimes called a *burned site*. If tenants keep opening and closing out in a specific property or specific unit, you deserve to know that history and why that's happening. It could happen to your business, too.

Who's Doing the Leasing for the Property?

What every landlord wants is stable and secure tenants — like strong national or regional name brand chains and franchise systems — who supply cash flow and security. Commercial landlords have several options for locating and securing these paragons, including the following two important ones:

- ✔ **Listing with a real estate brokerage.** The brokerage then puts up a "FOR LEASE" sign on the property and begins looking for tenants. In many cases, an outside agent brings forward a tenant and does a lease deal.

- ✔ **Having salaried employees do the leasing for a particular property.** This could be the property manager or an in-house salaried leasing representative who may work on multiple properties but effectively works for just one landlord. These individuals are often motivated by both salary and commissions — but ultimately their role is to secure quality tenants who can bring not only cash flow but greater value to the property. A proper tenant mix may be more important to in-house leasing reps than to random real estate agents, who don't have a long-term investment to maintain.

As with dealing with the landlord, find out as much as possible about the person doing the leasing, including their role and authority level, experience level, how long they have been working with *this landlord and this property*, and anything else you can dig up. *Know thy opponent.* If the leasing rep or agent just starting work on this property, they may hinder more than help you through the process.

Who Were the Two Most Recent Tenants to Move In and When?

When Jeff or Dale is coaching or negotiating for a tenant client interested in leasing space at a new location, or even on a renewal, we try to find out who the most recent tenants were to move in to a property. We can then call or visit these tenants and inquire about their leasing experience with the landlord.

By talking with these new tenants — or tenants who have recently renewed their lease — we can often learn what rental rate they are paying or whether they received lease inducements, such as a tenant allowance and free rent. We may find out whether they had to put down a deposit or a personal guaranty, and so on. If they received a tenant allowance, was it paid by the landlord on time or did the tenant have to wait months and jump through hoops to get it?

We've had tenants tell us how terrible their landlord or property manager were and express regret for leasing in that property. This information is extremely helpful in establishing a market rental rate for the property and how user-friendly the landlord is.

Knowing what rent other tenants recently agreed to pay on their new lease or renewal can help prepare you for your negotiations. If you find out that rents have increased substantially or are out of your budget, you may want to consider other properties. On the other hand, if you determine rents have gone down or are lower than you expected, that can keep you from overpaying on your lease or renewal.

Who Were the Last Two Tenants to Move Out?

When tenants move out of a property, learning why is extremely valuable. We call tenants and ask forthrightly why they moved. It may be that they needed a larger or smaller space that couldn't be provided in their current property. Or it could be that they didn't get along with the landlord — maybe the landlord wasn't properly maintaining the building or grounds. In some cases, a tenant moves because after they've been in the same location for five or ten years, the landlord tries to raise the rent to a level that they can't or won't pay.

Sometimes the last few tenants who moved out of a plaza didn't move out at all but closed out of business. Maybe the rental rates were too high, or there were insufficient parking spaces. In some cases, the reason for closing won't be relevant to you — but you may uncover other information that is. A restaurant client of The Lease Coach contacted the previous tenant to discuss challenges they had with the space — only to uncover an inadequate HVAC system, which would have cost our client tens of thousands of dollars had it not been discovered prior to signing the lease.

An excellent follow-up question for the agent (who may claim not to know) is which tenants, if any, are close to the end of their lease term and/or have expressed that they are not renewing their lease agreement? Just because a property is full today doesn't mean three or four tenants won't move out as their leases expire in the near future.

How Secure Are the Property's Anchor Tenants?

A second-generation commercial property about two miles from Dale's home was a typical strip plaza, with 12 tenants and a grocery store anchor. Dale was familiar with the plaza; he used the dry cleaner and often ordered takeout from the restaurants. Most family trips to this plaza were, however, primarily to buy groceries.

When the grocery store anchor relocated to a new property about two miles away, Dale stopped going to that plaza, found a new dry cleaner, and altered his family's shopping patterns permanently. To add insult to injury, the grocery store kept paying rent on the space it had vacated to prohibit competitors from taking over the unit — thereby making the property even less appealing.

A shopping mall a few miles from Dale's house had as one of its two anchor tenants a two-level department store offering mid-priced clothing and merchandise. For years, tenants at that end of the mall had a consistent traffic draw — until the anchor closed, making that end of the mall a ghost town for over a year. When Walmart took over the space, it was like Christmas every week for the other tenants close by. Shoppers flocked to that end of the mall. However, when Walmart built its own store property a few miles away and moved out of the mall, it was back to ghost town again. The landlord then secured a discount tenant for one floor and a sporting goods tenant for the other floor. Dale's wife, who previously visited the Walmart at least once a week, now only visited the sporting goods and discount store a couple times per year.

The point is, not all anchor tenants are created equal, and not all draw the same demographic or type of shopper. If you're dealing on a new property under development in the pre-leasing stage, don't take for granted that the specific tenants listed on the site plan are done deals. Ask and confirm.

Is the Property for Sale?

At The Lease Coach seminars, we often do a quick survey, asking tenants if they'd rather face a lease-renewal negotiation with their existing landlord or negotiate with a new landlord who is about to buy the property. The audience is usually split about 50/50.

We point out that no investor buys a property so they can lower rental rates. Landlords make the investment (often with renovation plans) so they can *raise* the rent on properties they buy.

If you're leasing space for a new location, in a property that's for sale, you may face delays. The selling landlord may be reluctant to close a deal for the new landlord at a rental rate lower than the new landlord thought they could get for the space a few months later. The combined rents paid by the tenants often determine the paper value of the property to a buyer or seller. It can also set a trend or market rental rate for a property.

A new landlord may be more picky or less in need of doing *any lease deal or renewal* than the previous landlord, who may have had few leasing inquiries, especially for certain units for lease because not all units are created equal.

What Were the CAM Charges for Previous Years?

You need to budget for increasing operating costs. The operating costs, or common area maintenance (CAM) charges, for past years are often a good indication of what may be repeated for future years. In other words, if operating costs have increased 10 percent per year for the past three years, they may continue to go up significantly after you move in.

You can also ask if the landlord has any major repair or replacement expenditures in their budget. One of our pharmacy tenant clients complained for some time until the landlord agreed to replace the cracked sidewalks with fresh concrete. This $35,000 expenditure will be borne by all the tenants — ideally amortized over many years — representing an increase in operating cost for some time.

On the other hand, if operating costs have gone down or stayed flat for a few years, that can indicate that the landlord has deferred maintenance on the property. If a property has a high vacancy rate (and the landlord doesn't want to put money into upkeep) — or if the landlord is planning to sell the property — they may avoid or put off necessary and routine management duties.

If the landlord normally cleans the parking lot twice a year or mows the lawn once a week, and cuts back on those activities, that's not really deferred maintenance, although it may bother tenants who are accustomed to a higher level of care. Deferring essential items like roof work, painting, HVAC systems, and asphalt repairs can be worrisome.

Chapter 20

Ten (or So) Warnings: What No One Ever Tells Tenants

· ·

In This Chapter

▶ Filling in the gaps when things start to go wrong

▶ Revealing some secrets not many tenants know

▶ Getting the train back on the track

· ·

*T*he Lease Coach is a magnet for tenants who are experiencing problems. On a weekly basis, we receive e-mails and phone calls from tenants who can't figure out why their train is going off the track and why they're having so many problems dealing with their landlords.

Dealing with landlords and their representatives can be challenging at any time, but when you're a novice or emotionally and financially attached to the deal (as tenants understandably are), the entire leasing process becomes much more difficult and treacherous. In this chapter, the wisdom we've acquired can help troubleshoot a few of the issues that you, as a tenant, may be experiencing.

Over the years Dale has developed a very no-nonsense, tell-it-as-it-is style and method of consulting to tenants. At The Lease Coach, we think it's our job to pull back the curtain and reveal the real reason that tenants and landlords struggle with communication and the deal-making process.

As a business owner and tenant, you may already have some preconceived notions about commercial leasing. For what it's worth, here are some of the things that no one (except us) ever tells tenants.

It's a Business, Not a Marriage

Opening a business and leasing space from a landlord may feel like a marriage, but it's not, and tenants need to get that notion out of their heads.

A typical landlord may have several hundred or even several thousand tenants, but the typical tenant has just one landlord. Furthermore, the landlord owns their property as an investment. The tenant is leasing the space as a means to an end. The landlord wants to own the property. The tenant doesn't really want to lease space — the tenant wants to operate a successful business.

The landlord for the most part is making business and leasing decisions with their head and their calculator. Tenants are well advised to do the same, keeping their emotions out of the deal-making process.

A tenant is not *in* business with the landlord; they are *doing* business with the landlord.

Not All Commercial Real Estate Agents Know What They're Doing

The commercial real estate industry (like every other industry) has its winners and its losers, its rookies and seasoned professionals. If the lease-making process isn't going the way you think it should, the problem may not be with you, the tenant. The problem may well lie with the commercial real estate agent who simply isn't very experienced or very good at their job or unknowledgeable about a property.

We estimate that 20 percent of all commercial real estate agents make 80 percent of all the money in the industry. If you happen to be working with a new agent who lacks experience, skill, or confidence, you can run up against one roadblock after another.

We're not taking a poke at the commercial real estate industry, but simply reflecting on the hundreds of business owners who have hired The Lease Coach to help them through the leasing process because the commercial real estate agent who was representing the landlord (or the tenant) didn't know how to put a proper deal together.

A tenant is well advised to check into the background and history of any real estate agent they're working with or coming up against in a lease negotiation.

Sketchy or Problematic Co-tenants

Take a good hard look at the tenants already in a property before you make a 5- or 10-year lease commitment. Are any of the tenants questionable?

When Dale used to work for landlords and do their leasing, the landlord received an offer to lease from an adult video store operator. Dale warned the landlord that if they accepted this tenant into the property, it would over time, hurt the long-term leasing program and drive away both existing and new prospective tenants. The landlord desperately needed the cash flow and did the deal with the adult video store anyway (against Dale's recommendation). Eventually, over the next 5–7 years, existing tenants started moving out instead of renewing because of this new tenant.

A problematic tenant can be noisy, smelly, or even intrusive to your tenancy. A client of The Lease Coach, a bookstore, eventually relocated away from a property because of the nightclub next door. Every morning, the bookstore tenant had to clean cigarette butts, urine, and vomit from its storefront sidewalk before opening.

Take a good look around at your neighbors.

Shabby Property Maintenance

Look around the property. What do you see? Nicely groomed landscaping or weeds?

When you tour a property for lease and see graffiti or broken signage, dirty sidewalks, and potholed parking lots, you can pretty much expect that it will stay the same way during your tenancy. When you're looking at leasing office space, look around as you walk through the lobby of a building: Is the floor clean? Do the walls show wear and tear and are they in need of repair? Are the finishings in the lobby dated or unattractive? Warning signs are everywhere when you tour a property, which is why we like to inspect properties for our clients whenever possible.

Absentee or Distant Landlords

The Lease Coach worked with a local chiropractor who was planning to sign a 10-year lease on a nice property that was turned into condominiums. The property was divided into units and been sold to various small local investors. To visitors, it looked like a nice normal plaza under one management, but underneath each tenant dealt with a different landlord/investor, each with different levels of interest or involvement with their condo property.

Here's how that situation played out: Once we had a deal essentially negotiated with the landlord's listing agent, we wanted the tenant to meet the landlord personally. When the landlord, who was a local investor, refused to meet the chiropractor, it sent out all kinds of signals. In fact, the landlord should have been insisting on meeting the tenant. Because of this and a few other reasons, we passed on the location and took her tenancy elsewhere.

If the landlord isn't visible and transparent during the offer-to-lease negotiation stage, don't expect anything more once you become the tenant. If the landlord is absentee or lives in a different city or state, try to find out how often they come to visit their property and their tenants.

Everything's a Battle with Them

In some cases, landlords and their management teams are professional and cooperative, but other times it's like fighting a battle over every single thing. If the landlord or their agents won't drop what they're doing and show the tenant space when it's convenient for the tenant, that's another warning sign.

Recently Dale had two opposite cases. The prospective tenant's wife hadn't seen the space yet, and Dale suggested he show her before working further on the deal. She was only available on Saturday, and the listing agent who normally worked Monday to Friday agreed to meet at the plaza on the weekend. The agent rolled out the red carpet and provided a lot of other information Dale had requested.

However, in another situation Dale's clients were two partners who also wanted their spouses to see a particular location, and 5 p.m. was the soonest any of them could meet there. The landlord's leasing representative outright refused to meet the prospective tenants at 5 because the property was an hour from his home and he didn't want to get home late.

Pay attention to patterns that develop early on. If that's the way they're treating you during the courtship, we doubt they'll be much more responsive once you've signed a long-term lease agreement.

The Location You Like is Simply Unrealistic

After giving a seminar to a business organization, we were inundated with questions, especially from the entrepreneurs in the room who were planning to open a business and who had just had their eyes opened regarding the leasing process.

One couple explained their business concept, which sounded reasonable, but then they told us about their choice of location. It was in a medium-sized bedroom community in a newly developed retail area designated primarily for big box stores. Their concept was unique and would appeal to a certain market segment, being office workers: They were selling office attire. When we asked why they weren't considering a downtown location in the city (near their future customers), their response was essentially that downtown was out of their comfort zone. They lived in the bedroom community and therefore, it was close to their home.

That was a terrible reason to pick the location they picked. And as far as we know, they never did get their business launched.

Ideally, you want to put your business as close to your core customers as possible, not necessarily expect them to travel a great distance to you or the place you've leased (for your convenience).

Many Landlords Don't Like Lawyers

For many years before becoming The Lease Coach, Dale worked for landlords. It might seem like strong language to state outright that landlords hate or at least have a strong dislike for lawyers, but many of them do. According to many landlords, lawyers are deal-killers.

Now, not all lawyers can be grouped into the same ring, and Dale has no personal aversions to lawyers. Many are extremely professional and serve tenants well. The problem occurs when a tenant gets a lawyer or uses an attorney who isn't "landlord friendly."

If the landlord is using a commercial real estate professional to lease the property, and the tenant turns their legal guns on the landlord, it's not surprising that a few landlords will push back unfavorably against the tenant.

You're Making Decisions for the Wrong Reasons

A franchise tenant in the gift retail business purchased the rights to a particular territory. The city or territory would ideally have three stores or locations within it. This type of store belonged in an enclosed shopping mall, which is where all the other franchise stores were located.

Doing their site selection was fairly straightforward, and it was easy for Dale to recommend the top three malls. He suggested they open their first store in the best mall and work their way down to the smaller malls. The logic was that if they couldn't make in it the best mall, they wouldn't have a chance in a smaller one.

Unfortunately, they insisted on leasing space in the smallest, least-desirable mall first, mainly because that was their comfort level. They didn't seem to realize that by the time they got around to opening store number two and store number three, same-industry competitors could claim those better malls for themselves and beat them to the customer.

Not All Landlords Are Litigious

Many tenants who could and should close their doors or negotiate a lower rental rate don't do so out of fear that the landlord may sue them.

However, many landlords are not litigious. Many even accept some responsibility for the low sales or demise of a tenant's business if it's due to high vacancy rates in the property, relocation of anchor tenants, or even a downturn in the economy.

Many of the landlords Dale worked for would never sue a tenant unless they felt the tenant had hurt or deceived the landlord.

It's All Negotiable if You Know What You're Doing

If there's one statement we hear most frequently from tenants, it's this:

The landlord is not negotiable.

The tenant has come to this conclusion either by trial and error and poor negotiating skills or by using the wrong professional to help them. Perhaps the tenant is simply repeating what the landlord's real estate agent has told him.

If you're a casual golfer, you know how hard it is to come close to scoring par. Yet professional golfers not only par, they birdie hole after hole. Don't be surprised if you can't get what you want for yourself, but a professional lease consultant can — because it is their business and their job.

It's all negotiable if you know what you're doing.

Glossary of Commercial Real Estate Terms

Abatement

Free rent provided to the tenant, at the beginning of your lease or throughout the lease term. Rent abatement can help reduce your start-up costs or carry you through a slow seasonal period for your business.

Absentee owner

A landlord who is based in a city other than where the property is located.

Addendum

A supplemental document within a lease containing unique terms and conditions negotiated for that specific agreement.

Additional rent

An amount beyond the minimum rent; this may include common area charges, real estate taxes, or reimbursements to the landlord for repairs or attorney's fees.

Advertising fund

A fund set up by the landlord for producing special campaigns or advertising for the shopping center.

Agent

A person or entity licensed under a governing real estate board to conduct real estate transactions as a representative of a client, such as a landlord.

Allowance

Money that the landlord gives the tenant for improvements to the tenant's space that doesn't have to be repaid by the tenant to the landlord.

Amendment

Changes, including both deletions and additions, made to a document after the original lease has been signed. Terms in the amendment negate the terms in the original lease.

Anchor pad

The land occupied by the anchor store in a shopping center.

Anchor store

The anchor store may own the land or have a ground lease, allowing them to control the property.

Anchor tenant

The largest tenant within a property, such as a shopping center. Major department stores and grocery chains are often anchor stores. Some office buildings also have anchor tenants.

Arbitration

A legal method for settling disputes between a landlord and a tenant using a third party as mediator. Often used as a way to avoid going to court.

Artificial breakpoint

The point in sales at which a tenant begins to pay percentage rent. Typically calculated higher than the natural breakpoint as a means of allowing for a higher sales volume before percentage rent becomes payable.

"As is" condition

An agreement by a tenant to accept property in its current condition, including any known or unknown defects.

Assignee

A new tenant who assumes the rights and responsibilities of the original tenant under the existing lease.

Assignor

A current tenant who wants to transfer the rights and responsibilities within an existing lease.

Assignment

A legal agreement or procedure transferring a lease from one tenant to another so a new lease agreement is not necessary. Commonly occurs when a business is sold.

Base rent

The amount of rent a tenant pays, excluding operating costs or percentage rent. Base rent is the most negotiable of all rents (synonymous with minimum or basic rent).

BOMA

Acronym for Building Owners and Managers Association, an international association for landlords and property managers.

Broker

A person licensed and paid to act as an owner's representative in real estate transactions.

Brokerage

A firm that acts as a representative for owners and receives a commission for their services.

Buildout

Upgrades to commercial space requested by the tenant to make a building suitable for their needs.

Build-to-suit

Building designed to meet the specific needs of a large tenant or anchor tenant who agrees to lease the site.

Business terms

The key points of a lease agreement originally outlined in the offer to lease such as the rental rate, term length, commencement date, and so on.

Buy out

A landlord pays off the remaining term of a tenant's existing lease agreement so the tenant can move their business to the landlord's building. May also apply to a landlord who pays a current tenant in their building to move, making room for a new tenant.

CAM

Acronym for Common Area Maintenance. All costs required to maintain a building or center's common areas. These costs, when charged back to the tenant in addition to the base rent, are called additional rent.

Chain store

A national or regional group of retail stores operating under the same owner.

Charge back

A way for a landlord to recover expenses such as CAM, real estate taxes, utilities, or work done to tenant space by billing the tenant for a percentage of the costs.

Closing

The signing of the final leasing documents by a landlord and tenant.

Cluster anchors

A group of complementary stores in close proximity selling merchandise similar to what a single anchor tenant sells.

Commencement date

The date a tenant's lease term begins.

CRU (Commercial Retail Unit)

A landlord's leased units within a building or center that conduct retail business.

Commission

A fee or percentage of the sale price paid to an agent from a leasing transaction.

Common area

The area of a building used by all tenants and their customers, such as lobbies, corridors, and restrooms. Parking facilities, malls, sidewalks, landscaped areas, public toilets, and truck and service facilities may be included as common areas when calculating the tenant's share of building operating expenses.

Concession

Benefits given by a landlord to encourage the leasing of new space or retaining a current tenant. Common concessions include a change of rent, cash, or cash equivalents given by the landlord as rental abatement, additional tenant finish allowance, or moving expenses.

Construction allowance

Money or other financial incentives given to tenants by the landlord to offset the cost of constructing their store space in a center.

Continuous occupancy clause

A lease clause stating that the tenant must occupy the premises for the entire length of the lease.

Contract

A legally binding agreement between two legally competent people.

Convenience goods

Goods bought frequently and with little effort, such as gasoline, groceries, or pharmaceutical supplies. Can also mean frequently used services such as beauty, barber and bakeshops, or laundry and dry-cleaning establishments.

Cooperating broker/agent

A broker/agent who brings a potential tenant to the broker representing the landlord or the site. Cooperating brokers share the commission with the landlord's broker. Also known as an outside broker.

Curb appeal

The visual appeal of a property from the outside.

Default

Not upholding the terms of the lease. Specific examples include failing to pay rent on time or not staying open for business during specific hours.

Delinquent

Being late in paying monies owed.

Demographics

Statistics that identify the characteristics of a specific group of people within a given area.

Depreciation

A decrease in the value of an asset over a period of time.

Distressed property

Property that has lost value due to neglect, or where less than 25 percent of a commercial property is occupied over a 12-month period.

Double net lease (Net net lease)

In a double net lease, the tenant pays a proportionate share of property taxes and property insurance in addition to base rent. The landlord pays all other operating costs.

Easement

The right to use property you don't own. Common reasons for granting easements include allowing access to adjoining land and access to public utility services/equipment.

Effective date

The latest date appearing on the signature page of the lease and the date the lease goes into effect.

Effective rent/rate

The actual amount of rent per square foot a landlord receives after deducting free rent, tenant allowance, landlord work costs, and realtor commissions. Also called new effective rent.

Enclosed center

A retail shopping center with common areas under one roof.

Enclosed common area

A term applied to enclosed malls and measured in square feet of floor area. It includes the mall, public rest rooms, receiving and distribution facilities used by tenants, and other enclosed common areas.

Enclosed mall

A mall that's enclosed, heated, cooled, insulated, and lighted.

Encroachment

Property use or structure that extends beyond the business's legal property line.

Encumbrance

Any claim, lien, charge, or liability that affects or limits the title to a property.

End cap

The ends of a strip center; regardless of the shape of the center, end caps are often considered premium locations due to their visibility.

Entertainment complex

Shopping center containing theaters, restaurants, or other entertainment facilities.

Equity

The difference between a property's current market value and the mortgages and liens owed on it.

Equity related loan

A loan that can be converted into equity ownership or collateralized with equity positions.

Escalation clause

A provision within a lease agreement allowing the present rent or operating costs to increase.

Escrow agreement

A contract describing how money placed into an escrow account is handled and distributed.

Estoppel certificate

A document commonly used to verify facts and information for a third party.

Exclusive broker/agency agreement

A real estate agent or broker, acting as the landlord's representative, who has the sole right to sell or lease a property.

Exclusive letter of representation

A tenant's written authorization specifying that a particular consultant or realtor act as the tenant's representative when negotiating a lease or renewal.

Exclusive use

A tenant's right or obligation to provide a particular service or product.

Exclusivity clause

A lease clause limiting the number of stores that can open in a shopping center that are in direct competition with a tenant for a specific type of business.

Exculpatory clause

A provision invalidating all previous agreements.

Executed lease

A lease that has been signed by all parties and delivered to each in its final form.

Expense recovery

Total receipts from tenants to recover operating expenses.

Expiration date

The date on which a tenant's lease term ends.

Face rate

The rental rate stated in the lease agreement, not including additional concessions or inducements.

Factory outlet

A store offering merchandise direct from the manufacturer at prices below retail.

Fair market value

The price an informed person is willing to pay on the open market for a property.

Financial statements

A summarized report of accounting transactions, consisting of the balance sheet, the operating statement, and the statement of cash flows.

First right of refusal

A tenant's right to lease other space within a building or shopping center if it becomes available.

Fixed assets

Things used in a business that are not for sale.

Fixed minimum rent

Also known as base rent. The amount of basic rent paid by the tenant, usually stated as an amount per square foot charged on an annual basis.

Fixturing period

The period of time prior to the commencement date that the tenant uses to build out or renovate the premises; usually free of minimum rent and operating expenses.

Flat CAM

A fixed tenant-occupancy charge in addition to base minimum rent, which may include additional costs, such as marketing and CAM. Excluded may be insurance, utilities, and real estate taxes. Flat Cam may be escalated on an annual agreed-upon rate such as the Consumer Price Index.

Flat rate

A rental rate that will not be lowered by any concessions from the landlord.

Flat rent

A specific rent on square footage paid by a tenant for a specified period of time.

Floor plan

A blueprint of a building's floor plan showing architectural details drawn to scale.

Force majeure

Any uncontrollable act that prevents a tenant or landlord from fulfilling conditions of the lease. A labor strike, weather, earthquake, or other natural disaster can be a force majeure.

Forbearance agreement

A lender's agreement to postpone foreclosure in order to give the borrower time and opportunity to pay any monies they owe.

Foreclosure

A legal process exercised by a mortgagee, franchisee, or landlord to gain lawful possession of a property if the tenant doesn't meet their financial obligations.

Formal lease agreement

A legal document outlining and defining all legal terms and conditions for a tenant to lease space for a given time period.

Franchisee

A person who buys a franchise and operates the business under the direction and regulations determined by the franchisor.

Franchisor

A corporation or person who sells their original business model, including the right to use the name, to other individuals, who must follow the seller's specifications for conducting business.

Free rent

Concession by the landlord to provide the tenant with space without paying base rent for a period of time. Also called rent abatement or abatement.

Frontage

The area of a store facing the street or the pedestrian walkway in a shopping mall. Often referred to as the window display and entrance.

Full service lease

A lease requiring the landlord to pay all the service costs required by the tenant throughout the lease term, such as taxes, insurance, and utilities.

General contractor

The overseer for a construction project. A general contractor will hire, pay, and oversee all sub-contractors working on a project.

Graduated lease

Rent that can vary over the term of the lease, depending upon future events such as tenant income, inflation, business expansion, or appraisal results.

Grantee

The person or legal entity receiving title to a property in a business transaction.

Grantor

The person or legal entity transferring title in a business transaction.

Gross

Total amount before deductions have been made; can refer to square footage, rental amounts, or profits.

Gross lease

With a gross lease, you pay a set amount of rent each month. The landlord pays all other expenses, including property insurance, taxes, and all maintenance on the property.

Gross margin

The difference between the amount earned from sales and the total cost of the merchandise sold.

Gross profit

A business's sales income after subtracting the cost of the goods sold. In some cases this includes the cost of merchandise returns, which is subtracted from the total.

Gross sales

The total sales a retailer makes during a specified financial period, such as on a daily, monthly, or annual basis.

Gross scheduled rent

The amount of rent that a landlord receives when a building is 100 percent occupied.

Ground lease

A lease that includes just the land; also called a land lease.

Guaranteed rent

The rent due each month as spelled out in a lease.

Guarantor

A person or entity whose credit standing is used to guaranty the tenant's monetary obligations if the tenant doesn't pay.

Guaranty

An agreement stating that if the tenant defaults, the money owed will be paid by the guarantor named in the agreement.

Heating, Ventilation, and Air Conditioning (HVAC)

The mechanical system of a building providing warm or cool air circulation. High rise office buildings and shopping centers have one or two main HVAC systems that supply all the tenants, whereas strip malls and industrial buildings often have small individual rooftop HVAC systems for each rental unit.

Holdover tenant

A tenant who remains in a leased premise after the lease has expired. Also known as the *over-holding period.* There is typically a holdover penalty or increase to the minimum rent during this period.

Incentive

A concession or allowance offered by the landlord to encourage the tenant to sign a lease or to renew a lease.

Inducement

An allowance, concession, or benefit offered by a landlord to a prospective tenant in order to encourage the prospective tenant to sign a lease.

Industrial space

The type of real estate suited to the needs of a manufacturing, assembly, warehousing, or distribution type of business.

In-house leasing broker/agent

A leasing representative working directly for a developer, owner, or retailer.

Initial assessment

A one-time assessment, equal to one year's dues, paid by new tenants in addition to the standard merchants' association annual dues.

In-line stores

Stores placed so that their frontages are in a straight line behind the lease line.

Insolvency

The failure to pay owed debts.

Intangible assets

Assets that are not physical in nature but that have benefits, such as brand names or trademarks.

Interest

Money paid for the use of money loaned, usually expressed as a rate or percentage of the initial sum loaned, called the interest rate.

Inventory

The goods in a specified accounting date.

Investor

A person who buys an existing business and retains ownership for a period of time with the expectation of earning a return on their initial investment.

Internal leasing organization

A group of leasing professionals hired by an owner to lease space.

Janitorial

An expense normally included as part of the CAM, net, or triple net costs. Janitorial generally includes emptying and removal of trash, light cleaning, or vacuuming of floors.

Kick-out clause

An option allowing either a landlord or tenant to terminate the lease early.

Kiosk space

A booth or stall set up in a property, often in an enclosed mall, to sell goods and services.

Land use regulations

Zoning regulations and ordinances that determine how land can legally be used.

Landlord

The owner of a property.

Landlord's floor area

The total leasable square footage in a shopping center.

Landlord's lease

A lease whose terms and conditions favor the landlord.

Landlord's work

Improvements and work done to a space by the landlord for the tenant as listed in the lease agreement.

Lease

A legally binding contract between a landlord and a tenant for a stated period of time as long as certain conditions are met.

Lease agreement

The contract between a landlord and a tenant describing the business, the legal terms of the contract, and the terms and conditions which both parties must adhere to.

Lease buyout

A payout by either the landlord or the tenant, which negates the terms of the lease.

Lease covenants

Clauses in a lease agreement detailing all promises to be carried out throughout the period of the lease.

Lease proposal

A written document listing the tenant's proposed terms and conditions for leasing a property.

Lease renewal

A clause giving a tenant the right to extend the term of their lease once the original lease term expires. The terms of the lease renewal may differ from those of the original lease.

Lease term

The period of time listed in the lease binding on both the tenant and landlord.

Leased space

The amount of space a tenant occupies in a center.

Leasehold improvements

Improvements that the tenant makes to the property with the landlord's approval. The landlord may contribute to these expenses and recover them as a portion of the rental rate during the tenant's lease term.

Leasehold interest

A tenant's legally binding rights.

Leasing agent/broker

The person responsible for the marketing and leasing of commercial property paid a commission by the landlord.

Lender

A company or person providing the tenant with financing.

Lessee

The term that describes the tenant in a lease agreement.

Lessor

The landlord or property owner.

Let

To rent or lease.

Letter of commitment

A formal letter issued by a lender to a tenant, committing the lender to provide a real estate loan.

Letter of credit

A commitment from a financial institute or other entity to a customer to provide a certain amount of money, so long as all terms and conditions within the note are met. Often used in lieu of a security deposit.

Letter of intent (LOI)

An informal offer to lease space from a landlord from the proposed tenant citing certain conditions, such as rent to be paid, before entering into any formal agreement with the landlord.

Lien

A legal claim against a property to satisfy an owed debt.

Liquidation

The sale of assets and the settlement of debts when closing a business.

Listing agreement

A contract between a property owner and real estate agent, giving the agent the right to lease the property in return for a fee or commission.

Listing broker/agent

The individual or real estate company given exclusive rights in listing and leasing space for a landlord.

Local tenant

A retail tenant operating one or more stores exclusively in a local market.

Long term lease

A lease term ten years or longer; in some areas, a lease term five years or longer.

Major tenant

The store that brings in the most customers to a shopping center.

Mall

The mall is typically an enclosed, climate controlled, and lighted structure containing multiple stores and surrounded by parking. The mall usually has entrances on all sides, with the largest nearest the anchor stores.

Mall manager

The person who supervises operations and maintenance of the mall's common area and parking lot, including managing personnel and coordinating with the developer, individual tenants and marketing director.

Management fee

The fee paid out to the company that manages a property for the landlord.

Market analysis

A tool to determine the demographics of a market in a certain area and the chances that a certain type of business will succeed there.

Market research

Information gathered to determine whether a business can do well within a certain market population, market economy, local industries, and competing businesses within the vicinity.

Market value

The price a property can sell for in a competitive and open market.

Mega mall

Often referred to as a regional or super regional shopping center, a mega mall is an enormous complex three to four times the size of a typical shopping mall. Mega malls generally contain a mix of businesses, including not only retail stores but also restaurants and movie theaters. The largest may even house, a hotel and amusement type facilities that make it a family vacation destination.

Merchants' association

A non-profit organization consisting of the landlord and the tenants of a shopping center. Landlords may require that all tenants belong to the merchant's association.

Minimum rent

The monthly rental rate for the property, not including operating costs. Also called basic or base rent.

Mixed use center

A center that houses a number of types of businesses, including office space, hotels, residential, recreation, a sports stadium, or other entertainment.

Modified gross lease

A lease where the tenant pays rent plus some portion of the operating expenses.

Mom and pop store

A place of business whose owners have only one location.

Monthly rent

The amount of rent due each month, generally at the beginning of the month. One-twelfth the annual rent.

Month to month lease/tenancy

An agreement between the landlord and tenant to rent space for no more than one month at a time. Normally the lease continues until either the landlord or tenant terminates it in writing.

Mortgage

The legal agreement in which the owner of a property uses the property as security while repaying a loan.

Moving allowance

Monies paid to the tenant by the landlord to help defray moving costs in or out of a location.

Natural breakpoint

The sales number at which time the tenant begins to pay percentage rent in addition to the minimum rent. This number is calculated by dividing the annual minimum rent payable by the percentage number. If the annual rent were $80,000 and the percentage rent 8 percent, then the tenant would pay 8 percent of every dollar over the natural breakpoint of $1,000,000 in sales.

Negotiation

The bargaining process between two or more parties to reach a mutual agreement. In commercial leasing, the amount of rent paid, length of the lease, and numerous other conditions or options are negotiated.

Net lease

In addition to the minimum rent, the tenant is responsible for their proportionate share of all other costs associated with operation and maintenance of the property.

Net profit

The amount of money left after a business owner pays all expenses.

Net rent

The rent the tenant pays to the landlord minus any operating costs.

Net sales

The total dollar amount of revenue received after deducting exchanges and refunds from the total gross sales.

Non-competition clause

A clause stating a tenant will be the only business within a building or location providing a certain type of goods or services. Also known as an *exclusive use clause* or *non-compete clause*.

Non-disturbance

A legal term that requires any mortgage holder to honor the lease agreement in the event of a foreclosure, provided that the tenant is not in default.

Non-exclusive authorization to lease

An agreement between the landlord and leasing agent that the landlord will pay a commission only if a tenant signs a lease within a set time frame.

Normal use

Using a site only for permitted purposes as outlined in the lease during normal building operating hours.

Occupancy

The percentage of space rented within a building or a location.

Offer to lease

A formal document binding tenant to a lease agreement if the landlord accepts the terms offered.

Open-air center

An attached row of stores or businesses managed as a unit, and not enclosed under a single roof, with on-site parking usually located in front of stores.

Opening contribution

A tenant's one-time contribution to the marketing fund for a center's grand opening or grand reopening.

Operating covenant

The promise of the tenant to open and operate its business for a certain number of hours in the day and days of the week as outlined in the lease.

Operating expenses

The cost of maintaining and managing a property, including property taxes, salaries, insurance, maintenance, utilities, and any additional costs.

Operation costs

The actual costs of maintaining and managing a property, including maintenance, repairs, management, utilities, taxes, and insurance.

Option to cancel/terminate

A clause within a lease that allows either the landlord or tenant to cancel the lease.

Option to renew

A lease clause giving the tenant the right to renew the current lease for an additional term, if he meets conditions specified in the lease agreement.

Outlet

A site which is not attached to a shopping center or mall but rather located on a peripheral area of the parking lot. Often called a parcel or pad site, these businesses and are often fast food restaurants, gas stations, drive up banking, or other services.

Outside broker

An individual or real estate company hired to lease space for a landlord.

Overhead

The expenses associated with running a business that don't generate a profit, such as utilities or wages.

Overholding period/clause

A clause stating what the rent will be if a tenant stays in a location without renewing his lease.

Owner

The person or corporation who has legal possession of a property.

Pad

The parcel of land under a department store's building.

Pad site

The land area available for a freestanding building at the periphery of the parking area of a shopping center or mall.

Parcel

A piece of land or property owned by a single person or corporation.

Parking area

The space in a shopping center devoted to parking, including walking aisles, walkways, islands, and landscaped areas.

Pedestrian flow

The direction and patterns in which customers move through a property, which can be influenced by the types of tenants on the site and the property design.

Pedestrian mall

An outdoor shopping location where vehicles are not allowed.

Percentage rent

Rent paid by the tenant in addition to the minimum rent calculated on a percentage of sales over a natural or artificial breakpoint.

Percentage rent only

The amount of rent a retail tenant pays based on a percentage of gross sales.

Permanent tenant

A tenant who has signed a lease with a term longer than one year.

Permitted use

The type of goods a tenant can sell.

Personal guaranty

The naming of a guarantor who will be held personally responsible for the payment of all the amounts for rent and additional rent if the tenant doesn't pay.

Phantom space

Space deemed to be unusable or unaccountable, though included in the total space being charged for. Often a result of a mistake or inaccurate measurement of the tenant's space.

Preleasing

The leasing of a real estate property before a property is fully constructed.

Pro forma rate

The projected or estimated rent determined by the landlord.

Profit

The amount of money a business makes after paying all its business-related costs.

Property manager

The individual who manages and supervises all day-to-day operations of a property for the landlord or management company.

Proportionate share

Each tenant pays a proportionate share of the total cost, based on the amount of square footage they inhabit.

Quiet possession/enjoyment

The right of the tenant to operate his business without interference from the landlord during the lease term.

Radius clause

A restriction in the lease preventing the tenant from opening another business within a certain distance of the property.

Rate of retention

The rate at which current tenants renew their leases and stay in a location.

Rate of return

The percentage of income earned compared to the outgoing expenses.

Real estate taxes

Charges imposed on all owners of real estate by the local government, usually based on the assessed value of the property.

Recourse

The right of a landlord or property manager to hold the guarantor of an agreement liable for any costs not paid as agreed upon by the tenant.

Redevelopment

Renovation, expansion, or reconfiguration that substantially changes the marketing direction of an existing shopping center.

Regional analysis

A study of the general economic and demographic conditions of the surrounding areas of a property to determine what trends may affect it.

Relocation clause

A lease clause which gives the landlord the right to relocate the tenant within the property.

Remodeling allowance

An allowance offered by the landlord to the tenant to help the tenant with the costs of moving in and setting up business.

Renewal option

An agreement giving the tenant permission to extend the term of the lease.

Rent

The amount of rent paid to the landlord during the term of the lease.

Rent abatement

Free rent provided to the tenant at the beginning of their lease or throughout the lease term. Rent abatement can help reduce start-up costs or carry the tenant through a slow seasonal period for their business.

Rent acceleration

The right of the landlord to collect rent for the balance of the term of the lease in one lump sum if the tenant defaults on his obligations.

Rent commencement date

The first day that the tenant pays rent.

Rent relief

A reduction of the tenant's rent, which is typically repayable by the tenant to the landlord at a future date.

Rent-free period

Period of time where the tenant doesn't have to pay rent.

Rental area

The amount of square footage available for rent in a building or unit.

Request for proposal

A written request from the tenant to the landlord for information on the lease and the building.

Rider

A specific agreement within a supplement document in a lease. Also known as an _addendum_.

Right of first negotiation

An option giving a tenant the right to negotiate for a space before the landlord offers the space to another tenant.

Right of first offer

A provision requiring the landlord to offer vacant space to the tenant before leasing it to anyone else.

Right of first refusal

A right granted to a party to enter into a contract with the same terms as those offered by a third party.

Right to terminate

A clause in the lease agreement giving the tenant the right to cancel the lease.

Sale projection

A tenant's estimate of his monthly and yearly sales.

Security deposit

Money the tenant pays the landlord before the tenant takes up occupancy in the new leased space. The security deposit can be returned at some point negotiated by the tenant.

Shell space

A vacant space that's enclosed but not finished.

Site

A tract of land that meets certain conditions for development, such as size, shape, and location plus accessibility and zoning and suited for the proposed use.

Specialty center

A building designed with a certain image or theme that caters to a certain population, often those who live or work around the building.

Specialty store

A store that carries just a few types or categories of merchandise and usually provides a high level of service.

Speculative space

Space built by the landlord before he has any signed tenants for the area.

Square footage

The measurement standard used in the real estate industry.

Standard form lease

A basic and uniform lease that a landlord uses with all of his tenants.

Step-down rents

An agreement that the percentages paid on total sales will decrease as the tenant's sales increase.

Step-up lease/rents

An agreement that allows set increases in basic rent at pre-set times during the lease term. Also known as a *graded lease*.

Staightlining

Averaging of the tenant's rent payments over the life of the lease.

Strip center

A property containing various businesses that are not part of an enclosed structure. Each business has parking in front and an outside door.

Sublease

A lease that allows a person to take over the original tenant's space and pay rent to the original tenant directly. The original tenant is still responsible for the lease. Generally, the landlord must approve the sublease.

TMI

Acronym for *Taxes, Maintenance, and Insurance*. This is used interchangeably with Common Area Maintenance, abbreviated CAM.

Take back clause

A special provision in the lease that allows the landlord to take back sub-leased space in order to rent to a new tenant.

Target market

A specific group of consumers and clients that the tenant hopes to draw to his business.

Temporary tenant

A tenant who rents a property for a short period of time.

Tenancy in common

A form of co-ownership in which there is individual ownership by the district owners; there are several vendors who own the property in such a way that each has a definite and separate but un-partitioned share in it.

Tenant

The person or entity responsible for paying rent to the landlord or management company in order to set up business in a specific location for a specific amount of time.

Tenant allowance

Concessions made by landlords to help a tenant build out his space or other inducements to lease, such as a period of free rent.

Tenant eviction

Legal removal of the tenant from a property, usually for non-payment of rent or failure to follow the landlord's rules and regulations.

Tenant improvement allowance

Monies paid or credited to the tenant by the landlord to help the tenant with the cost of improvements to the property.

Tenant trade name

The legal name a tenant does business under.

Tenant's lease

A lease that gives a tenant more rights than the landlord.

Term

The amount of time a property is leased for.

Termination

Negation of the lease before the end of the lease term.

Title

A document verifying the legal ownership of a real property.

Title report

A report describing the current status of the title, including any easements, restrictions, liens, covenants, or any defect in the title.

Total rent

The sum of all the types of rent the tenant will pay. Total rent includes common area maintenance expenses, or CAM, minimum rent, and percentage rent.

Traffic

The volume of people at a commercial property at any given time.

Triple net lease (Net net net lease)

In a triple net lease, the tenant pays a proportionate share of all operating costs, which can include not only property taxes and property insurance, but also repairs, elevator maintenance, parking lot maintenance, security, and snow removal, to name a few.

Unanchored shopping center

A shopping center that has no anchor tenant such as a major department store occupying at least 50,000 square feet. See *anchor tenant*.

Use clause

A lease provision that restricts the type of goods a retail tenant can sell.

Vacancy rate

The ratio of vacant space to the total space available for rent.

Valuable consideration

The granting of some right, interest, profit, or the suffering of loss or default by one party in exchange for the service or performance of another.

Vanilla box

A space partially completed by the landlord when turned over to the tenant. This typically includes a bare concrete slab with demising walls, dry-walled, and ready for paint.

Waiver of subrogation

An agreement signed by both the tenant and landlord stating that they agree not to sue one another for property damage.

Warm brick

Unfinished space in a shopping center; the tenant must pay all construction costs.

Zoning

The limits placed by local government on the type of construction or land usage permitted within a certain area.

Index

• C •

ple & Mac

ad For Dummies,
h Edition
8-1-118-49823-1

hone 5 For Dummies,
h Edition
8-1-118-35201-4

acBook For Dummies,
h Edition
8-1-118-20920-2

X Mountain Lion
r Dummies
8-1-118-39418-2

ogging & Social Media

cebook For Dummies,
h Edition
8-1-118-09562-1

m Blogging
r Dummies
8-1-118-03843-7

nterest For Dummies
8-1-118-32800-2

rdPress For Dummies,
h Edition
8-1-118-38318-6

siness

mmodities For Dummies,
d Edition
8-1-118-01687-9

vesting For Dummies,
h Edition
8-0-470-90545-6

Personal Finance
For Dummies,
7th Edition
978-1-118-11785-9

QuickBooks 2013
For Dummies
978-1-118-35641-8

Small Business Marketing Kit
For Dummies,
3rd Edition
978-1-118-31183-7

Careers

Job Interviews
For Dummies,
4th Edition
978-1-118-11290-8

Job Searching with
Social Media
For Dummies
978-0-470-93072-4

Personal Branding
For Dummies
978-1-118-11792-7

Resumes For Dummies,
6th Edition
978-0-470-87361-8

Success as a Mediator
For Dummies
978-1-118-07862-4

Diet & Nutrition

Belly Fat Diet For Dummies
978-1-118-34585-6

Eating Clean For Dummies
978-1-118-00013-7

Nutrition For Dummies,
5th Edition
978-0-470-93231-5

Digital Photography

Digital Photography
For Dummies,
7th Edition
978-1-118-09203-3

Digital SLR Cameras &
Photography For Dummies,
4th Edition
978-1-118-14489-3

Photoshop Elements 11
For Dummies
978-1-118-40821-6

Gardening

Herb Gardening
For Dummies,
2nd Edition
978-0-470-61778-6

Vegetable Gardening
For Dummies,
2nd Edition
978-0-470-49870-5

Health

Anti-Inflammation Diet
For Dummies
978-1-118-02381-5

Diabetes For Dummies,
3rd Edition
978-0-470-27086-8

Living Paleo For Dummies
978-1-118-29405-5

Hobbies

Beekeeping
For Dummies
978-0-470-43065-1

eBay For Dummies,
7th Edition
978-1-118-09806-6

Raising Chickens
For Dummies
978-0-470-46544-8

Wine For Dummies,
5th Edition
978-1-118-28872-6

Writing Young Adult Fiction
For Dummies
978-0-470-94954-2

Language & Foreign Language

500 Spanish Verbs
For Dummies
978-1-118-02382-2

English Grammar
For Dummies,
2nd Edition
978-0-470-54664-2

French All-in One
For Dummies
978-1-118-22815-9

German Essentials
For Dummies
978-1-118-18422-6

Italian For Dummies
2nd Edition
978-1-118-00465-4

Available in print and e-book formats.

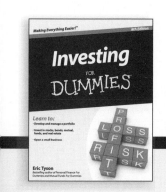

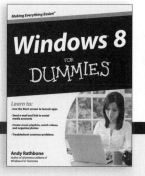

Math & Science

Algebra I For Dummies,
2nd Edition
978-0-470-55964-2

Anatomy and Physiology
For Dummies,
2nd Edition
978-0-470-92326-9

Astronomy For Dummies,
3rd Edition
978-1-118-37697-3

Biology For Dummies,
2nd Edition
978-0-470-59875-7

Chemistry For Dummies,
2nd Edition
978-1-1180-0730-3

Pre-Algebra Essentials
For Dummies
978-0-470-61838-7

Microsoft Office

Excel 2013 For Dummies
978-1-118-51012-4

Office 2013 All-in-One
For Dummies
978-1-118-51636-2

PowerPoint 2013
For Dummies
978-1-118-50253-2

Word 2013 For Dummies
978-1-118-49123-2

Music

Blues Harmonica
For Dummies
978-1-118-25269-7

Guitar For Dummies,
3rd Edition
978-1-118-11554-1

iPod & iTunes
For Dummies,
10th Edition
978-1-118-50864-0

Programming

Android Application
Development For
Dummies, 2nd Edition
978-1-118-38710-8

iOS 6 Application
Development For Dummies
978-1-118-50880-0

Java For Dummies,
5th Edition
978-0-470-37173-2

Religion & Inspiration

The Bible For Dummies
978-0-7645-5296-0

Buddhism For Dummies,
2nd Edition
978-1-118-02379-2

Catholicism For Dummies,
2nd Edition
978-1-118-07778-8

Self-Help & Relationships

Bipolar Disorder
For Dummies,
2nd Edition
978-1-118-33882-7

Meditation For Dummies,
3rd Edition
978-1-118-29144-3

Seniors

Computers For Seniors
For Dummies,
3rd Edition
978-1-118-11553-4

iPad For Seniors
For Dummies,
5th Edition
978-1-118-49708-1

Social Security
For Dummies
978-1-118-20573-0

Smartphones & Tablets

Android Phones
For Dummies
978-1-118-16952-0

Kindle Fire HD
For Dummies
978-1-118-42223-6

NOOK HD For Dummies,
Portable Edition
978-1-118-39498-4

Surface For Dummies
978-1-118-49634-3

Test Prep

ACT For Dummies,
5th Edition
978-1-118-01259-8

ASVAB For Dummies,
3rd Edition
978-0-470-63760-9

GRE For Dummies,
7th Edition
978-0-470-88921-3

Officer Candidate Tests,
For Dummies
978-0-470-59876-4

Physician's Assistant Exa
For Dummies
978-1-118-11556-5

Series 7 Exam
For Dummies
978-0-470-09932-2

Windows 8

Windows 8 For Dummies
978-1-118-13461-0

Windows 8 For Dummies
Book + DVD Bundle
978-1-118-27167-4

Windows 8 All-in-One
For Dummies
978-1-118-11920-4

Available in print and e-book formats.

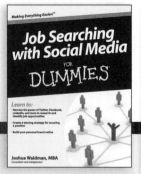

Take Dummies with you everywhere you go!

Whether you're excited about e-books, want more from the web, must have your mobile apps, or swept up in social media, Dummies makes everything easier .

Dummies products make life easier

- DIY
- Consumer Electronics
- Crafts

- Software
- Cookware
- Hobbies

- Videos
- Music
- Games
- and More!

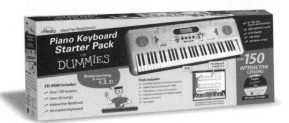

For more information, go to **Dummies.com**® and search the store by category.

FOR
DUMMIE
A Wiley B